SECOND
FRONT

JOHN R. MacARTHUR

SECOND FRONT

Censorship and Propaganda
in the 1991 Gulf War

UPDATED WITH A NEW PREFACE

Foreword by
Ben H. Bagdikian

UNIVERSITY OF CALIFORNIA PRESS

Berkeley • Los Angeles • London

University of California Press
Berkeley and Los Angeles, California
University of California Press, Ltd.
London, England
Published in 2004

Library of Congress Cataloging-in-Publication Data

MacArthur, John R.
Second front : censorship and propaganda in the 1991 Gulf War /
John R. MacArthur ; foreword by Ben H. Bagdikian.—Updated with a new pref.
p.   cm.
Includes bibliographical references (p.   ) and index.
ISBN 0-520-24231-9 (pbk. : alk. paper)
1. Persian Gulf War, 1991—Press coverage—United States.
2. Persian Gulf War, 1991—Censorship—United States.
3. Government and the press—United States. I. Title.

DS79.739.M33   2004
956.7044'28—dc22   2004041412

The author is grateful to the following for permission to reprint from already published material: Columbia Journalism Review, for Michael Massing's "Another Front," copyright © May–June 1991; Naval War College Review, for "Two Routes to the Wrong Destination: Public Affairs in the South Atlantic War" by Lt. Cdr. Arthur A. Humphries, USN, May–June 1983; New York Newsday, for Susan Sachs's "End of the War: Allies Faced Ghost Army," copyright © 1991 by the Los Angeles Times Syndicate International; The New York Times, for R. W. Apple, Jr.'s "The Confrontation in the Gulf: Oil, Saddam Hussein and the Re-emergence of America as the Superpower" and William Safire's "Essay, The Hitler Analogy," copyright © 1990 by the New York Times Company; Newsweek, for Tony Clifton's "Frustrations for a Veteran Correspondent," copyright © 1991 Newsweek Inc.; Paul William Roberts, for "Inside Iraq," originally published in Saturday Night, May 1991; Hutchinson, for an excerpt from John Simpson's From the House of War, copyright © 1991 by John Simpson; The Spectator, for Paul Johnson's "Kindly Leave the Pulpit," copyright © 1991 by The Spectator; The Voice (New Baltimore, MI), for excerpts from Dick Runels's letters from the Gulf; Time Insider, for Jay Peterzell's "Inside the Pentagon Press Pool," copyright © 1990 Time Inc. Magazine Co.

The above has been reprinted by permission of the publishers. All rights reserved.

13 12 11 10 09 08 07 06 05
10 9 8 7 6 5 4 3 2

Printed in the United States of America

The paper used in this publication meets the minimum requirements of ANSI/NISO Z39.48-1992 (R 1997) (Permanence of Paper). ∞

For Renée

Simple, plain Clarence! I do love thee so
That I will shortly send thy soul to heaven,
. . . .
With lies well steel'd with weighty arguments.

—SHAKESPEARE, *Richard III*

CONTENTS

CONTENTS

FOREWORD

HISTORICALLY, when clans, kingdoms, and nations have gone to war, whoever brought information to the public—bards, town criers, and the press—have been full-throated cheering squads for the home army. As Phillip Knightly and others have shown, modern nation-states with supposedly free, democratic news media are no exception.

The United States has suffered from the same compliant news. Of all countries of the world, ours gives the news media the most complete protection from government pressures. Our news regularly proclaims its power to remain independent from officialdom. Yet with rare exceptions, the American mainstream news during combat has been much like the hired bards of medieval monarchs: when war has come, our journalists have become propagandists.

An exception sometimes cited was the American war in Vietnam. Many of those who still support the validity and military success of that war have spread the notion that "the news media lost the war in Vietnam." In that view, American journalists reported the war at such odds to the official version that the public lost faith in the enterprise and forced military withdrawal on the verge of victory.

That notion is, of course, groundless. American involvement in Vietnam began in 1954 and continued with escalating intensity for more than a decade, all the while with almost unanimous support—or indifference—from the main media of the country. When in the 1960s it became a major military effort, almost all mainstream reporting—which is the source of news for most Americans—continued dutifully to take at face

value the official government line that the war was vital to
American interests, that the enemy was on the verge of collapse, that our strategy and tactics were effective, and that each
year would end in victory. The standard news based almost all its
reporting on the official claims despite mounting evidence to the
contrary on the battlefield and even in underlying official data.

Only after many years of this kind of reporting did a handful, and only a handful, of American mainstream correspondents begin to report what they were finding from officers in
the field. These few reporters found the realities—outcomes of
battles, data on progress of the war, and the basic nature and
failure of tactics and strategy—to be fundamentally different
from the official announcements coming out of the Saigon high
command and Washington.

By the time this tiny band of establishment journalists
broke ranks with the mass of their colleagues, there had been
years of military failures, hundreds of thousands of civilians at
home had spontaneously taken to the streets in protest, and the
fabric of the American consensus toward the war had been
irretrievably shredded.

Though this more realistic reporting was very late in the
war and involved only a few non-conformists in the major news
operations, their work was utterly unexpected in the traditions
of war reporting. They were immediately accused by many
officials of hating their own govenment and of trying to aid the
enemy—an accusation that has always been the first anti-news
weapon of government. Yet in the wars of the last fifty years,
no American correspondent has significantly endangered plans
or troops by accurate reporting, including reporting on wars
with relaxed censorship.

The nature of "small" wars in the last half of this century
has departed from what most of the public considers the
urgency of any war.

With modern travel and communication, it is increasingly
difficult for any government to place an effective news shield
around extended distant military operations. Other nations not

involved in the war have their own sources of information, including their own mainstream journalism unhampered by the wishes of governments active in the war. More multinational reporting of news is available to ever larger audiences everywhere, especially to the most educated and cosmopolitan population of a country like the United States, whose most influential citizens travel internationally and have routine professional access to foreign news accounts.

There has also been a change in the causes of "small" wars that nullifies the arguments by which countries and kingdoms historically mobilized and controlled their press and people during military engagements.

Governments at war depend, implicitly or explicitly, on the classical model that unifies the society in supporting conscription of troops and ceasing independent reporting: the fear that a vicious enemy is about to invade our shores, rape our women, kill our children, pillage our cities and towns, and enslave our survivors. But in our generation of contemporary ideological and colonial wars, there is a more abstract basis for military action: the fear that a distant hostile force will damage "our interests" abroad. Or that unless military action is taken now in a pre-emptive war against the other country, that country will soon send its troops to invade and destroy our homeland.

"Our interests" abroad is not always enough to obtain overwhelming public support. Many citizens will not be willing to pay added taxes or sacrifice their sons and daughters in order to protect distant oilfields, air bases, or corporate investments. And this country has sent too many frantic and, for the United States, implausible alarms, that unless, for example, the Sandinistas are stopped in tiny Nicaragua, their soldiers, with Soviet support, will soon march down Main Street in Texas or fire missiles into New York.

The longer a distant war is fought on the basis of a particular theory of American—or British, or French, or Soviet, or Chinese—distant "interests," and the more distorted or false official reporting of results, the more likely that returning combat veterans' stories of blood, terror, mutual brutality—the stuff of all wars—will paint a less neat picture of what constitutes "victory" and "defeat." Inevitably, the new picture will raise public questions about the price paid for those "interests."

Thus, the more we have learned about the American war in Vietnam, the more we have seen the questionable basis of "vital American interests." Despite our failure to defeat the North Vietnamese, communism did not march in victory down our Main Streets. It did not expand into the rest of Asia. It did not unite the Soviet Union, China, and the Indochinese into an overwhelming anti-American bloc. It did not paralyze us with nuclear blackmail.

A lesson we should have learned in the 1960s and 1970s is that when governments, including our own, become desperate over a failing policy, they are tempted into that historic folly of nations, self-delusion. The more frustrated the leader becomes, the more the leader is likely to see subordinates who report bad news as disloyal or not sufficiently zealous about the official enterprise. Bad news is filtered out before it reaches the top. Official channels of information become corrupted. In the end, as always, the propagandist government becomes the victim of its own propaganda.

With a compliant news system there is little or no effective information free of government beliefs, so official failures go uncorrected, faulty strategies continue, incompetents remain in leadership, and there is growing likelihood of public demoralization and civil disorder. Even the old USSR, usually seen as having the "advantage" of a totally controlled news system, had to wind down its war in Afghanistan because the public sacrifice for dubious "interests" was so great that returning Soviet veterans plus foreign news sources and an underground news system created overwhelming public opposition and contributed to the unraveling of the government itself.

In democracies, the self-destructive process of governmental delusion and deception is supposed to have a remedy in independent news. This is why the press of a democracy has been called "The Fourth Estate," the unofficial source of public information that tests the validity of official words and deeds.

In the United States more than in any other nation, journalists are asked to view the world without political orientation or other preconceptions, including the rightness or wrongness of official actions. The basic premise is that democracy succeeds to the degree that government has an outside source of information about its own weaknesses and the public has sufficient valid information to judge government performance and reports. The result is supposed to give the public a greater chance to pursue its own self-interests knowledgeably and to hold the government accountable.

For years the main body of our democratic balancing force in Vietnam failed. When the war ended, one and a half million southeast Asians had been killed, a rich region of the globe had been devastated, 58,000 American soldiers had died, and the war had started its crippling infection of the American economy. The price of that national tragedy has been painfully high. For the news media, it was supposed to be The Great Lesson. Never again would journalists look the other way or accept at face value official civil and military claims without careful examination.

But the lesson failed. Something went terribly wrong.

The military learned its own lesson from Vietnam: keep wars short and keep the news media completely controlled in the opening days of the engagement. By maintaining total control of the initial image in a military action, the government can create the framework into which the public thereafter fits subsequent information. By severely limiting reporting by journalists, the government can prolong that controlled public image of a military action until the media move to something else and lose interest in the event.

What went wrong is that the standard news media conformed to the military's expectations.

In 1983 the United States, the world's most powerful military machine, invaded a tiny, virtually defenseless island named Grenada under rules that kept all reporting away until the scene had been made neat. The cause of invasion was largely fallacious and its execution extraordinarily inept. But the news media were sequestered from the early days of the invasion while a largely false picture of the "national interest" and "the enemy" were implanted by undiluted official propaganda.

By the time the shooting was over, the main body of American journalism, as the Pentagon had predicted, had gone off to some new, unrelated excitements. The news system did not go back to Grenada when all controls had been lifted, or if some organizations did, they did not present the new, more valid picture with the same emphasis with which they had spread the earlier flawed governmental version.

Undoubtedly, the government duly noted the news media's failure to straighten the record effectively.

The government invasion of Panama repeated much of the same level of military fiasco and news control. After the smoke had cleared, the main media once more did not reconstruct a more accurate picture with sufficient emphasis when the real facts became known.

When, in 1991, the United States went to war in the Persian Gulf, the news media paid the price for its weak response in Grenada and Panama and repeated its inability to prevent unprecedented censorship. Long before action started, but after announcement of the new draconian censorship policies, smaller news organizations challenged the severity of the censorship in court action. Every major news organization refused to join in the challenge. So in the opening days of the Gulf War, American newspeople were sequestered and forced to transmit totally controlled military versions of what was happening. After the shooting was over and reconstruction of the realities known, once again, the major news media failed to collect all the facts and present them in a coherent way that would effectively correct the misleading and inadequate information the public had been given earlier.

How does one explain these repeated failures by the world's most powerful and free news operations? In Vietnam, Grenada, and Panama the lessons of news failures were too dramatic to escape any mainstream news organization whose memory is not limited to the last five minutes. But in the Gulf War, something like that seemed to happen. There are many intelligent and experienced journalists in our major news organizations. And while the news system is, in fact, regrettably limited in its memory and attention span, something other than a collective desire to mislead is at work.

John MacArthur in this book has laid out in enormous detail how all this happened in the Gulf War. He reports in copious interviews with important actors in both the reporting of the war and in the intricate government planning to control images of the war. One hopes that as a result, our major media, four times burned, will be four times shy in accepting future official releases and briefings at face value without adding their own independent and rigorous examination of the realities. As MacArthur demonstrates, our military understands the bad habits of the news system better than the news system does itself. One hopes that his detailed account of how the news and the government interacted during the Gulf War will help bring the news system's actual operations closer to the high-sounding rhetoric of its leaders and make the government less confident that almost any strategem of information control will be accepted.

Ben H. Bagdikian
Berkeley, California

PREFACE TO THE
2004 EDITION

In descriptions of battles it is generally said that such and
such armies were sent to attack such and such points and
were then ordered to retire and so on. . . . Anyone who has
been in a war knows how untrue that is, yet the reports are
based on that assumption, and on them the military descriptions. Make a round of the troops immediately after a
battle, or even next day or the day after, before the reports
have been drawn up, and ask any of the soldiers and senior
and junior officers how the affair went: you will be told
what all these men experienced and saw, and you will
form a majestic, complex, infinitely varied, depressing,
and indistinct impression; and from no one—least of all
from the commander in chief—will you learn what the
whole affair was like. Two or three days later the reports
begin to be handed in. Talkers begin to narrate how things
happened which they did not see. . . . Everyone is glad to
exchange his own doubts and questionings for this decep-
tive, but clear and always flattering, presentation.
—LEO TOLSTOY
Afterword to *War and Peace,* 1868

NOT LONG AFTER the official conclusion of "Operation
Iraqi Freedom"—the Bush family's military and propaganda
sequel to "Operation Desert Storm"—I went looking for real
news in the cramped, third-floor Montmartre apartment of a
young French television journalist recently back from the
front. By tradition and training, I normally would have pursued
my inquiry in New York or Washington, D.C., in the company

of a grizzled American reporter who had witnessed many wars. But at twenty-nine, Vincent Nguyen of France 2's foreign staff had come to represent for me the profound contrast between the more aggressive European culture of reporting on war and disinformation and the contemptibly passive U.S. version. Moreover, Nguyen's half-Vietnamese parentage and distinctly Vietnamese features couldn't help but evoke the last war in which American journalists did their jobs the right way.

In 2003, twenty-eight years after the fall of Saigon, Vietnam remained the mirror and the benchmark for all subsequent war coverage of U.S. troops—the raw, uncensored exception to the sanitized treacle that followed. Vietnam was the crucible, the defeat that caused future presidential administrations to vow that the people of the United States would never again see human combat in all its ugliness, gore, and chaos—that Americans, in their diminished capacity as citizens, would never again witness their political leaders, their generals, or their soldiers caught up in a very big lie.

Not that Nguyen had witnessed any carnage during the twenty-one-day military campaign to overthrow the dictatorship of Saddam Hussein (and, not coincidentally, to remap the Middle East and secure Iraqi oil fields for the U.S., Britain and friendly nations other than France and Russia). Indeed, he hadn't seen a single corpse. Assigned to the smaller, less publicized northern front, in the autonomous region of Kurdistan, Nguyen had found himself in the town of Kalak, just a few hundred meters from Iraqi troops guarding the border with Iraq proper. He watched daily bombardments of the Iraqi position by U.S. warplanes that "made the walls tremble" in his temporary residence, but every morning the Iraqi soldiers popped up again, alive—at least until they abandoned their posts on April 3.

Just before midnight on March 25, U.S. airborne troops, eventually numbering about two thousand, began parachuting onto an abandoned landing strip near the village of Hareer and set about making a base for humanitarian aid and combined U.S.-Kurdish military operations. Always up for a good story,

Nguyen had already encountered (and unsuccessfully pursued at high speed) a late-model white Toyota Land Cruiser carrying U.S. Special Forces, whose mission was to head off conflict between the Turks—fearful that overthrow of Saddam's Baathist Party apparatus would propel Kurdish ambitions for full independence across the border into the Kurdish region of Turkey—and Iraqi Kurds—who feared preemptive Turkish military action inside Iraq to suppress possible Kurdish agitation.

So, six days after the parachutists of the 173rd Division arrived on the scene, Nguyen and about twenty other journalists eagerly approached the new base and asked for a tour. What followed was utterly unexceptional—that is, if you had followed the evolution of press-military relations since Vietnam. Nguyen and his colleagues, including the legendary Vietnam War photographer Don McCullin of Great Britain, were politely told that they couldn't enter the base. Instead, the Army press officer presented the newspeople with ten rifle-toting American soldiers, forming a sort of military chorus line, who had clearly been coached to say nothing of interest. (The media-trained equivalent of name, rank, and serial number in Gulf War II was "I'm here to help liberate the Iraqi people" or, as two paratroopers in the 173rd put it, "The Kurdish people are nice," and, "It's all good now.")

"Somewhat annoyed" by the emptiness of the interviews, Nguyen did something that no ordinary American television reporter would even think to do—he instructed his cameraman to back away from the standard close-up of soldiers talking, so that viewers at home would be able to see the choreographed nature of a "completely organized" media event "in the middle of nowhere," with hand-picked G.I.s "trained in two things: parachute jumps and talking without saying much," surrounded by a mini mob of reporters.

Not very newsy in the conventional sense, but, as Nguyen put it, "It was so strange, I had to show it." One might ascribe his innate skepticism to the French educational system, steeped as it is in philosophy, argument, and critical thinking, or simply to the overwhelming opposition in France to the invasion. But I prefer to think that Nguyen was merely innocent, in the best sense of the word. While the great mass of American and other reporters cynically or passively submitted to a Pentagon program called "embedding"—a kind of censorship by envelopment instead of by force—the young Frenchman had entered the theater of war unsupervised by any national authority.

Thus, when I asked Nguyen how he and his colleagues referred to themselves—to distinguish themselves from the "kept" press traveling with the U.S. and British military in the south—he expressed genuine puzzlement. (Twelve years earlier, reporters who wouldn't cooperate with the government's tightly controlled "pool system" were dubbed "unilaterals.") "It wasn't an issue," Nguyen replied. "We just called ourselves journalists." Never having been exposed to the American approach to propaganda and press-release journalism, Nguyen was taken aback to find such sophisticated public relations practices at work in a remote part of the world, far from the media centers of Paris, New York, and Qatar.

Qatar? Yes, the little emirate on the Persian Gulf had subverted Western-imposed rules of war TV with its quasi-governmental, twenty-four-hour news channel, Al Jazeera. In the second Gulf War, the Arab world (indeed most of the world outside the United States) could view its own victims and perpetrators through the eyes of Arab editors, producers, and retired military pundits instead of through the ever more stridently patriotic lens of CNN and its chief cable rivals, MSNBC and the Rupert Murdoch–owned Fox News Channel. (All three cable channels adopted the government slogan "Operation Iraqi Freedom" as their basic war-coverage logo.) Al Jazeera had already distinguished itself to such a degree in Afghanistan, during the U.S. campaign to oust the Taliban and avenge 9/11, that the U.S. Air Force paid the Arab version of CNN the compliment of bombing its Kabul bureau. A regrettable mistake, according to the United States.

But on April 8, 2003, when U.S. warplanes blasted Al

Jazeera's Baghdad bureau, killing journalist Taraq Ayyoub and wounding cameraman Zouhair al-Iraqi, an accident seemed an unlikely explanation. In contrast to the real CNN, the Arab TV channel had continually shown images of bloody corpses (military and civilian), wounded and dismembered women and children, and even Iraqi government footage of dead American soldiers and U.S. prisoners of war, very much alive and very much afraid. Time and again, state-financed and state-supervised Al Jazeera showed up the American media, which, though formally free of government control, often behaved as if it were indeed state-run—on the Soviet model, not the Qatari, British, or French one. Should anyone ever have questioned the existence of a second front in wartime—propaganda and the battle to control information, as opposed to soldiers killing other soldiers—the martyrdom of Al Jazeera should have laid such doubts to rest.

If, by April 2003, war news could be effectively managed in the wilds of Kurdistan, in contemporary Washington the packaging of propaganda had reached an apotheosis. When George Bush Sr. first sold a war against Saddam Hussein, he did so with the assistance of a PR team from Hill & Knowlton, broadcasting gruesome allegations of Kuwaiti babies being torn from incubators by Iraqi soldiers. Twelve years later, the Bush media plan may have lacked what salesmen call the "touchie-feelie" dimension, but it was just as effective in the end. On the second go-round, the casus belli against the Iraqi dictator was presented to a largely unwitting public (and witless media) encased in the cold alloy of 81mm, high-grade aluminum tubes, double-wrapped in the apocalyptic imagining of nuclear holocaust.

Comparing the advertising techniques of 1990–91 and 2002–3, I found nothing in the latter campaign that was as viscerally powerful as the fabrication of the great baby incubator atrocity. But one could cite numerous fraudulent assertions—aluminum tubes in particular—by a Bush II public relations team that scattered Enlightenment notions of reason and logic (to paraphrase Bush I's baby-killing metaphor) like so much firewood across the U.S. Capitol floor.

By the new millennium, government manipulation of public opinion was an old story, but the new President Bush seemed especially gifted in the black arts of publicity and sloganeering. In 1990, Bush I—with brilliant support from a Kuwaiti "witness" named Nayirah, who turned out to be the daughter of the Kuwaiti ambassador to the United States—had harnessed the fake baby-killing story to help drive a reluctant Senate and public into rescuing the Kuwaiti royal family (and, as Bush I's U.S. Trade Representative Carla Hills told me, "to guarantee the right to import oil"). The "liberation" of a tiny emirate that had never known genuine liberty remains one of the great propaganda coups of recent times, and its lessons were not lost on Bush II. But in seeking to "liberate" (and "disarm") Iraq itself from Saddam Hussein and his Baathist Party, the younger Bush and his counselors showed themselves every bit the equals of the father.

In August 1990 the case for war was easier to make—Saddam had, in fact, invaded Kuwait. In 2002, Bush II possessed no such advantage. Except for the far-fetched (and ultimately refuted) connection between the 9/11 hijacker Mohammed Atta and the Iraqi government, the forty-third president's team began its race for congressional war authorization from a standing start. Calling Iraq, Iran, and North Korea the "axis of evil" in his 2002 State of the Union address was catchy, but Bush II had a long way to go to convince the American people—and the United Nations Security Council—of the urgency of his mission.

Fortunately for the president, he was blessed with two of America's best marketing men, Senior Advisor Karl Rove and White House Chief of Staff Andrew Card. So accepted, so ingrained in the culture was the practice of political public relations by 2002 that, unlike in 1990, the White House saw nothing unseemly about running its advertising campaign almost entirely in-house. Thus, it was Card, the former General

Motors executive (rather than a phony spokesman for a front group called, say, Citizens for a Free Iraq), who reminded an impatient media—eager to see the president make good on his menacing remarks back in January—that "from a marketing point of view, you don't introduce new products in August."

With this dictum in mind, Bush's men launched their efforts on September 7 with a story that was a near-total fabrication. The first TV spot of the ad campaign called Regime Change featured George W. Bush and British Prime Minister Tony Blair at Camp David, together asserting the existence of a "new" report from the United Nations International Atomic Energy Agency allegedly stating that Iraq was "six months away" from building a nuclear weapon. Inarticulate to a fault, Bush backtracked moments later from "new" and stated that "when inspectors first went into Iraq and were . . . finally denied access, a report came out of . . . the IAEA that they were six months away from developing a weapon. I don't know what more evidence we need."

For public relations purposes, it hardly mattered that no such IAEA report existed, because almost no one in the press bothered to check out the president's claim. (In the twenty-second paragraph of her account of the press conference, the *Washington Post*'s Karen DeYoung did quote an IAEA spokesman saying, in DeYoung's words, that "the agency has issued no new report," but she didn't confront the White House with this terribly interesting information.) What mattered was the unencumbered rollout of Card and Rove's marketing plan.

Millions of TV viewers saw Bush, tieless and tongue-tied, but nevertheless determined-looking and self-confident, making a completely uncorroborated case for preemptive war. While we contemplate the irony of Bush quoting a United Nations weapons inspection agency that he would later dismiss as ineffective, we need to ask why no more evidence was required than the president's say-so—and why no reporters asked for any.

But the next day more "evidence" suddenly appeared, on the front page of the Sunday *New York Times*. In a disgraceful

piece of stenography, Michael Gordon and Judith Miller inflated
an administration leak into something resembling a prediction
of nuclear armageddon: "More than a decade after Saddam
Hussein agreed to give up weapons of mass destruction, Iraq
. . . has embarked on a worldwide hunt for materials to make
an atomic bomb, Bush administration officials said today."

The key evidence of this reborn A-bomb program was the
attempted purchase of "specially designed aluminum tubes,
which American officials believe were intended as components
of centrifuges to enrich uranium." Mysteriously, none of these
tubes had reached Iraq, but "American officials" wouldn't say
why, citing "the sensitivity of the intelligence."

Gordon and Miller were careful to attribute their information to anonymous "administration officials." But in keeping
with the promotional tone adopted by the media over the next
eight months, the *Times* people couldn't resist crossing the line
into commentary. After nodding to administration "critics"
who favored containment of Hussein, they wrote this astonishing paragraph:

> Still, Mr. Hussein's dogged insistence on pursuing his nu-
> clear ambitions, along with what defectors described in in-
> terviews as Iraq's push to improve and expand Baghdad's
> chemical and biological arsenals, have brought Iraq and
> the United States to the brink of war.

That same Sunday, Card's new product introduction moved
into high gear when Vice President Dick Cheney appeared on
NBC's *Meet the Press* to brandish Saddam's supposed nuclear
threat in front of an audience of more than four million viewers. Prompted by a helpful host named Tim Russert, Cheney
cited as supporting evidence—what else?—the aluminum tubes
story in that morning's edition of the *New York Times*—a story
leaked either by Cheney himself or by his White House associates. Russert: "Aluminum tubes." Cheney: "Specifically aluminum tubes." This gave the allegations about Hussein's nuclear

program a certain ring of independent confirmation: "There's a story in the *New York Times* this morning," said Cheney. "And I want to attribute *[sic]* the *Times*."

Did it matter that in the following months, aluminum tubes as weapons of mass destruction were discredited time and again? Did it matter that former U.S. weapons inspector David Albright told CBS's *60 Minutes* on December 8 (during a program in which I participated) that "people who understood gas centrifuges almost uniformly felt that these tubes were not specific to gas centrifuge use [for production of enriched uranium]"—that the administration was "selectively picking information to bolster a case that the Iraqi nuclear threat was more imminent than it is, and, in essence, scare people"? Would the *Times* publish one of its famous "clarifications" (as it did for its erroneous coverage of accused spy Wen Ho Lee)* based on IAEA chief Mohamed ElBaradei's January 9 and March 7 reports insisting that there was no evidence that the 81mm tubes were intended for anything other than conventional rocket production?

As for "defectors" with special knowledge of Saddam's elusive chemical weapons stockpile, did Miller and Gordon— or indeed anyone in the mainstream U.S. media—take proper note of *Newsweek*'s exclusive on March 3, 2003, just before the outbreak of war? In it, John Barry reported that Iraq's most important defector, Hussein Kamel, who had run Saddam's nuclear and biological weapons program, had told the CIA and UN weapons inspectors in the summer of 1995 "that after the gulf war, Iraq destroyed all its chemical and biological weapons stocks and the missiles to deliver them" because they wanted no evidence lying around if American troops drove all the way to Baghdad.

---

* Lee, a Chinese American scientist, was fired from the Los Alamos nuclear weapons laboratory in March 1999 and imprisoned for 283 days after being falsely accused of spying for the Chinese government. The journalist Lars-Erik Nelson denounced the *Times*'s role in railroading Lee, and on September 25, 2000, the paper published a long apology, of sorts.

And what of Saddam's overall nuclear procurement program? When ElBaradei told the UN Security Council on March 7 that supporting documents (presumably supplied by the U.S. and Britain) detailing Iraqi attempts to buy uranium from Niger were forgeries, the *Times* offered no correction of the Gordon-Miller report. Perhaps the reporters still believed their own scare story: "Hard-liners are alarmed that American intelligence underestimated the pace and scale of Iraq's nuclear program before Baghdad's defeat in the gulf war," they wrote in their September 8 article. "The first sign of a 'smoking gun,' they argue, may be a mushroom cloud."

The nuclear red herring wasn't the only weapon in George W. Bush's arsenal of mass deception. Following his father's example, he floated his own uncorroborated stories of atrocities. On October 7, 2002, in a widely covered speech in Cincinnati, he declared that "on Saddam Hussein's orders, opponents have been decapitated, wives and mothers of political opponents have been systematically raped as a method of intimidation, and political prisoners have been forced to watch their own children being tortured."

None of these sensational accusations appeared in the dossiers of Human Rights Watch, the most reliable of the humanitarian watchdog organizations present in Iraq. I had to go to the politically self-interested State Department human rights report to find anything approaching Bush's lurid description, and then I found only references to alleged prostitutes being decapitated. The State Department did mention the rape of "female relatives" as a method of political intimidation, but the backup looked shaky.

Effective propaganda relies on half-truths as well as fabrications, and on the conflation of disparate "facts." Saddam did indeed have a horrible and well-documented record of human rights violations, which were ignored by the American government in the years when he served as a U.S. client. But in Gulf War II, human rights seemed played out as an effective tool for mobilizing public opinion. Who cared about some foreigners' dead babies when you feared for your own babies at home? In the era of post-9/11 panic, the A-bomb, the anthrax canister, and the smallpox shell received top billing in the president's PR theatrical.

As a consequence, tall tales designed to frighten the public onto a war footing (rather than to prick their consciences) proliferated during the prewar sales season. When one story failed to stick, another was quickly put forward. To list the most important:

> Secretary of State Colin Powell tells the Security Council of a "poison factory" in northern Iraq linked to Osama bin Laden's al Qaeda organization. When reporters visit a compound of crude structures and find nothing of the kind, an unidentified State Department official responds by telling the *New York Times* that "a 'poison factory' is a term of art."

> Powell cites new "British intelligence" on Saddam's spying capabilities; British Channel 4 reveals that this new dossier is plagiarized from a journal article by a graduate student in California.

> Just days before a massive series of antiwar demonstrations, the administration raises its terrorist threat level to "orange," causing widespread anxiety and frantic purchases of duct tape to seal homes against gas attacks; *ABC News* reports that the latest terror alert was based largely on "fabricated" information provided by a captured al Qaeda informant who subsequently failed a lie-detector test.

> Powell announces a new threat from an Iraqi airborne "drone"; the drone, patched together with tape and powered by a small engine with a wooden propeller, turns out to have a maximum range of five miles.

> Apparently fresh out of ideas, Powell returns to the Security Council on March 7 brandishing . . . aluminum tubes! "There is new information . . . available to us and . . . the IAEA about a European country where Iraq was found

shopping for these kinds of tubes . . . [tubes] more exact by
a factor of 50 percent or more than those usually specified
for rocket motor casings." When I inquire at the State
Department about the name of the European country, I am
informed that said country wishes to remain anonymous
(as did Nayirah al-Sabah twelve years earlier). When I ask
the IAEA about Powell's "new information," I am told that
ElBaradei's analysis, presented before Powell's declaration,
was unchanged: "Extensive field investigation and document analysis have failed to uncover any evidence that Iraq
intended to use these 81mm tubes for any project other than
the reverse-engineering of rockets."

Powell's and the administration's relentless disinformation
campaign prompted a career U.S. diplomat, John Brady Kies-
ling, to resign in protest. In a letter to Powell, he wrote that
"we have not seen such systematic distortion of intelligence,
such systematic manipulation of American opinion, since the
war in Vietnam."

The few corrections and refutations of the White House
line were too little and too late for American democracy. Enter-
prising reporting was needed from the moment of the Bush-
Blair PR gambit on September 7 until the early hours of
October 11, the day Congress abdicated its warmaking authority and essentially told the president he could attack Iraq whenever he felt like it. During that crucial period, I was able to find
only one newspaper story that straightforwardly countered the
White House nuclear propaganda; it appeared, of all places, in
the right-wing pro-administration *Washington Times,* owned
by the Reverend Sun Myung Moon. On September 27, a very
competent piece by Joseph Curl pointed out not only that there
was no "new report" by the IAEA saying Saddam was six
months away from making a nuclear weapon but also that the
agency had never issued a report predicting any time frame.
What's more, when IAEA inspectors pulled out of Iraq in December 1998, after a U.S.-provoked dispute between Iraq and

the UN over the makeup of inspection teams, spokesman Mark Gwozdecky told Curl, "We had concluded that we had neutralized their nuclear-weapons program. We had confiscated their fissile material. We had destroyed all their key buildings and equipment." Curl's scoop was buried on page 16. Better play might have qualified him for a journalism prize.

How did the Bush administration get away with it? George Orwell would likely have blamed "slovenliness" in the language, as in the phrase "weapons of mass destruction." As the Iraqi nuclear threat evaporated and attention shifted to biological weapons and poison gas, Bush continued to assert the existence of a hidden arsenal of "weapons of mass destruction." Less sophisticated citizens thought the president was still talking about the kind of bomb that destroyed Hiroshima and Nagasaki, as though all "weapons of mass destruction" were the same. Lethal as they are, biological and chemical weapons are very unlikely to kill in the same numbers as nuclear weapons, but Bush got a free ride on sloppy English—and sloppy journalism.*

Slipshod reporting did not end with the removal of Saddam from power. After the war, when chemical and biological weapons appeared impossible to find in post-Saddam Iraq, the *Times*'s Judith Miller continued her crusade to prove the White House case against Saddam, on this occasion in the company of a newly formed investigative "team" calling itself Mobile Exploitation Team Alpha, attached to the 101st Airborne Division. Miller's first dispatch was printed on the front page of the paper on April 21—headlined "Illicit Arms Kept Till Eve of War, An Iraqi Scientist Is Said to Assert"—and it was extraordinary, not for what it revealed about Iraqi chemical weapons but for showing how far the media had stooped to do the gov-

---

* Survivors of the World War II Allied bombings of Hamburg, Dresden, and Tokyo might also have wondered how "conventional" bombs came to be exempted from the "weapons of mass destruction" category.

ernment's bidding. Acknowledging that "the failure to find such weapons has become a political issue in Washington," the article described how Miller came to be the journalistic confidante of "MET Alpha":

> Under the terms of her accreditation to report on the activities of MET Alpha, this reporter was not permitted to interview the scientist or visit his home. Nor was she permitted to write about the discovery of the scientist for three days, and the copy was then submitted for a check by military officials.
>
> Those officials asked that details of what chemicals were uncovered be deleted. They said they feared that such information could jeopardize the scientist's safety by identifying the part of the weapons program where he worked. . . .
>
> While this reporter could not interview the scientist, she was permitted to see him from a distance at the sites where he said that material from the arms program was buried.
>
> Clad in nondescript clothes and a baseball cap, he pointed to several spots in the sand where he said chemical precursors and other weapons material were buried. This reporter also accompanied MET Alpha on the search for him and was permitted to examine a letter written in Arabic that he slipped to American soldiers offering them information about the program and seeking their protection.

Gone were minimal standards of corroboration and skepticism (what danger did the "scientist" face with Saddam removed from power and possibly dead?); indeed, gone were minimal levels of journalistic pride.

Perhaps it was asking too much to expect the media to halt the tidal wave of disinformation before the Iraq war, particularly in the absence of organized opposition from the Democratic Party (although someone might at least have thought to question the Bushes' switch from Hitler to Stalin as the metaphor for ultimate evil).* With or without the Judith Millers of the press, it has always been easy for politicians to have their way with the public. Peter Teeley, Bush I's press secretary when he was vice president, explained it this way: "You can say anything you want during a [televised] debate, and 80 million people hear it." If "anything" turns out to be false and journalists correct it? "So what?" says Teeley. "Maybe 200 people read it, or 2,000 or 20,000."

Adolf Hitler's henchman Hermann Göring was more specific. "Why, of course, the *people* don't want war," he told the U.S. intelligence officer G. M. Gilbert at the Nuremberg war crimes tribunal. "Voice or no voice, the people can always be brought to the bidding of the leaders. . . . All you have to do is tell them they are being attacked and denounce the pacifists for lack of patriotism and exposing the country to greater danger. It works the same in any country."

The invasion of Iraq began on March 20 with a bombardment of Baghdad, apparently intended to kill Saddam Hussein in the first hours of battle. But the assassination attempt failed, and a joint American-British ground invasion proceeded from bases in Kuwait. Things did not go quite as smoothly as planned.

Coming up the elevator of my office building toward the end of the first week of "Operation Iraqi Freedom," a slightly crazed-looking bicycle messenger spied me and, perhaps sensing a sympathetic ear, blurted out: "We're getting our asses kicked over there, and they're not telling us what's going on."

I have never been much for man-in-the-street generalizations, but my excitable new acquaintance was clearly expressing something significant about the media coverage of Gulf War II; namely, that expectations and reality had collided in a way not seen in America since the fall of Saigon in 1975.

---

* This tactical propaganda shift—Bush the Elder had repeatedly compared Saddam to Hitler in the period leading up to the Gulf War—was test-marketed in Bush the Younger's Cincinnati speech on October 7, 2002. The White House may have feared that overuse of the Hitler-Saddam comparison, given Bush the Elder's notable reluctance to overthrow the Iraqi dictator in 1991, would invite ridicule.

Except for the brief moment of clarity brought on by the photograph of a U.S. Army Ranger's corpse being dragged through the streets of Mogadishu, Somalia, in 1993, Americans had pretty much forgotten that war is about death—the bloody kind. And that the natives, whoever might be their rulers, often don't take kindly to the presence of foreigners with guns.

Which isn't to say that the United States and Britain were ever losing the battle in a conventional military sense, nor that the coverage by embedded reporters was particularly penetrating or accurate. (Indeed, embedded reporters blew the story out of proportion when the drive for Baghdad briefly stalled.) But so much PR effort had been devoted to promoting American military invincibility during the prewar sales campaign that the ordinary citizen (and journalist) could have been excused for forming the impression that "shock and awe"—a Pentagon slogan for the psychological effect of massive aerial bombardment—could, all by itself, conquer another country.

Certain things hadn't changed about American war correspondents since the first gulf conflict. Credulity and misplaced patriotism remained the rule; dispassionate reporting meant to inform rather than inspire remained the exception. In the first few days of fighting, I happened to be on the French side of the Caribbean island of St. Martin and was able to compare coverage by the BBC, two French channels, and CNN. Invariably, the French and British approach was suitably sober, while the CNN reporters and anchors often seemed juvenile in their enthusiasm, thrilled to be along for the ride.

On the first Saturday of the war, Walter Rodgers of CNN actually said he was having "great fun," in response to anchor Aaron Brown's unwarranted praise for Rodgers's "terrific . . . reporting." (This included such extrasensory observations as "There were whole families standing up there waving white pieces of cloth that looked like pillow cases indicating they surrender. They had no hostile feelings.") Indeed, it must have been exhilarating to be racing northward in the company of General George Custer's storied 7th Cavalry Regiment with the desert wind in your face—as long as no one was shooting at you. (Like Rodgers, Custer enjoyed the adrenaline rush of battle, right up to the bitter end. Like Custer, Rodgers didn't speak the language of the natives.)

But on March 22, with sandstorms and counterattacks by Saddam's paramilitary *fedayeen,* came shock, if not awe. Even skeptics like myself had expected to see at least some Iraqis welcoming GIs with grateful smiles; instead we were shown a surprisingly hostile landscape. (They're shooting at our guys? They don't love us? Why isn't there a Shiite uprising in Basra?)

In spite of all the "embeds," most American war reporting was, by government design, remote from combat—as-told-to reconstructions by spokesmen in the rear. These "briefings" took place mostly on a stage set in Doha, Qatar, which seemed custom-built, at the reported price of $250,000, for U.S. Central Command's new media star, the distinguished-looking and telegenic Brigadier General Vincent Brooks. As handsome and unflappably media-trained as Brooks was, and no matter how many videos of smart bombs were shown precisely hitting their targets, the absence of hard news forced the media to run endless tape loops depicting lonely soldiers far from home, supplies being loaded and unloaded, and armored vehicles and infantry moving from hither to yon. For the most part, the "news" was uninformed speculation by ex-generals and talking heads doing their best to emulate the color commentators of the National Football League. (Underscoring the lack of real news about fighting, the *New York Times* reported on April 11, in a story with a Washington dateline, that "out of sight of television cameras, some of the heaviest fighting in Iraq has been raging for nearly three weeks near the town of Qaim on the Syrian border, where American Green Berets and British commandos have been attacking units of Iraq's Special Republican Guard and Special Security Services.")

Nevertheless, Ted Koppel's presentation of two Iraqi corpses on ABC television revealed more about the consequences of organized, state-sponsored violence than was seen in all six weeks of the first Gulf War, with its tightly controlled pool coverage. And a few reporters, like *Newsday*'s Letta Tayler, actually described combat and death the way it's supposed to be done: "It was kind of nice to get it out of the way," Marine Cpl. Mark Hylen told her when she asked about his first killing of an Iraqi. She observed, "He paused for a minute, then appeared to dismiss whatever thought was emerging. 'Screw him,' he said. 'He died.'"

Tayler even dared to quote U.S. Marines the way they really talked, citing frequent references to "nuking" Iraqis, who were known as "ragheads" and "camel jockeys." In one choice interview, Lance Cpl. Christopher Akins sang, "Raghead, raghead can't you see? This old war ain't ——— to me." Tayler wanted to know what constituted a raghead, and Akins replied, "Anybody who actively opposes the United States of America's way. . . . If a little kid actively opposes my way of life, I'd call him a raghead too."

Gems like Tayler's were a rarity, and they didn't go unnoticed by the officers entrusted with her supervision. "I chalked up most of these comments to youthful machismo," she later wrote with touching primness. "But because the remarks suggested an enormous cultural chasm between invaders and invaded, I reluctantly felt obliged to report them. After my article was published, Capt. Myle Hammond, the Golf Company commander, threatened to kick me out of his unit in a move I interpreted as an attempt to soften my reporting."

Although the American media might have been a little freer to show Iraqi corpses than they were in 1991, American casualties were another matter altogether. The Pentagon's hosting of about six hundred reporters evidently engendered enough goodwill, or gratitude, with the media bosses stateside that self-censorship seemed to accomplish the same public relations mission that overt censorship had during Gulf War I. Little wonder, then, that Secretary of Defense Donald Rumsfeld remarked after the war that manipulating the media was a simple matter of carrot and stick: "I think there's not anything you can do, with our Constitution, which is a good one, that allows for free speech and free press, about [negative war coverage] except to, you know, penalize the . . . television [news shows] and the newspapers that don't give good advice and reward those people that do give good advice."

The new public relations strategy of welcoming reporters at the front—rather than arresting them—worked brilliantly overall. Embedded reporters were invited to join their units well before the war started, a tactic that not only promoted feelings of comradeship but also resulted in dozens of positive feature stories about the rigors of military training.

The collaborative spirit of the embedding system lasted throughout the war. Except for ABC, which obscured the faces of the corpses, American TV networks and newspapers declined to show the gruesome and upsetting Iraqi government footage (broadcast on Al Jazeera) of dead American soldiers caught in an ambush on March 23. Live POWs got somewhat more play, most notoriously in the made-for-TV, utterly fraudulent "rescue" of Private Jessica Lynch. But in the main, the U.S. media treated war reporting less as a constitutional responsibility to inform the citizenry than as a matter of taste. The exception proved the rule. The media's repeated depiction of a horrifically mutilated survivor of the war, a twelve-year-old Iraqi boy named Ali Ismail Abbas—"Stumpy," as he was privately referred to by reporters—served two purposes: to give a false impression that gritty, realistic reportage was the norm, and to ease the guilty consciences of Americans. Stumpy's missing limbs paradoxically offered hope and redemption; this innocent victim would be "rescued." He would receive the best possible medical care from the very people who had disfigured and orphaned him.

TV was easy to ridicule, but the highbrow press was similarly squeamish about showing the viscera of war. On March 27, morning newspapers everywhere carried front-page stories about the explosions (likely caused by errant American bombs) in a working-class neighborhood of Baghdad that killed at least seventeen civilians and wounded forty-five. The *New York Times* and Paris's *Le Figaro* both ran photographs of the devastation taken by Goran Tomasevic of Reuters. For its front page, the *Times* selected Tomasevic's color picture of an anguished young man, very much alive, in front of the burning wreckage of two cars; on page 3 *Le Figaro* ran a different shot by Tomasevic in black and white, this one of a hideously charred corpse, the face partially visible, prostrate in front an anguished child.

As if to compensate, above its Tomasevic photo the *Times* printed a staff photographer's image of a dead Iraqi soldier, lying on a dirt road, with a U.S. Marine in the distance, back to the camera. The Iraqi was fully clothed, wearing a headdress and scarf, almost picturesque in death. But the *Times*'s artistically rendered corpse carried none of the brutal impact of the one published in *Le Figaro*. Once again, self-censorship obviated official censorship. (In another example of U.S. media fastidiousness, photographs of GIs frisking Shiite women in their black robes, which outraged Arab newspaper readers, never appeared in mainstream American news outlets.)

Moreover, the *Times*'s John Burns demonstrated that operating free of U.S. military pressure guaranteed neither good journalism nor good writing. Burns had apparently defied his bosses by staying in Baghdad after the Pentagon warned reporters to get out. As a result, he became the most institutionally important (and self-important) newspaper reporter in the Iraqi capital, as well as the one most often interviewed by American television networks with no correspondent in place. Burns was subject to Iraqi government control of his movements, but if the following passage from his April 3 dispatch is any indication, he was free to write all manner of purple promotional copy for the U.S. imperium. "To have been in Berlin or Dresden or Hamburg in the last months of World War II would surely have been more ghastly," he wrote, "but American air power, as the 21st century begins, is a terrible swift sword that strikes with a suddenness, a devastation and a precision, in most cases, that moves even agnostics to reach for words associated with the power of Gods."

Paradoxically, war reporting tends to improve if the military situation stagnates or deteriorates, in part because G.I.s, officers, and military bureaucrats start to worry out loud within earshot of journalists. This is good news for the American people. Realistic war coverage is the best war coverage, not just because it has the potential to horrify, and thus make future wars less likely, but because it's better for soldiers and civilians alike. Candor can save lives because it puts political pressure on the civilian commanders back home to fight more intelligently and at least to think about trying to minimize casualties.

For a time, candor was seeping out everywhere, as in the March 27 admission by Lt. General William Wallace that "the enemy we're fighting is a bit different from the one we wargamed against." Wallace's remark startled the civilian establishment in Washington and emboldened the normally docile Pentagon press corps into challenging the military strategy of Donald Rumsfeld, who responded as petulantly as any dictatorial CEO contradicted by a subordinate. As with other government bureaucrats, when military officers start complaining to journalists (as they did to Seymour Hersh in the *New Yorker*), it usually means they're covering their backsides by talking over their bosses' heads to the politicians and the people.

Although things never reached the point of Vietnam-style five o'clock follies (as U.S. reporters dubbed the daily military press briefing in Saigon), the nervousness of the military began to show. All the kindly treatment of the "embeds" began to look a little hollow after four "unilateral" journalists (two Israeli and two Portuguese) were roughed up and expelled from Iraq by the U.S. Army because they supposedly posed a "security threat." On the same day that the U.S. Air Force killed the Al Jazeera reporter, an American tank fired at the Palestine Hotel—known to be full of reporters—killing Taras Protsyuk of Reuters and Jose Couso of Spain's Telecino television. In response to a protest letter from the Committee to Protect Journalists, Pentagon spokesperson Victoria Clarke denied that the journalists were fired on intentionally, repeating the military line that the troops in both cases were returning hostile fire. Then she condescendingly reminded Joel Simon of the CPJ that life is unfair. "War," wrote Clarke, "by its very nature is tragic and sad." Such meaningless prose explained why Clarke's last job, prior to becoming Assistant Secretary of Defense for Public Affairs, was as general manager of Hill & Knowlton's Washington, D.C., office.

During Vietnam, a "credibility gap" developed when military claims diverged more and more widely from the obvious reality on the ground. With dozens of reporters in Baghdad and hundreds more with the American military, such a gap developed only briefly in the second Gulf War—at least until the president declared the "end of major combat" on May 1.

Skepticism—indeed standard reporting—in the U.S. media may well have gone the way of the passenger pigeon. Why do I say this? Because that putatively tough liberal, Dan Rather of CBS News, often uses bird-extinction metaphors (see chapter 6 below) to decry the decline of contrarian reporting over the past thirty years. His criticism rings a little false, since Rather largely ceased posing difficult questions to politicians after the resignation of Richard Nixon in 1974. After the events of 9/11, Rather fell completely into line, declaring his unquestioning fealty to President Bush on the David Letterman show, offering a quasi-religious homily to U.S. troops stationed in Kuwait after Bush's January 2003 State of the Union address, and, during the fighting, emphatically reminding the public that he was unashamed of his pro-American bias.

After the war symbolically ended on April 9, 2003—with the staged-for-TV toppling, by a U.S. armored vehicle, of a statue of Saddam Hussein in central Baghdad—Rather earned an accolade that earlier in his career might have embarrassed him. It was the grade assigned to his coverage of the Iraq invasion by the prowar, right-wing Media Research Center. Jingoistic viewers inclined to think of Rather as a dangerously liberal subversive were no doubt surprised to learn that the media icon received the highest grade of any journalist or network, a B-plus. Even Rupert Murdoch's flag-wavers at Fox got only a B. Surely, it pays to do what Rather once pejoratively referred to as suck-up journalism.

I've long resisted overarching left-wing theories about the editorial motivations of the American media (allegedly conservative and usually progovernment), preferring to examine individual cases. But on April 21, after weeks of "support the troops" propaganda on television and in the newspapers, I started to think that perhaps the leftists had a point. How else to explain the advertisement printed at no cost in that day's edition of the *New York Times,* sponsored by the 9/11 PR concoction known as the Office of Homeland Security? Topped by a photograph of Homeland Security majordomo Tom Ridge, the headline read: "You've probably wondered, 'Is there anything we can do to protect ourselves from the threat of terrorism?' Here's your answer." The ad appeared the same day as Judith Miller's fable about the Iraqi scientist in the baseball cap who supposedly pointed to evidence of chemical weapons. Both were free advertising for the Bush administration and its public rationale for war.

But the disarmament of Iraq to achieve domestic security was never more than a pretext; the real motivations were conquest, geopolitics, and oil. And Ridge's new bureaucracy was little more than an advertising slogan, just as Miller's news story was little more than government propaganda. So what were the *Times* and its publisher, Arthur Sulzberger Jr., doing, if not turning over its good name for use by the state? Always jealous of its position as the paper of record, the ultra-respectable paragon of objectivity seemed to be leading the rest of the media over a precipice, to a land of somnambulance from which it might never return.

It was this sense of a hypnotized press that caused a troubled Ellen Goodman, without naming names, to raise a singularly important question about the Bush administration's propaganda campaign for war in her column in the *Boston Globe* —"how we got from *there* to *here.*" Writing shortly before the invasion, the syndicated columnist explained that "there" was innocent 9/11 victimhood at the hands of religious fanatics; "here" was a bullying superpower bent on destroying a secular dictator. I assumed that a journalist as astute as Goodman would reveal at least part of the answer—that the American media provided free transportation en route; that the success of "Bush's PR War," as her column was titled, was largely dependent on a compliant media that uncritically repeated every fraudulent administration claim about the threat posed to America by Saddam Hussein. But she didn't.*

It was left to a foreigner to sum up the precepts of American war journalism. Russell Smith of the Toronto *Globe and Mail* was writing about the combat coverage, but he could just as well have been describing the propaganda-soaked prelude to war. Smith's was as good a critique as I could find, and it deserves special mention:

> The coverage of this war in the press and on television has been disgusting. North American reporting, and in particular on the US television stations, has been cravenly submissive to the Pentagon and the White House.
>
> The worst culprit was also the one with the most "embedded reporters" and the most exciting live footage, and so it was, sadly, the one I watched most of the time: CNN, the voice of Centcom [U.S. Central Command]. CNN was more irritating than the gleefully patriotic Fox News channel because CNN has a pretense of objectivity. It pretends to be run by journalists. And yet it dutifully uses all the language chosen by people in charge of "media relations" at the Pentagon. It describes the exploding of Iraqi soldiers

---

* Also absent from Goodman's account was any mention of Saudi Arabian religious fanatic Osama bin Laden, the CIA client turned revolutionary, who stood to gain the most—in recruits and stature—from the overthrow of his secular enemy Saddam Hussein.

in their bunkers as "softening up"; it describes slaughtered Iraqi units as being "degraded"; some announcers have even repeated the egregious Pentagon neologism "attrited" (to mean "we are slowly killing as many of them as we can"). I don't know if I'm more offended by the insidiousness of this euphemism or by the absurdity of its grammar.

After noting that "the graphic reality of 'degradation' is a large pile of dismembered bodies," Smith reminded his readers that "there were no embedded reporters with the Iraqi troops. It's hard to get a TV camera into a line of trenches that is being pureed by bombs. Instead of reporting that this peripeteia in the war's narrative was happening, and that it entailed thousands of deaths leading to the rapid collapse of the Iraqi regime, the television and the press simply downsized the story. This is the real meaning of 'degradation.'"

Not quite the whole meaning, though. In both gulf wars, the degradation unto sleep of the U.S. media was largely self-inflicted. So, when al Qaeda struck the Western residential compound in Riyadh, Saudi Arabia, on May 12, killing thirty-four people, including at least eight U.S. citizens, the question could be asked: was there any American reporter awake to cover the real story?

By December, with the number of U.S. war dead approaching five hundred, the total of wounded topping two thousand, and an Iraqi guerrilla movement seeming to grow stronger by the day, it finally dawned on some in the media that "liberation" might actually mean occupation and a very long and violent conflict. Nobody was yet seriously counting the thousands of deceased Arabs—innocent noncombatants as well as anti-U.S. rebels—but the outline of a new "Vietnam Syndrome" had clearly emerged on the political horizon, most obviously in the newest version of Pentagonspeak.

During the Vietnam War, Johnson administration officials, particularly in the Pentagon, frequently employed euphemisms—"protective reaction," "body counts," "kill ratios," and the like—to obscure the failures and destructiveness of the U.S. military. This mangling of political language was most famously crystallized in the metaphoric slogan, often attributed to General William Westmoreland, that the government could see "the light at the end of the tunnel" of the U.S. war effort—when precisely the opposite was true.*

Such fantasy phrasing was encouraged by Lyndon Johnson's supreme arrogance—an arrogance that, ironically, permitted a great deal of truth to come home from the front. LBJ seemed really to believe that he was entirely in the right; thus, according to someone who knew him well (but prefers anonymity), "it would never have occurred to him" to impose formal censorship on war reporters, to cover up the daily reality of mass death in an overt way.

Now, in Iraq, American corpses are being repatriated not in body bags or coffins but in aluminum "transfer cases," which some Pentagon officials loosely refer to as "transfer tubes." Bush I had banned photographers from the U.S. military morgue at Dover Air Force Base during the first Gulf War in order to diminish unpleasant associations between the video reenactments of battle shown on television and the real thing. At the end of 2003, I hadn't found anyone in the press who had actually seen these high-tech caskets, so no one could tell me if they had observed any light at the end of the tube.

New York City, December 12, 2003

* Historians disagree on whether Westmoreland, supreme commander in Vietnam, ever uttered the phrase "light at the end of the tunnel." Don Oberdorfer's book *Tet* reports that the general used it in an internal memo to his staff. Professor John F. Guilmartin of Ohio State University calls the phrase "essentially, an urban legend" that was exploited by the antiwar movement once it entered the public domain. He says "light at the end of the tunnel" first surfaced in connection with Vietnam in a May 1953 issue of *Time* magazine, when it was the French who were trying to talk their way out of the quagmire. The *Time* dispatch quoted an officer on the staff of General Henri Navarre.

ACKNOWLEDGMENTS
TO THE FIRST EDITION

I could not have written this book in the time allotted without the help of my extraordinarily talented researcher, Scott Anderson. Besides collecting information, conducting interviews, and checking facts, Scott made important suggestions that improved the manuscript. I'm also greatly indebted to Diane Kraft, my assistant at *Harper's Magazine*. Diane performed the difficult tasks of keeping me organized and maintaining her sense of humor while under intense deadline pressure. (She turned out to be a pretty good reporter as well.)

Sara Blackburn edited the manuscript thoroughly and intelligently, and the copy editor, Angela Palmisono, did crucially important work for which I'm very grateful. Erika Goldman gave me the original idea, and my close friends Vince Passaro and Dan Janison provided moral support and useful criticism of my second draft. Beth Passaro contributed research, and Sally Singer of Hill and Wang and Helene Atwan at Farrar, Straus and Giroux expertly guided me through the unfamiliar terrain of book publishing. My agent, Denise Shannon, supported this project enthusiastically from the start.

Every writer can benefit from a mentor; I'm fortunate in having had three: Lewis Lapham, Earl Shorris, and the late Walter Karp. They gave me the inspiration that made it possible to complete this undertaking. But inspiration without complementary tools can be next to useless, and I came to this task at least partially equipped thanks to a variety of newspaper people who taught me the reporter's trade and

gave me the chance to practice it. They include Jonathan
Laing, Frederick C. Klein, the late John McWethy, Dennis
Stern, Stuart Loory, Terry Shaffer, the late Charles (Chip)
Magnus, Leon Pitt, Anne Henderson, Gerald Loughren, and,
not least, my friends on the *Columbia Daily Spectator*. Spe-
cial thanks go to Tom Moffett, Paul Varian, and Bobby Ray
Miller, who forced me to become a faster writer when I
thought I was already pretty fast.

Journalists dream of working for a publisher who backs
them up and gives them encouragement at just the right
moments, but few of us ever get that lucky. On this book I
was privileged to have the best: Arthur J. Rosenthal.

As a publisher myself, I have the advantage of working
at *Harper's Magazine*, where the existence of a supportive
and highly competent staff permitted me to take the time I
needed to write. Ellen Ryder and Ellen Rosenbush helped
especially by reading the manuscript and the galleys.

Finally, I'd like to thank my parents. From them I received the habit of independence—without a doubt, a reporter's best friend.

SECOND
FRONT

CHAPTER 1

Cutting the Deal

Some men are pleased to give orders and some men are pleased to take orders.

—EARL SHORRIS
Scenes from Corporate Life

ON A DRIZZLY August morning in 1990, eight days after Iraqi forces invaded Kuwait, the Washington bureau chiefs of the four major U.S. television networks presented themselves at the imposing Virginia home of His Royal Highness Prince Bandar Bin Sultan Bin Abdul Aziz, Saudi Arabia's ambassador to the United States. In another era, such a meeting might have been construed as an offer of tribute from grandees representing the commercial interests of the civilized West in exchange for trade concessions from a primitive Oriental despot. But by the fifth decade of the post-1945 American republic, the power balance had shifted to the detriment of the West, and the representatives of CBS, NBC, ABC, and CNN possessed considerably less leverage—and proportionately less money—than their forebears.

To be sure, the visiting potentates—Barbara Cohen of CBS, Timothy Russert of NBC, George Watson of ABC, and Bill Headline of CNN—were still very important people. The networks' nearly $10 billion in revenue in 1990 and their combined evening-news audience of forty million voting-age Americans were enough to make even a sheikh stand up and take notice. But these grandees were neither—as William Randolph Hearst might have been—in the position nor in the mood to dictate terms to the prince. Rather, they were in the uncomfortable posture of "pleading," in the words of ABC's Watson, for visas to Saudi Arabia so that their correspondents might be allowed to witness the largest American military intervention since the war in Vietnam.

In Washington, in 1990, this should not have been surprising to anyone. Prince Bandar, a nephew of King Fahd, was rich in his own right, and the income of the four networks hardly compared with his country's $45 billion in oil revenue that year. Moreover, King Fahd was paying hard cash for the luxury of securing an American defense against a possible invasion by Iraqi forces, and nothing in Saudi tradition called for the attendance of reporters at royal spectaculars. Not a single foreign journalist was based in Saudi Arabia when Saddam Hussein's tanks rolled into Kuwait on August 2; foreign news agencies always relied on heavily censored stringers to get news from the realm of the al-Saud family. Saudi Arabia could be accurately described as one of the most hostile nations in the world to the notion of press freedom. The kingdom never signed the United Nations' International Covenant on Civil and Political Rights, and its own media are as tightly controlled as Cuba's. In short, according to the censorship monitoring group Article 19, Saudi Arabia is a place where "freedom of the press is totally absent."

Such conditions do not and did not make for a congenial environment in which to practice journalism, a reality that could scarcely have escaped the notice of the television bureau chiefs. What they perhaps did not know as they entered the prince's foyer that August day was the extent to which their own government admired the press policies of the Saudi monarchy. For as the media managers would learn to their dismay five months later at a stormy meeting in a Pentagon auditorium, the U.S. Department of Defense (and the White House) had more in common with their Saudi brothers-in-

arms—at least where freedom of the press was concerned—
than anyone would then have dared to suggest.

As befits a wealthy political aristocrat, Prince Bandar
lives in a Georgian-style mansion on Chain Bridge Road in
the exclusive Washington suburb of McLean, Virginia, just
down the street from Senator Edward M. Kennedy. The
prince received the bureau chiefs in his double-height drawing room and seated them around a large coffee table
crowded with silver trinkets of the sort found in a catalog
from Asprey. A servant appeared and took orders for re-
freshments. By all accounts, the prince, who dresses in Western raiments, is thoroughly versed in the ways of the capital.
A former fighter pilot and the son of the Saudi defense minister, Prince Bandar has a grasp of military affairs that is
similarly well informed. His English is excellent, and with
the help of his expensive American lobbyist, Fred Dutton,
so is his understanding of the Washington media.*

For the visitors, the issue was straightforward. The television people wanted more visas, and Bandar was ostensibly
the man who could persuade the government in Riyadh, the
Saudi capital, to grant their request. One may ask why the
media representatives of a nation of 250 million people,
which had offered to spill its citizens' blood in defense of a
kingdom of 16 million subjects, needed to plead for tickets
to the coming conflict. The answer is simple: President Bush,
Secretary of Defense Dick Cheney, and U.S. Central Command wanted the networks to beg on Bandar's doorstep. It
was convenient for the Administration, and would set the
tone for all that was to come.

From the moment Bush committed troops to Saudi Arabia on August 7, the Administration never intended to allow
the press to cover a war in the Persian Gulf in any real sense,

---

* The Saudis paid Dutton about $1.4 million in regular compensation and a
bonus from December 1989 through December 1990.

and it intended to tightly manage what coverage it would permit. The meeting on Chain Bridge Road was thus the opening gambit of a grand ploy, a second front. Strategically, this first move was a brilliant success. In addition to making the newspeople beg, it initiated a program of playing off the various media companies against one another—newspaper against newspaper, network against network, and television against print—all of whom were competing for the meager, carefully doled out table scraps to be known thereafter as "access."

Bill Headline of CNN had requested the meeting with Prince Bandar—after consulting with his colleagues on the television bureau chiefs' special hotline—because Cheney had announced that the American government couldn't simply insist that the Saudis provide more visas for journalists. After all, Cheney pointed out, Saudi Arabia was a sovereign state with its own rules about such matters. And although the Pentagon was preparing to transport to Dhahran, Saudi Arabia, a small national press "pool" with representatives from each news medium—seven from television, five from the news wires, two from newspapers, two from newsmagazines, and one from radio—applications for other journalists would have to be made to the Saudi government.

The four network representatives were cordial and deferential upon entering Bandar's home. As Barbara Cohen remembered it, Fred Dutton and the prince were friendly and cooperative.

"I think [the prince] believed that to get public support in America for this venture, he needed the press to generate public support," she recalled. The prince, as it turned out, need not have worried. He had powerful allies in the government, the U.S. public relations industry, and the media, who were already hard at work in Tampa, Washington, D.C., and New York City on manufacturing enthusiasm for greater American intervention.

But why were the media envoys so willing to plead with

the prince? Why didn't they bring the formidable and collective weight of the American journalism establishment to bear on a U.S. Administration that had regularly professed devotion to the First Amendment and the importance of an informed citizenry? For now it is sufficient to know that they did not, and that the rendezvous at Bandar's home set the stage for the media's colossal defeat at the hands of the United States government.

Around the time the network bureau chiefs were chatting with Prince Bandar in McLean on August 10, navy captain Ron Wildermuth was seated in his office at U.S. Central Command in Tampa drafting a secret ten-page memo soon to be known as Annex Foxtrot. In a belated story the following May, *The New York Times* explained that Annex Foxtrot "laid out a blueprint for the [military] operation's public information policy." This policy, the *Times* reported, "began with a decision by the Administration's most senior officials, including President Bush, to manage the information flow in a way that supported the operation's political goals and avoided the perceived mistakes of Vietnam."

Captain Wildermuth was General H. Norman Schwarzkopf's chief public relations man, and Annex Foxtrot emphasized one rule above all others for media coverage of what was then known as Operation Desert Shield: "News media representatives will be escorted at all times. Repeat, at all times."

The military would stick unyieldingly to the basic principles of Annex Foxtrot in the coming conflict. And while it may be an overstatement to call the Administration's plan for censoring the media unprecedented, the *Times* was largely correct in its much-after-the-fact assertion that "the Gulf War marked this century's first major conflict where the policy was to confine reporters to escorted pools that sharply curtailed when and how they could talk to the troops."

A reading of the now-declassified Annex Foxtrot con-
firms the *Times*'s explication of the text and shows clear
evidence of the Administration's hostile intentions—from
the very beginning of the military intervention—toward the
media's desire to report what was occurring around the rhetorical "line in the sand" that George Bush drew on August
8. What is not clear is why the nation's newspaper of record
and its powerful corporate neighbors in New York and Washington fell so readily into line with the goals of Wildermuth
and his colleagues. For in the weeks and months of postwar
wailing and self-criticism by the media, it was difficult to find
anyone who didn't, at least officially, count Desert Storm as
a devastating and immoral victory for military censorship and
a crushing defeat for the press and the First Amendment.
Yet, as the media critic Norman Solomon remarked in a
postmortem *Times* op-ed piece, "albeit with some grum-
bling, the big media went along to get along with the war-
makers . . ."

Back in August, not a single newshound even growled;
they made polite inquiries, held informal meetings, and sent
respectful letters, but they voiced no strong objection. By
August 14 the first group of reporters from the Pentagon's
permanent revolving pool had already checked into the
Dhahran International Hotel to observe, under military escort, the arrival of troops and matériel. Among the media
and the Pentagon bureaucrats in Washington, the argument
was not about constitutional principles but about the number
and the duration of visas to be made available for each news
organization. In the words of retired *Washington Post* executive editor Benjamin Bradlee, the posture of the individual newspapers and networks in that period was all "me, me,
me, me, me . . ."

The Department of Defense's National Media Pool was
a leftover from the carefully managed invasion of Panama
eight months earlier; it had been fashioned in response to

protests over the news blackout effected in the first two days of the invasion of Grenada. Although reporters had bellowed long and loud about the restrictions of the pool system in Panama—which prevented any coverage of the first thirty-six hours of fighting—the pool arrangement remained fixed in place on August 2, 1990.

After the Gulf War, *Time* magazine Washington bureau chief Stanley Cloud—a pre-war critic of pooling—would say that by consenting to the National Media Pool in the first place, the journalists had already lost the game.

"The DOD National Pool is the mother of all pools," he remarked in a postwar mockery of Saddam Hussein's pathetic war cry. "The rules agreed to [after Grenada], erroneously in my view, by a lot of bureau chiefs are the basic rules we lived under in the Gulf War. They were amplified and they grew from little seedlings into jungles in the Gulf War, but it's the basic system . . . and it is membership in that pool that gave the Pentagon the opening to allow them to control everything we did in the Gulf War."

Nevertheless, in the late summer and early fall of 1990, as the President began revving up for armed conflict, the media grandees would be busy setting a new standard for credulity. Experience, evidently, is not always the best teacher.

In terms of lobbying for "access," television, while it had been quicker off the blocks, was no less obedient to the Administration's wishes than were its print counterparts. Print and television bureau chiefs joined forces in a letter faxed to the President at Kennebunkport dated August 22, which expressed concern about the Saudi restrictions on reporters. Bush was "relaxing" at his summer house in Maine by racing around in his speedboat and playing golf in the driving rain. The letter, signed by eleven of the major news bureaucrats, would do nothing to exacerbate the President's as yet undiagnosed thyroid condition.

Dear Mr. President,

Those of us listed below, representing the nation's major media organizations in Washington, are deeply concerned about current limitations on open press coverage in Saudi Arabia.

The American press has been allowed minimum access to Saudi Arabia in the form of the DOD Pool, and extremely limited unilateral representation.* While we appreciate what the Saudis have done in recent days to allow more journalists into their country, we now understand that access may be cut back, leaving, at best, a small media pool.

Never in American history has this country been faced with as large a commitment of manpower and equipment with as little opportunity for the press to report. There has been no parallel situation and there can be no justification for further restrictions.

We respectfully request that the Administration do everything in its power to gain full media access to Saudi Arabia and to the American presence there. Perhaps accreditation through the American military would be the correct solution.

In the quietly reassuring style that would typify the Administration's tone for the next few months, the President's press secretary, Marlin Fitzwater, replied to each of the eleven news managers on September 6:

Dear [Bureau Chief]:

Thank you for your letter to President Bush concerning press coverage in Saudi Arabia. The President is aware of your interest in this matter and shares a strong sense of responsibility for reporting to the American people on

---

* "Unilateral representation" was a term coined by the military that meant unescorted reporting.

events related to our military forces in the Middle East. He discussed this matter with Secretary Cheney and General Powell.

As Secretary Cheney said at the President's press conference Wednesday, August 22, we believe deeply in the rights of the press and your right to report on our military forces. I understand your access in Saudi Arabia is now much improved.

We all understand, government and media, that the best approach is full and open coverage at all times. The various necessities for pool arrangements, which we have learned to live with in every aspect of journalism today, are never the desired course. Yet, we know them to be necessary in certain circumstances. There will always be disagreement between us about those circumstances and about the size and access of pools. Nevertheless, please be assured that we will do everything possible to help meet your needs.

Fitzwater's comments about the "necessities for pool arrangements" should have set off alarm bells, but the media hardly stirred. Thanks to the helpful Fred Dutton—"the most sought-after man in town," according to ABC's George Watson—just enough extra reporters were getting into Saudi Arabia to calm the bureau chiefs. And that the escorted DOD National Media Pool members were being allowed to file even the most routine of stories somehow served to placate both them and their bosses. Stanley Cloud of *Time* recalled with dismay how his own pool correspondent, Jay Peterzell, "normally the most sane of journalists and the most skeptical of all . . . found himself a complete apologist for the pool system. [Peterzell] even sent a memo, to his undying discredit, which [Pentagon spokesman] Pete Williams goes around quoting all the time, saying, 'You want to know how good the early use of the national pool in the Gulf War was? Here's Jay Peterzell of *Time* magazine [praising it].' He would be the first to admit to a serious case of the Stockholm syndrome while he was over there."

Not until October 9, nearly two months after Bush's call to arms, and with more than 150,000 U.S. troops already in place, did the dukes of print begin to display genuine anxiety over limited access to the Gulf theater. Significantly, the first rumblings were heard from the middle managers in Washington, not their bosses. Michael Getler, *The Washington Post*'s assistant managing editor in charge of foreign news, collected the signatures of five other print colleagues on a letter to Pete Williams at the Pentagon requesting more visas than the one visa per corporation then being issued by the Saudis. The six signatories represented the elite of the national press corps. Jack Nelson, bureau chief of the *Los Angeles Times*, and Albert Hunt of *The Wall Street Journal* were the most visible because of their regular appearances on television talk shows. Thomas DeFrank of *Newsweek* (standing in for bureau chief Evan Thomas), Stanley Cloud of *Time*, and Bernard Weinraub of *The New York Times* (standing in for bureau chief Howell Raines) completed the list.

Considering the media's angry postwar criticism of Gulf War restrictions, the letter is illuminating to read today. After the war, journalists invoked words like "censorship," "democracy," "independent journalism," "the public," and "press freedom," albeit cautiously. The pool system was widely denounced. On October 9, only the languid voice of bureaucracy could be heard:

Dear Pete,

As you know from earlier conversations, we are all greatly concerned about the prospect that we will have less than adequate coverage from the Persian Gulf, under conditions that currently exist, should fighting begin.

At this time we all are limited by the Saudi government to one visa per organization. That simply is not acceptable for us under war-time conditions in which more than 200,000 American troops are committed to the defense of Saudi Arabia and perhaps the broader Gulf region.* For many reasons, there is no way that a single correspondent will be able to provide comprehensive coverage from the scene for major print news organizations such as ours, with collectively many millions of readers. Since it will presumably be impossible to get into the region by commercial air transport once a conflict begins, we are all essentially running the risk now of being caught with just the single reporter in-country.

Our proposal is as follows:

1) We urge you and the Secretary of Defense to urge the Saudi authorities to allow at least two visas for each of the major American newspapers, news magazines and other large news organizations, effective immediately. It may be that some organizations will choose not to keep two people there all the time. We believe, however, it is essential for us to have that option. Considering the size of the American military deployment to the region, what would amount to probably a few dozen more reporters would not seem to add much strain.

2) Because we are not likely to be able to enter the war zone by any commercial means once fighting starts, we are requesting that the Defense Department include in its plans some form of a military, or military-approved commercial press charter, that news organizations would pay for, that would leave the U.S. on day one of the conflict and take a pre-selected group of military reporters—one per organization—from the Pentagon press corps—into the region. This would require a third

* The Pentagon said there were 150,000 U.S. troops in Saudi Arabia on October 9.

visa from the Saudis, one that could be pre-approved and either be made available on the plane or upon landing. We believe it is going to be essential to have some way to augment our correspondents once fighting begins, and also to get reporters with experience covering the military there promptly.

We are sending a copy of this proposal to Saudi officials, and their representatives in Washington are urging their cooperation.

Thank you for your assistance.

The cover note to Bandar, who was sent a copy, was even more polite. It read in part: "We appreciate your assistance in providing *access* [emphasis added] to the Kingdom thus far but we urge you to allow some expansion, especially for large news organizations, which would involve approval of a second visa now and a provisional third visa for a Pentagon press charter if and when combat gets under way."

These letters make no mention of pools or censorship. What they demonstrate is that at this early stage of the conflict, "access" became a euphemism for freedom of the press, and "visas" a substitute for journalism. Moreover, the system of confining reporters to military-escorted pools was already in effect on the day the letter was sent to Williams. The status quo was not being challenged here, merely the limit on passes to the theater.

In the end, Prince Bandar, his lobbyist Fred Dutton, and the Pentagon smoothly managed the matter by producing complimentary tickets and the desired plane. As expert practitioners of public relations, they understood the benefits to be gained by parceling out favors, as well as the value of delay.

As the fall wore on, a series of meetings with television and print representatives was scheduled at the Pentagon, the first two at the request of the bureau chiefs. At the initial meeting, which took place on October 25 at Pete Williams's Pentagon office, limited seating was provided and the tone was still confidential and clubby. The Pentagon had combined the competing groups of four television bureau chiefs and six print men plus Steve Kurkjian of the *Boston Globe*, Clark Hoyt of Knight-Ridder, and Andrew Glass of Cox Newspapers. Williams, with his principal deputy, Bob Taylor, taking notes, took the cordial and sympathetic tone which persists to this day in his official communications with journalists. Ever since the Panama invasion, the Pentagon's chief spokesperson had been busy mollifying anxious news bureaucrats about censorship, and by the fall, he had achieved a rather pleasing drone; journalists and their bosses genuinely seemed to like him—to the extent that many actually even ascribed the Pentagon's most restrictive policies to other, more sinister figures. How much more successful could any public relations operation be?

To characterize Williams's double-talk as Orwellian would be to exaggerate his powers as a manipulator. It is his bland and unaggressive style that is the key to his success. In the familiar law-and-order scenario, he plays the quintessential good cop, eager to demonstrate his sensitivity to his charges' needs. His March 30, 1990, letter to bureau chiefs enclosing the Hoffman Report (the Pentagon's summary of the pool operation in Panama) is both typical of his prose and outstanding in its banal deceptiveness.

"It is important to remember," Williams wrote, "that the President personally made the decision to deploy a pool of reporters to cover Just Cause with the agreement of the Secretary of Defense and the Chairman of the Joint Chiefs of Staff. Their decision should dispel the fear that the media pool would never be used in actual combat. Every decision that we made during Just Cause was intended to facilitate open, timely media coverage of the operation."

This, of course, was a lie. What the Administration prevented during the first thirty-six hours of the Panama invasion were any eyewitness accounts or photographs of the shelling of El Chorrillo, the desperately poor neighborhood in Panama City where General Manuel Noriega's headquarters were located. At least three hundred civilians died in the attack and resulting crossfire, some of them burned alive in their homes. But no one was able to observe these events, except the victims and U.S. Army film crews. (When he asked to see the army pictures, Patrick Sloyan, a reporter for *Newsday*, was referred to the Freedom of Information Act.)

At the October 25 meeting in his office, Williams was at his most unflappable. This was the man who would write in *The Washington Post* after the war—presumably with a smirk—that "the press gave the American people the best war coverage they ever had." Giving the appearance of Pentagon cooperation with the thirteen* news executives assembled that afternoon seemed to come naturally to Williams. One who attended, Kurkjian of the *Boston Globe*, was preoccupied with his own fear of being shouldered aside by "the big guys" from the larger media companies—the six "pals around town" from the print side who had signed the letter to Williams, and the network bureau chiefs.

"These are the media moguls who decide what's going to go on the nightly news or what's going on page one tomorrow," Kurkjian said later. "When they write a letter, as informal as it might seem to me, Pete Williams is going to pay attention." Having been excluded from the original pool, he complained in the meeting that the *Globe* and other papers like *Newsday* were "getting screwed by the present arrangement."

During the two-hour meeting Williams seemed ready to help, according to Kurkjian. "It was a very substantive meeting. Pete said he'd work on our requests; he was very co-

---

* There might have been one or two more, but no one, including Williams, seems to have kept an exact record of who attended the meeting.

operative on those individual requests. Basically he said, 'Yes, I see no problem in getting a plane to go over there once the war goes off. Get your people ready. Give us names, rank, serial number of all the people you would want to send. I could imagine it being a big plane and every one of you here would be able to get one, two, or three people on the plane.' "

Cox Newspapers bureau chief Andrew Glass recalled that "there was a lot of touch-me-feel-me stuff over who was standing in the way of the visas. These organizations, with the exception, I think, of the L.A. *Times*, had only one ticket to Saudi Arabia." Glass claims he understood the shifting alibis by Williams and the Saudis for what they were.

"The Saudis were saying, 'One news organization, one visa,' and saying that's the way the Pentagon wanted it. The Pentagon people were saying, 'No, no, we don't have any problem with it. It's the Saudis.' So they were playing Alphonse and Gaston over visas."

The question of a Pentagon-chartered plane (soon to be dubbed "Bigfoot") upon the outbreak of war had arisen, according to Glass, because the bureau chiefs "feared that when the fighting started, the Saudis would close their airspace to commercial air traffic, which in fact occurred. So they wanted the Pentagon to give them assurance that in that situation, on a contingency basis, the Pentagon would either charter an airplane which the Saudis would agree to, or a military aircraft would be used to get people in shortly after the war began . . . That, in fact, occurred. It was a C-141."

Glass said the issue of pools did come up, but only, "as the lawyers say, inter alia . . . It was a peripheral issue."

George Watson's memo to his boss, ABC news division president Roone Arledge, reveals better than anything else the cordial atmosphere that prevailed at the meeting and the passivity of those present. After reporting that Williams had agreed to provide the airplane, Watson went on to discuss the issues of pooling and censorship, using language that makes Williams sound like a scoutmaster and the bureau chiefs like Boy Scouts preparing for a camping trip:

> Williams asserted that if we expect to cover the first part of any fighting, the pool must be deployed in advance. Nobody disagreed.

> The Pentagon would supply necessary gear to poolers, including helmets, flak jackets, chemical warfare suits, web gear, etc. They would also brief pool reporters on the use of chemical antidotes and special equipment.

As a good molder of young men, Williams offered the scouts the opportunity to demonstrate leadership skills by running their own show, with appropriate adult supervision:

> The pools would remain in the field for five to seven days at a stretch. In the pre-war period, with four pools in the field, ABC News would be continuously responsible for one pool. If the additional four pools were activated, ABC would be responsible for two during the initial stage of the conflict.

Watson's earnestly trusting report continues:

> These pools do not replace or preclude unilateral coverage. Williams says he wants unilateral as soon as possible . . . People who remember "hitching a ride to Da Nang" and other such places during Vietnam wondered why unilateral coverage seems so restricted. Williams says he is talking only about the very early stages of a conflict. When "maturity of the theatre" is achieved—meaning supply lines and transportation systems are established—then the Pentagon, he says, will welcome unilateral requests.

In a third section titled "Reporting Restrictions," Watson relayed the news that "[Pete] Williams says the Pentagon

is not thinking about censorship which, he said, would require congressional action . . . So, at this stage, we are not
talking about guys with green eye shades and blue pencils."
Watson summed up by explaining that "Williams seemed to
be saying let's not pick a fight over this now, and that mood
prevailed at the meeting."

But Williams, Watson said, was "intentionally . . .
vague" about the ground rules already in effect for correspondents in Saudi Arabia. Reporters there were required
to sign the ground-rules document before they could receive
credentials. In doing so, they gave away their right to do any
serious reporting of the military buildup; off-the-record interviews, a necessary arrow in any reporter's quiver, were
also forbidden. To make certain that nobody tried to break
the rules and to guarantee "security at the source," Williams's office had inserted the following sentence of
doubletalk:

> You MUST remain with your military escort at all times,
> until released, and follow their instructions regarding
> your activities. These instructions are not intended to
> hinder your reporting. They are only to facilitate troop
> movement, ensure safety, and protect operational
> security.

To be fair, no one at the meeting knew about the Wildermuth memo dictating perpetual escorts, and participants
like Kurkjian had the impression that Williams and his colleagues were still "in the drawing-up stage" of handling the
war coverage. But given the ground rules in Dhahran, the
bureau chiefs were surprisingly gullible. Later, in a candid
January 12 telephone conference with his subordinates at
U.S. Central Command's Joint Information Bureau in Dhahran, a tape of which was obtained from the Pentagon, Williams would explain the real role of the escort: "You're the
one who keeps [journalists] out of areas they shouldn't be

[in] . . . Your job is to get them to where the action is, make sure they get moving, be the housemother to them, and the den mother . . ."

As a reporter, Kurkjian noted only one newsworthy comment from Williams during the meeting. "He said, 'When we go to war, all these questions will be resolved about coverage.' It was 'when,' not 'if.' No one followed up on it, which is interesting for a bunch of newshounds . . . No one said anything."

Were the bureau chiefs simply corporate managers trying to make it through the day? If the quantity of visas, rather than liberty, was their greatest concern, the cynic might conclude that they were motivated principally by economic needs imposed on them by their corporate masters. But such analogies between the rigid world of the corporation and the workings of the news media are dangerous. Old-fashioned ideals and practices that would never be tolerated in a company that was operated solely for profit do exist in the media. (The three major television networks lost money on the war.) Some measure of pride in the news trade does manage to survive within the corridors of CBS (controlled by Loews Corporation chairman Laurence Tisch), NBC (owned by General Electric), and ABC (a subsidiary of Capital Cities/ABC, Inc.). *The New York Times*, *The Washington Post*, and the *Los Angeles Times* do, from time to time, exhibit an interest in the principle of freedom of the press in their editorial pages.

Nevertheless, who *is* responsible for policy and for negotiating strategy within the megaliths called media? If the bureau chiefs were to be compared with middle management at IBM, then one would logically want to know where their bosses stood on the question of Pentagon press policy, just as one would ask where the chairman of IBM stands on matters of antitrust law in regard to cooperation with Apple. This is a difficult issue to address, for the subject of responsibility seems to make everyone in the news business nervous. In media companies, as in other corporations, higher-ups are famous for leaving middle management holding the bag.

But while news can be defined as a product, the First Amendment cannot. And in the run up to the Gulf War, the effort to distinguish product from principle appears to have sown confusion in the ranks of media middle management and group heads. This was best exhibited by Robert Ingle, executive editor of the Knight-Ridder chain's *San Jose Mercury News*, in a postwar forum at Stanford University. Asked by former congressman Pete McCloskey why the major press failed to join or promote a lawsuit challenging the constitutionality of the Pentagon's pooling system, Ingle replied: "I cannot exactly tell you why we did not participate in the challenge to the censorship . . . But I can tell you that as the editor of one of the larger Knight-Ridder newspapers, I'm not even aware that there was any discussion of that." When panel member Judith Coburn inquired why not, Ingle said, "I don't know. I can only pose a possible theory and that is [that] newspapers all over the country, including *The New York Times*, the *Los Angeles Times*, and all the others, are terribly concerned about losing touch with their readers and losing the support of their readers . . . You have to keep in mind that this was a terribly popular war by all of the polls I've seen . . . I think the conflict between needing to stay relevant and in touch with readers, and independent of those readers, is a terribly difficult one."

Ingle's comments, although remarkable because they are so candid even as they avoid assigning responsibility for the media's pitiably weak response to military censorship, are not altogether surprising considering the editor's middle position within the Knight-Ridder hierarchy.

Nicholas Horrock, Washington bureau chief at the *Chicago Tribune*, said that Tribune Company president Charles Brumback and his top managers appeared unconcerned with the Pentagon press restrictions. "I don't think they see it,

and I don't think the management at *USA Today* or other
people see a relationship between First Amendment rights
and moving their product."

Today, according to Horrock, a publisher is less likely
than his reporters to rely on constitutional principles. Instead, he is more apt to be busy catering to the needs of
anxious stockholders. "I think what you have now are people
responding to stockholders once a year at an annual meeting.
They're thinking much more about practical short-term
causes . . . Brumback is a more successful employee than I
am, and that's his real job. He sees himself running a company and not running the First Amendment."

At the highest levels of television news operations a
similar murkiness exists. Peter Jennings, the anchor for
ABC's "World News Tonight," remembered fielding the
telephone call from the Center for Constitutional Rights inviting ABC's participation in the lawsuit that it would bring
against the Pentagon's censorship policy in January 1991.
But Jennings was vague on the details of the internal debate
that followed.

> I almost haven't got the time to pay attention to issues
> of the press. Some will regard it as an abrogation of
> responsibility, but I'm going to worry about Eastern Eu-
> rope, and child care, and children in poverty, and drugs
> in California . . . You embarrass me to the extent that
> someone as senior as I should probably have a more
> vigorous role to play. I should play a more vigorous role
> in the question of censorship. I tend to let my manage-
> ment do that.

Thus, in their own postwar embarrassment about how
they had cooperated in the Pentagon's successful censorship
campaign, the bureau chiefs were understandably equivocal
about the roles of their superiors. Bill Headline of CNN,
when asked if more firepower—such as direct intervention

from CNN owner Ted Turner—could have been brought to
the table in the negotiations with Williams, volunteered to
take the blame for not sounding the alarm loud enough.

> I accept some of the blame for not screaming like a
> wounded eagle when we were in trouble, that we were
> being had . . . I guess there's a reluctance to admit that
> you misunderstood or were led astray.

Barbara Cohen said she kept her immediate boss, CBS
News president Eric Ober, informed of the negotiations, but
that in the end Ober decided CBS could not afford to opt
out of the pools for commercial and competitive reasons; the
network had to be seen with reporters "on the ground."
Stanley Cloud of *Time*—among his colleagues the most persistent opponent of pooling—enlisted the help of *Time* managing editor Henry Muller, who did write a letter to Williams
in January, protesting the censorship shortly before the war
began.

But Cloud faced the same dilemma as everyone else.
Muller, while an important man at Time Inc. Magazines, was
still merely the managing editor of a single publication. No
formal pressure or public complaint came from Time Warner
chairman Steven Ross, Time Warner president Nick Nicholas, or Time Inc. Magazines editor-in-chief Jason McManus.
"Who the hell is the owner?" asked Cloud in some frustration after the war. "Steve Ross isn't really the owner
either. Frankly, I'd rather have a letter to Cheney from the
editor of *The New York Times*, *The Washington Post*, and
Time magazine, which is going to get more attention than a
letter from Steven Ross, who is a Democratic contributor."
Ross declined to be interviewed, and McManus told me he
did not complain directly to the Administration because such
an aggressive action would have been "counterproductive."[1]
Michael Getler of *The Washington Post* said he sent
copies of all his correspondence with Williams to Ben Brad-

lee, the executive editor at the time, and Donald Graham, the publisher. But Graham declined to be interviewed for this book and instead, in a letter, passed the buck to Getler. It remains unclear what, if any, role he played in opposing the Pentagon restrictions.

From the Pentagon point of view, this confusion was ideal. "I don't think the Pentagon did any of this without having thought it through," said Cloud. "I think they realized that by dealing with middle management they could whipsaw us around a lot and that we had little recourse. So I think they preferred to keep things at the bureau-chief level. We've been aware of that weakness in our position from the beginning and it became acute during the war. That's when we got our higher people to write letters." But "higher people" meant last-minute objections from Muller and the presidents of the network news divisions. It evidently never meant owners or chief executive officers.

In any event, Pete Williams had more candy in his suitcase; there would be more come-ons, more enticements, more rewards, more obfuscation, and, of course, more meetings and memoranda. In retrospect, it appears that Williams intended to create the feeling among the news executives that coverage of the Gulf conflict was a joint production of the Pentagon and the media. At the same time, like any good public relations man, he was carefully feeling out his target, moving stealthily, and trying hard not to offend. It is ironic how the intelligent press agent uses precisely the technique most cherished by reporters to get their way: "I understand your problems and I sympathize. I'm really on your side." From the first meeting on October 25 to the end of the war four months later, Williams became an expert at sympathizing with his counterparts in the Washington media establishment. All requests from the bureau chiefs were taken under studious advisement and all complaints about the most outrageous restrictions were received with compassion and care.

Yet behind the safe, fortified walls of the Pentagon,

Williams was less charitable toward the media's concerns. In his January 12 telephone conference with public affairs officers in Dhahran, Williams cynically divided the objections of the press into three categories:

> One is an objection to almost anything we're going to do from a segment of the news media that never supports military operations in the first place . . . That's how I would characterize one of the legal actions being pursued against us . . . which I'm not too concerned about . . .
>
> There's another segment of people who are genuinely torqued—are absolute freedom of speech and First Amendment people. I would include in this Michael Gartner, the president of NBC News, who has been critical of every time the military in the past has ever used ground rules. He's an absolutist. He doesn't believe the government has any right at all to interfere with what people report in any way . . . and there's no way to satisfy that . . .
>
> The third category of objections is people who understand exactly what we're trying to do here, who will tell you offline they understand why it is we're doing what we do. They will even give us a little advice on how we can tweak it up a little better, but who feel they must publicly take a position against us. But I think where it boils down is in an editorial that was in *The New York Times* the other day about our guidelines saying they don't know quite what to make of [the restrictions], but they think we are making a good faith effort and so they'll play along.

Williams's hypocritical treatment of what he perceived as a hypocritical press paid handsome dividends before, during, and even after the war, when the media realized that "Pete," as they all called him, had taken them for a long and dusty ride. That he so easily convinced dozens of veteran journalists into thinking he was on their side, and successfully guaranteed the Administration favorable news coverage of the war, did not go unappreciated by NBC News president Michael Gartner, the First Amendment "absolutist." "I'd hire Pete Williams tomorrow as a reporter," Gartner told me after the war. "He'd be every bit as good a journalist as he is a spokesman."

With all this, as late as the spring and summer months of 1991, it was impossible to find a major-league bureau chief prepared to call Williams a liar. And yet Williams's essential lie—that reporters would be allowed to cover the Gulf War without substantial impediment—lay, like Poe's purloined letter, in plain sight for all to see. Access was all, and it would continue to be. But access to what?

If the bureau chiefs were credulous to a fault on October 25, they were only somewhat more skeptical at their next meeting with Williams, on November 28. Once again they traveled to the Pentagon, and once again an atmosphere of trust seemed to prevail. But the world had changed in the meantime. Between the two meetings, President Bush had announced the doubling of American troop strength, had heightened his anti-Hussein rhetoric, and had begun to pattern himself after the wartime Winston Churchill. With the midterm elections safely past, the President was free to act without fear of immediate political consequence. Operation Desert Shield was looking more and more like Operation Desert Saber. With Hussein's continued cooperation, it seemed increasingly likely there might be real bloodshed. But the U.S. media and military were still barely skirmishing. No one had even been scratched.

The second meeting was again small, with the same thirteen news bureaucrats and Bob Taylor, Williams's assistant, attending. The event was evidently not newsworthy, at least to the newspeople, and no stories about the conversation appeared the next day. Williams was conciliatory as always, assuring the bureau chiefs of his desire to cooperate and his commitment to freedom of the press, if not freedom of movement. By most accounts, the journalists were somewhat more suspicious. They nonetheless appreciated Williams's supposed efforts on their behalf to convince Secretary of Defense Cheney, General Powell, and General Schwarzkopf of the importance of unescorted coverage. The important thing was that Williams remained vague, and his professed adversaries from the Fourth Estate remained polite, if slightly petulant. Getler of the *Post* expressed his fear that Williams would fail in his mission to persuade the higher-ups, but no one accused Williams of anything short of good faith. The good cop persona had seldom been so deftly executed.

On December 14, some people might have gotten an inkling that Williams was not so friendly to the concept of unilateral coverage of the war. In a memo issued that day, he began sounding very much like the Assistant Secretary of Defense for Public Affairs he was and far less like a benevolent scoutmaster. For the first time, Williams said that combat "pool material" would be subjected to "security review at the source." Translated, this meant a censor would read and edit the pool reports before they were released to the rest of the press corps. "Security review" had never been mentioned in the two meetings between Williams and the bureau chiefs. It would seem that such an announcement—of the first official wartime censorship since Korea—would have sent shock waves through the Washington media establishment and finally caused it to sound a public alarm. Nothing of the kind occurred. Indeed, Williams's surprise attack on the bureau chiefs elicited little comment. Indeed, his effrontery—and public relations skill—was so polished that he succeeded in presenting the matter as if he were performing a great favor for his friends in the media, when in fact he had taken the first critical step in handcuffing them. The favor came in the form of "Bigfoot," the C-141 airplane, which the bureau chiefs had so earnestly sought since September. Yes, said Williams, the Pentagon would supply the media a plane when the war broke out. Meanwhile, he wanted to hear "comments and questions" on the "concept of combat pools," an idea which was "the result of a month of planning and discussions" within the Pentagon.

Williams earned his year's salary with the following sentence, which ranks as a classic in deadpan chicanery. In explaining Cheney's and Powell's approval of the airplane he said, "The objective is to help prevent the pool operation from breaking down through a lack of news media representatives necessary to make it work—the editors, producers, technicians, writers, and pool coordinators who will be essential to successful pool operation." Despite the bureaucratese, the message was very clear: "The Pentagon wants to help you tell the Pentagon's story."

Most of the media scouts who read page 2 of the Williams memo were further lulled by the promise of something called "three-phased" coverage of the war, culminating in their being allowed "unilateral coverage of activities." Very few seemed to have questioned whether "activities" meant woodworking classes, nature lore, or combat, but the words "Phase III" had a reassuring ring. Only the most analytical scouts—let's call them the foxes—protested the blatant contradiction in the last paragraph of the memo:

> Phase III would begin when open coverage is possible and would provide for unilateral coverage of activities. The pools would be disbanded and all media would operate independently, although under U.S. Central Command escort.

The notion of a reporter working independently while escorted by a military public relations officer was a curious one. But few of the bureau chiefs contributed to the comments-and-questions period allowed for by Williams because they apparently understood Phase III to be a genuine commitment to wide-open coverage, Vietnam style, where you could "hitch a ride to Da Nang" whenever you felt like it.

Technically, as George Watson has pointed out, the Vietnam reporters were "escorted" to the extent that they were attached to military units. There was, however, a big difference between reporters selecting a combat platoon and accompanying it freely through the Mekong Delta and being assigned to a unit by U.S. Central Command and having a public affairs officer attached to your side.

Just two bureau chiefs saw fit to lodge serious objections to the Pentagon's new restrictions. Chuck Lewis of Hearst Newspapers wrote to Williams that Phase III was an "oxymoron," and Howell Raines of *The New York Times* complained that it "flies in the face" of the "agreement" reached at the meeting on November 28. As for "security review," Lewis said he was "sorry" to see it and Raines sarcastically called it "an innovation to which no one agreed."

Williams was stringing the bureau chiefs along, of course. Yet, aside from Raines, no one accused him of bad faith, at least not until their next and final meeting with him on January 4. By then the United Nations Security Council had set a January 15 deadline for Hussein to withdraw from Kuwait and authorized military force by the American army and its smattering of "allies" if he failed to obey the ultimatum. The only remaining obstacle to the President's first step in creating a "new world order" was the U.S. Congress, just then trying desperately not to debate a war resolution.[2] In Washington and New York the media had been preoccupied with last-minute diplomatic initiatives, and the challenge of covering an actual war had receded from its collective consciousness.

An unpleasant surprise greeted the original thirteen media managers as they entered the Pentagon auditorium to which they were assigned on January 4. Unbeknownst to them, Williams had decided to expand their number considerably. The cozy meetings were over, and the media grandees found themselves lost in a mob of more than fifty of their lesser-known colleagues. Williams had effectively arranged a press conference where no negotiating could be done. In the heated atmosphere, "comments and questions" were reduced to posturing and speechmaking. Early in the meeting, Stanley Cloud noticed that a Pentagon bureaucrat was taping the event and asked if the meeting, like the others, was off the record. Williams, taken aback, acknowledged he was recording the meeting, and in the end everyone agreed to allow the taping to continue.*

At last, many of the journalists understood that they had been entirely taken in, and some even became angry. The most memorable speech of the day, by many accounts, betrayed the weakness of the journalists' position. It was delivered by Andrew Glass of Cox Newspapers and came to be known as the "trust us" speech. While Glass made passionate reference to the principle of freedom of the press, he sabotaged his argument by asking the government to trust in the patriotism of the press. American journalists, he promised, would never violate military security and, by implication, would never expose any secrets. Effectively, Glass was promising to play ball with the government in the name of the First Amendment. In doing so, he further and foolishly compromised what remained of the shredded integrity of the national journalism establishment. It was a patently absurd plea. Of course the government didn't trust the media. Why construct such elaborate methods of information control if the politicians and generals considered reporters trustworthy? Evidently the Pentagon public relations team possessed a clearer understanding than the bureau chiefs of the role the Founding Fathers had assigned to the press. Wasn't the granting of special protection in part to encourage press exposure of government secrets?

It was too late, in any case, and Glass's supplication

---

* A Freedom of Information Act request and repeated inquiries to Williams's office failed to produce the tape or a transcript. This is odd, given the much more sensitive material the Pentagon released for this book.

merely added to the dismal record of capitulation by the media. From January 4 to the beginning of the bombing campaign on January 16, the Pentagon PR men rolled up the carpet. Williams continued to play the game, asserting that the latest rules were merely for "talking purposes," and promising revised rules, which were duly circulated. After the success of the deception and manipulation became obvious, some bureau chiefs attempted to protest in letters and phone calls. Howell Raines of *The New York Times* revealed his sense of betrayal when he wrote Williams on January 8 after he received yet another version of the ground rules:

> Suffice it to say that the core problems are obvious and remain uncorrected in this latest rendition. The idea of a constant "escort" was never accepted by or even discussed with our group. Indeed, the representation was that you would move as quickly as possible to disband the pool and leave us to undertake what you called "unilateral coverage" from the battlefield on the Vietnam model.

Raines's protest showed a sudden awakening:

> As for the various stipulations on what can be reported, this can only be interpreted as an effort to impose rigid censorship in place of a common-sense understanding about specific disclosures that would endanger lives. *By combining these categories of reportable information with the requirement for a "security review," you have created a system of censorship* unlike anything in recent combat history. The idea that officers on the scene should be involved in any such review process adds complications that boggle the mind. [Author's italics]

In spite of this protest, Raines clung with childish faith to a pool system that had already succeeded in muzzling the press in Grenada and Panama:

> Operating under the informal understandings that have prevailed since 1985, we had a pool agreement that might have worked. In trying to fix something that was not broken, the Department of Defense has produced an arrangement that is riddled with pitfalls for you and for us. I urge you and the Secretary to scrub this rule-making exercise and return to the common-sense arrangement that we had to begin with.

The Pentagon had experienced spectacular success in Grenada, first by creating a pool and then by sending it to the island too late, and in Panama by virtually imprisoning the pool on an army base. In both cases, reporters missed the fighting entirely, and the American public was treated to antiseptic military victories minus any scenes of killing, destruction, or incompetence. In protesting the Gulf War censorship, why did Raines propose returning to the censorship status quo?

On January 9, some top management in the media finally acted. The network news division presidents signed a protest letter, which was hand-delivered to the Secretary of Defense's office by George Watson. In the original draft of the letter, the presidents included a sentence of extraordinary servility that was later modified. In the first version, it read: "[W]e think the existing proposals go far beyond what is required to meet the goals we share with the military." Evidently this was deemed too craven, and the sentence became "We think the existing proposals go far beyond what is required to protect troop safety and mission security." Here again the strictures of the institutional "go along to get along" voice rendered the prose impotent:

> "Security review" may not be censorship in its purest form, but it compromises the free flow of information with official intrusion and government oversight.

> The long years of war in Vietnam clearly proved that journalists can be relied on to adhere voluntarily to appropriate security ground rules.

Trust us, pleaded Roone Arledge of ABC, Eric Ober of CBS, Tom Johnson of CNN, and Michael Gartner of NBC. According to Watson, Cheney didn't bother to reply.

Time managing editor Henry Muller's letter to Cheney the same day wasn't any tougher:

> Mr. Secretary, *Time* wants to cooperate in every way possible during these difficult times. But I most urgently request that you and your aides reconsider these infringements on the press's freedom to cover hostilities in the Persian Gulf.

Also that day, Jonathan Wolman of the Associated Press wrote Pete Williams a cheerful "protest" letter:

> Thanks for providing a copy of the new proposed guidelines for combat coverage in the event of hostilities in the Gulf. We welcome the improvements over previous versions, yet I wanted to express my hope that you will modify several troublesome provisions . . .

It has been argued that Ronald Reagan debased the English language to a degree greater than any politician in

American history, and it may be asking too much of the media bureaucrats to deliver Jeffersonian rhetoric after eight years of mind-numbing subjugation. But they had an alternative to polite persuasion. On January 10 a group of small, primarily left-wing weeklies and monthlies and four prominent writers (represented by the Center for Constitutional Rights) sued the Pentagon in New York federal court claiming that the Pentagon rules were unconstitutional. Some of the big media were invited to join the action, which was brought by *The Nation*, *Harper's Magazine*,* *Newsday* columnist Sydney Schanberg, *The Village Voice*, *LA Weekly*, and others. The big three television networks, as well as *The Washington Post*, *The New York Times*, and *Newsday*, all declined either to join the suit or to contribute friend-of-the-court briefs once the suit was filed. After the war, amid all the handwringing about censorship, media executives resorted to the institutional voice when asked to explain their decision to avoid the lawsuit.[3] In a letter to Joan Coffey, a Long Island radio talk-show host, *Washington Post* publisher Donald Graham explained:

> No media organization argued more vociferously than *The Washington Post* against the restrictions placed on the press by the military during the Gulf crisis. We also reported extensively on this issue. Ultimately, we did not feel that a lawsuit would improve this situation any more than we could through other channels.

Since Graham declined to be interviewed for this book, it may never be known what vociferous arguments were brought to bear. The editor of *Newsday*, Anthony Marro, was more specific. After noting his columnist Schanberg's participation in the lawsuit, he wrote:

---

* As publisher of *Harper's Magazine*, I played a minor role in publicizing the lawsuit and attempting to correct inaccurate reports about its purpose.

We didn't join the lawsuit as a newspaper for a number
of reasons, one of them being my concern that a loss in
the courts would make a bad situation worse by affirming
the legal right of the Pentagon to exclude reporters and
to limit them to press pools.

In a letter to Sumner Rosen of the Columbia University
School of Social Work explaining his newspaper's decision
not to join the lawsuit, *New York Times* managing editor
Joseph Lelyveld conceded a major portion of the Pentagon's
justification for establishing combat pools:

The First Amendment gives us the right to publish just
about anything. It doesn't give us the right to go just
about anywhere.

Judicial politics being what they are, participation
and financial support from the big media—even with friend-
of-the-court briefs—would likely have strengthened the
plaintiffs' case: Leonard B. Sand, the federal judge who
heard the arguments, is considered one of the strongest defenders of the First Amendment in the Southern District of
New York. The media bosses might have heeded Schanberg,
who pointed out that "there was nothing left to lose," since
military censorship had triumphed completely over the media.* As Howell Raines told Peter Schmeisser in *The New
Republic*, "We lost. They managed us completely. If it were
an athletic contest, the score would be 100 to 1." Stanley
Cloud of *Time* put it this way: "Throughout the long evolution of the Department of Defense pool, the press willingly,
passively, and stupidly went along with it. That is the original

---

* Schanberg was well qualified to comment on censorship and war reporting.
While a correspondent for *The New York Times*, he covered the Vietnam War
and won a Pulitzer Prize for his dispatches about the fall of Phnom Penh.

sin which got us here, and I don't blame anybody as much as I blame us."

Thus, when American bombs started dropping on the evening of January 16, the media were tied up in the knots of their own collusion with the government. At least, that is the charitable explanation.

CHAPTER 2

Selling Babies

> For to say the press *does* things conceals the fundamental
> truth that the press, strictly speaking, can scarcely be said
> to do anything. It does not act, it is acted upon.
> —WALTER KARP
> "All the Congressmen's Men"
> *Harper's Magazine*, July 1989

MUZZLING THE MEDIA during wartime was one thing.
Using the media to start a war was quite another, though
just as important to the White House. While one public
relations specialist, the Pentagon's Pete Williams, was lulling
the bureau chiefs to sleep, a host of others worked tirelessly
to awaken the docile journalists to a previously little known
danger named Saddam Hussein. This was no easy task. The
Canadian military analyst Gwynne Dyer was largely correct
when he remarked in the fall of 1990 that "Saddam Hussein
was not a problem that kept anybody awake in July." Before
his seizure of Kuwait, the Iraqi dictator was regarded by
many politicians and journalists as merely another unpleasant
Third World strongman for whom the U.S. foreign-policy
establishment had a necessary affinity. From 1980 to 1988,
Hussein had shouldered the burden of killing about 150,000
Iranians,* in addition to at least thirteen thousand of his own
citizens, including several thousand unarmed Kurdish civil-

* This number is an Iranian government estimate. In his book *The Longest
War*, author Dilip Hiro cites conservative Western estimates of 260,000 Iranian
dead.

ians, and in the process won the admiration and support of elements of three successive U.S. Administrations. While it might overstate the case to suggest that in 1980 the Carter Administration encouraged Hussein to attack Khomeini's Shiite legions, one can safely say that no one in the Carter camp seemed to object very loudly. In those days (and through most of the eighties), Khomeini's Islamic revolution was regarded by the U.S. as the greatest threat to peace in the Middle East and to a steady supply of cheap oil. The semisecular Hussein, cognizant of his own restive Shiite majority, viewed Khomeini with equal unease, and he hungered after Iranian oil and ports. This happy confluence of interests, coming on the heels of the Iranian kidnapping of the U.S. embassy staff in Tehran, guaranteed at the very least official U.S. neutrality in the Iran–Iraq war.

In this case, however, neutrality rapidly metamorphosed into quiet backing for Iraq, which eventually led to military support. At first, practical dealings and the hostage crisis were thought to require military aid for Iran as well, but by 1984 the Reagan Administration "tilted" toward Iraq and against Iran.[1] Better the mustachioed Saddam, with whom one could deal, the thinking went, than the bearded Khomeini, who actually meant what he said when he called America the "Great Satan." As Germaine Greer put it in London's *The Independent Magazine*, the West "saw Iraq as a sort of repulsive friend in that it was slaughtering the sons of a worse enemy."

Outside the Washington establishment, there was genuine concern about Hussein's penchant for killing people without due process. Human rights groups were well aware of the Iraqi President's violent behavior and had carefully documented his crimes. In March 1990, for example, the Committee to Protect Journalists expressed its alarm when Hussein hanged Farzad Bazoft, an Iranian journalist who was arrested after taking soil samples from the grounds of an Iraqi weapons plant in full view of Iraqi soldiers. Bazoft was said to be investigating a massive explosion at the facility for the *Observer* of London.

Hussein also periodically made threats to annihilate Israel, but this sort of rhetoric hardly distinguished him from most of his fellow Arab leaders. At such behavior official Washington yawned. Human rights groups were always yowling about this or that Middle Eastern despot; whether it was Hafez Assad of Syria or Khomeini or Hussein or the Emir of Kuwait or King Fahd of Saudi Arabia made little difference to the realpoliticians. What mattered was "What have you done for me lately?" and lately Iraq had done a lot to check Iran. As a consequence, meetings like the one on April 12, 1990, between a group of five U.S. senators (led by Robert Dole) and Hussein in Baghdad were bound to take place. This meeting, in retrospect, was rich in irony, because the most outspoken member of the delegation was Wyoming senator Alan K. Simpson, the future point man in the Administration's assault on CNN's Peter Arnett. An excerpt from a CIA transcript of the meeting reveals Simpson's contempt for "Western"-style media. Remember that Bazoft, the journalist, had been executed four weeks earlier, on March 15.

> SIMPSON: I enjoy meeting with frank and direct people. It is difficult for us in the wild West—the cowboys —to understand that when we lose a case sometimes, we do not lose our life. This was one of the reasons that made the five of us . . . call the President yesterday. We told the President our visit to Iraq will cost us dearly, as it will make us lose popularity and so many people will attack us for visiting Iraq . . . President Bush told us, however, "Go. I want you to go. There are so many topics that we must raise with the Iraqis . . . If you are criticized for visiting Iraq, I will defend and speak out for you."
> . . . Democracy is a very irksome and confusing thing. I believe your problem is with the Western media, not with the U.S. government, because you are isolated

from the media and the press. The press is spoiled and conceited. All the journalists consider themselves brilliant political scientists. They do not want to see anything succeeding or achieving its objectives. My advice is that you allow those bastards to come here and see things for themselves.

HUSSEIN: They are welcome. We want them to come and see, and then let them write freely . . . I wish the media men would come . . . [But] if governments are not responsible for disseminating what happens—or, let us say, if the U.S. government is not responsible for propagating what happened, how then was this huge amount [of negative coverage of Iraq] produced in such a short time?

SIMPSON: It is very simple . . . They feed on each other. Each one of them eats part of the other. A front-page report in *Newsweek* is taken by another reporter and published by him in turn.*

The willingness to give Hussein the benefit of the doubt extended into the higher echelons of the Bush Administration, which often seemed devoted to cleaning up his bad-boy image. Sometimes the Administration offered direct advice to its vilified client. In her famous meeting with Hussein on July 25, 1990, U.S. Ambassador April Glaspie tried her best to help out with the dictator's questionable reputation. After consoling Hussein over a "cheap and unjust" profile by ABC's Diane Sawyer, Glaspie wished out loud for an "appearance in the media, even for five minutes," by the Iraqi President that "would help [the Administration] explain Iraq to the American people." She also noted wistfully that if George Bush "had control of the media, his job would be much easier."

* The Iraqi government's version of the conversation quotes Simpson citing *The New York Times*, not *Newsweek*. The CIA may have mistranslated an Iraqi radio broadcast of the meeting transcript.

Another example of Administration PR support for Hussein concerned Iraqi use of chemical weapons. As recently as May 1990, he had been portrayed by the Pentagon as a rather ordinary Middle Eastern dictator who happened to kill political opponents with poison gas. Just four months later he was cast by the Administration as the uniquely evil equivalent of Adolf Hitler; suddenly the Iraqi President relished the use of gas on ethnic minorities, particularly Kurds and—if he could get away with it—Israeli Jews.

Among those who actually cared about such things, Hussein was, in fact, infamous for his use of chemical weapons against rebellious Iraqi Kurds who exploited the Iran–Iraq war to further their dream (doomed as always) of independence. The most notorious of these Iraqi massacres occurred at Halabja, in March 1988. There, according to human rights monitors, about four thousand Kurdish civilians, including women, children, and the elderly, were killed in a chemical attack allegedly ordered by Iraqi forces to punish the Kurds for helping Iran. But in spring 1990, Pentagon leakers appeared eager to convey another perspective: they said the victims at Halabja were killed in a crossfire of Iraqi and Iranian gas. The new version of events suggested you could flip a coin when it came to atrocities by the two combatants. Such are the rules of realpolitik.[2]

Later, in the summer, the Bush Administration would cynically beat back attempts by members of Congress, disturbed by Hussein's violent conduct and belligerence toward Israel, to place stricter controls on U.S. trade with Iraq. And in the July 25 meeting between Ambassador Glaspie and Hussein, the U.S. strongly suggested it would not intervene in a conflict between Iraq and Kuwait.[3]

But on August 2, when Hussein grabbed Kuwait, he stepped beyond the imaginings of the practitioners of realpolitik. Suddenly more was required than manipulation by leak. Convincing Americans to fight a war to liberate a tiny Arab sheikhdom ruled by a family oligarchy would require the demonization of Hussein in ways never contemplated by human rights groups. It called for a frontal assault on public opinion such as had not been seen since the Spanish–American War. The war had to be sold. Fortunately for the President, there was talented help at hand.

It may be argued effectively that when politicians refer to American ingenuity, they're really talking about American salesmanship. Romantics might insist that the American experiment in self-government is the Republic's crowning glory. But in the Reagan–Bush era, democracy was eroding from within: the Iran-contra scandal had shown clearly how secret government policies could easily subvert the principle of popular sovereignty. Meanwhile, American industry was collapsing in the face of competition from Japan and Germany. The U.S. was still the number-one military power, but with the Soviets quitting the battle, it hardly seemed to matter anymore. Throughout the 1980s, outside of weaponry, America maintained its unchallenged lead in one area: advertising and public relations. So dominant was the U.S. in this field that an academic "discipline" called "marketing" was popularized to lend an aura of sophistication to the grubby business of promotion and sales. After years of suffering so many American tourists in search of culture, the French began coming to America to study *le marketing*. It was no wonder. A culture that could produce a marketing genius of the caliber of Roger Ailes was surely a culture to be emulated by ambitious foreign businesspeople. Ailes had helped perform the marketing miracle of the century: reinventing in 1968 the once unelectable Richard Nixon and getting him elected President. He repeated the feat in 1988 for the somewhat more attractive George Bush by running him against the decidedly unattractive rapist/murderer Willie Horton, rather than the Democratic nominee. Thus, it seems perfectly sensible that the eminent American historian Daniel Boorstin has pronounced advertising "the characteristic rhetoric of democracy."

But, as any good promoter will tell you, advertising often works best when someone else does it for you for free. For this one needs what once was known as a press agent and today is called a public relations firm. The former term is more to the point, because it suggests a relationship between the agent, who "sells" information, and the newspaper, which "buys" it. In August 1990, the Bush Administration's task was to sell two images—an ugly one of Hussein and a handsome one of Kuwait—to the American media. Then, God willing, the media would help sell it to the American people. For this formidable enterprise, the Administration required the best press agents money could buy.

On August 3, 1990, it must have been obvious to anyone paying attention that Kuwait had an image problem in the United States. Given the American citizen's famous ignorance of world geography, a substantial number of Americans probably couldn't find Kuwait on the map. Those who could probably knew that it was not a democratic country and that it had a lot of oil. Few were aware that since independence in 1961, the tiny emirate had been a remarkably free country by comparison with its immediate neighbors—Saudi Arabia, Iran, and Iraq—but that in 1986 the ruling al-Sabah family had dissolved the National Assembly. Even when the Assembly had been functioning, voting privileges were limited to about sixty-five thousand males (out of a total population of about two million people) who could prove Kuwaiti ancestry before 1920. None of the elected members of the National Assembly—who made up 50 percent of the body—could belong to a political party, and the nation's executive power was vested in the Emir, who was selected by and from the al-Sabah family. Women were entirely excluded from the formal political process and, according to the censorship monitoring organization Article 19, the remaining residents were considered second-class citizens.

Kuwait's reputation as a U.S. ally was also rather shaky. From January 1989 to June 1991, Kuwait voted with the United States in the United Nations General Assembly just nineteen times, which was three times less often than the Soviet Union did. In his speech during the Senate debate on war authorization, Senator Daniel Patrick Moynihan recalled Kuwait as having been "a particularly poisonous enemy of the United States" during his service as U.S. ambassador to the United Nations in the 1970s. "One can be an antagonist of the United States in a way that leaves room for further discussions afterward," Moynihan said. "But the Kuwaitis were singularly nasty. Their anti-Semitism was at the level of the personally loathsome when Resolution 3379 equating Zionism with racism passed the General Assembly."

The Kuwait government could be quite nasty with its own citizens as well. As recently as January 22, 1990, police had broken up a pro-democracy opposition gathering of six thousand using tear gas and batons. In the process, several politicians, including a seventy-year-old former member of the Assembly, were beaten. Afterward, political assemblies were banned. In regard to noncitizens, particularly those impoverished foreigners employed as domestic servants, the Kuwaitis could be worse than poisonous. Germaine Greer explained their plight in *The Independent Magazine*:

> When foreign workers arrive [in the Persian Gulf states], their passports are taken away; they sign documents in Arabic, which they neither speak nor read, and find themselves bound to hard labor for years. Those who refuse to sign are told they must leave at once and pay their own fares home. Some who think that they are going to exercise the professions for which they are qualified

find themselves scrubbing floors for half the pay they
were promised.

Foreign workers in the Gulf have no rights and no
representation. Their fate is entirely in the hands of the
employer and his family. Children are taught to
discipline—that is, to insult, pinch, slap and pull the hair
of—servants who displease them . . .

Now and then the *Kuwait Times* reported spectacular cases of servants thrown from roof-tops, burnt or
blinded or battered to death; the systematic abuse they
endured every day was unworthy of remark . . .

Greer explained that this form of de facto slavery extended to England, where "the Home Office makes it easy
for Gulf Arabs to import slavery by issuing their servants
with visitors' visas and denying them the right to work for
any other employer." She cited the case of a woman servant
who was imprisoned and brutalized over the course of four
years in her Kuwaiti mistresses' London apartment. The servant endured lack of food and daily whippings and had her
two gold teeth and passport stolen by the two Kuwaiti prin-
cesses, who kept her locked up. The case came to light only
because of a successful lawsuit by the servant after she escaped through the cat flap in the apartment door.

The unsavory facts about Kuwaiti society made the task
of presenting a martyred nation to the American public a
delicate one. The selling of Kuwait as a modern-day analogy
to pre–World War II Czechoslovakia would take some doing.

Kuwaitis were "great travelers, even before oil [was dis-
covered]," Dr. Hassan al-Ebraheem told me in his office.
"This explains why more than three hundred thousand Kuwaitis [close to half the nonforeign population] were outside
Kuwait when the invasion took place." Kuwaitis are also
immensely wealthy because of their vast oil holdings, and

can easily afford to spend the hot summer months in cooler climates, far away from their desert home. Dr. al-Ebraheem was one of those lucky enough to be out of the country on August 2; by fortuitous coincidence he was in Washington attending a conference in his capacity as professor of international politics at Kuwait University. Dr. al-Ebraheem was also a former government education minister and well placed among the Kuwaiti elite. Years of study at Indiana University had, he said, taught him "the American way of thinking," and made him the natural choice for president of Citizens for a Free Kuwait (CFK), which came into being shortly after the Iraqi invasion of his country. The Kuwaitis who gathered at their embassy on Washington's International Drive the morning of August 2 were understandably shocked and demoralized by what had happened, but unlike most political refugees they had the money to do something about their predicament.

The Kuwaitis in Washington also understood the power of public relations. One of Dr. al-Ebraheem's first moves, he says, was to hire Hill and Knowlton (H&K), one of the largest and most politically connected public relations firms in America. If in fact it had been his to make, it was probably the smartest decision of his life.

Dr. al-Ebraheem is a cheerful, upbeat man of middle age. He was ebullient when I visited him at CFK's Washington headquarters, located in a small shopping mall on upper Connecticut Avenue, a few months after the liberation of Kuwait. Packing boxes filled with now useless CFK propaganda littered the floor, as the organization prepared to transform itself into the new Kuwait–America Foundation, "truly the first people-to-people organization of its kind between the United States and Kuwait," according to its literature. Although his country had been returned by the United States, and Hill and Knowlton no longer represented CFK, Dr. al-Ebraheem was still unable to relax and stop selling his story. Iraqi "atrocities" in Kuwait were still very much on his mind, and he said he wanted to show me some shocking photographs.

"I don't want to upset you by showing pictures," he said, "but I will be glad if you want to." The pictures, at first glance, were horrifying. Some were amateurish out-of-focus shots of human figures covered with bloody gashes. A couple of figures had metal shafts driven through their chests, and some were trussed with straps. Another picture showed "torture" instruments. For a few minutes my skepticism about Dr. al-Ebraheem was checked, but on closer examination I realized the human figures were actually mannequins. Someone had reconstructed the alleged results of the Iraqi occupation for public relations purposes. The significance of this little pantomime cannot be underestimated; vaguely documented photographs and testimony from unidentified Kuwaitis provided some of the staples of the Hill and Knowlton campaign throughout the late summer and fall.

Dr. al-Ebraheem was evasive about why his committee of thirteen had turned to an American public relations firm (H&K has a British owner) except to say that his organization was overwhelmed and needed help. In the first few days after the invasion, CFK busied itself, according to Dr. al-Ebraheem, with organizing the approximately five thousand Kuwaiti citizens living in the United States, "asking our people to stick together, supporting each other emotionally, sending them policy guidelines . . . ways and means of contacting their friends, and how to behave in a rally. I mean, we have spent a long time in the United States and I was in school in the sixties, I've been to rallies."

Dr. al-Ebraheem was presumably referring to *antiwar* rallies, protesting the American intervention in Vietnam. But CFK/H&K had made the case *for* American military intervention in Kuwait. Despite his clear sophistication, Dr. al-Ebraheem maintained a straight face throughout our interview, which was no mean accomplishment on June 4, 1991. Three weeks later, even the stridently pro-war *Economist* was criticizing the "feudal, vengeful behavior" of Kuwait's rulers and their "noxious martial-law trials of suspected collaborators." Amnesty International reported on government torture of suspects. And on June 30, in perhaps the greatest of all postwar ironies, *The New York Times* described how more than twelve hundred Bedouin refugees—panicked by the death sentences meted out against alleged collaborators—fled into Iraq from Kuwait, rather than risk returning to their homes in Kuwait.

After CFK went into action on August 2, Dr. al-Ebraheem said, "We worked almost twenty-four hours a day [out of an embassy office]. Our young people were manning the telephones to answer phone calls for all our citizens . . . We were completely overwhelmed by the media." This last remark is easily understood given that Kuwaitis are not used to working long hours or very hard; they generally have foreigners to do that. In an article in London's *Independent Magazine*, the American Middle East expert Milton Viorst explained that Kuwaiti citizens held only 19 percent of their country's jobs. (Before the Iraqi invasion there were 500,000 foreign workers in Kuwait.) He quoted the secretary-general of Kuwait's Higher Planning Council, Fuad Mulla Hussein, on the difficulty of creating a Kuwaiti work ethic:

> Kuwaitis have neglected to work for more than 30 years . . . In the Fifties and Sixties, we acquired the luxury of employing others to execute our massive development programs, which in any case we could not do by ourselves. But the price we paid is that Kuwaitis have become spoiled children . . . the truth is that we're not sure how to get Kuwaitis back to work. How do you motivate someone who has everything?

Fortunately, there was plenty of money available to hire foreigners to do the work of Citizens for a Free Kuwait. Not surprisingly, the "Citizens" part of the organization was a fiction, as was the pretense of being an ordinary nonprofit charity. After the war, when it grudgingly owned up to its true status, CFK reported to the Justice Department receipts of $17,861 from seventy-eight individual U.S. and Canadian contributors and $11,852,329 from the government of Kuwait.

In any case, Dr. al-Ebraheem said, "[We] found that we needed some advice," and CFK signed up Hill and Knowlton. He said this occurred in September; the contract was actually signed earlier, on August 10, just one week after the invasion. The principal reason for engaging H&K so quickly becomes apparent when one looks at the roster of the firm's senior executives. The contract was signed by H&K chairman Robert K. Gray, a powerful fixture in Republican politics who was active in the two Reagan Presidential campaigns. Craig Fuller, the firm's then Washington-based president and chief operating officer, was Vice President Bush's chief of staff. According to *O'Dwyer's P.R. Services Report*, Fuller was "on the Kuwaiti account at H&K since the first day," and *The Washington Post* said H&K's efforts on behalf of CFK bore the "imprimatur" of the White House. (After the war, Fuller told the BBC, ". . . I think almost spontaneously, as the Kuwaitis were talking to us, we [H&K] were also talking to people in the Administration to find out how we could be supportive with respect to the President's program.") Not that H&K lacks bipartisan clout. H&K vice chairman Frank Mankiewicz was a close aide to Robert F. Kennedy and a top official in George McGovern's Presidential campaign in 1972, and senior vice president Thomas Ross was Pentagon spokesman in the Carter Administration. In all, according to H&K's Justice Department registration papers, 119 H&K executives in twelve offices around the U.S. were working on the Kuwait account. *O'Dwyer's* said, "H&K's registration as a foreign agent at the Justice Department [for CFK] is one of the largest ever submitted by a public relations firm for one client."

Quality work costs money; in the first ninety days H&K racked up fees of $2.9 million and expenses of $2.7 million. By the end of the war, H&K had collected nearly $10.8 million from the Kuwaitis. The expense breakdown for the initial three months makes interesting reading: "research" cost $1,114,850; "video production" (likely for video news releases) ate up $644,571; and "printing" (in part for public relations kits on Kuwait) cost $436,825. Significantly, "advertising" took only $43,217 (the point, after all, is to get the *free* advertising supplied by newspaper and television coverage).

It's difficult to know precisely what the $5,640,000 total bought in the first phase of the campaign. We do know that the H&K team, headed by former U.S. Information Agency officer Lauri J. Fitz-Pegado, organized a Kuwait Information Day on twenty college campuses on September 12. Later that month, on Sunday, September 23, churches nationwide observed a national day of prayer for Kuwait. The next day, thirteen state governors declared a national Free Kuwait Day. H&K distributed tens of thousands of Free Kuwait bumper stickers and T-shirts, as well as thousands of media kits extolling the alleged virtues of Kuwaiti society and history. Fitz-Pegado's crack press agents put together media events featuring Kuwaiti "resistance fighters" and businessmen and arranged meetings with newspaper editorial boards. H&K's Lew Allison, a former CBS and NBC News producer, created twenty-four video news releases from the Middle East, some of which purported to depict life in Kuwait under the Iraqi boot. The Wirthlin Group was engaged by H&K to study TV audience reaction to statements on the Gulf crisis by President Bush and Kuwaiti officials. The Kuwaiti ambassador to the U.S., Saud Nasir al-Sabah, appeared several times on television pundit shows, including "Crossfire," and Tom Brokaw said Allison delivered "the Emir's principal fixer" for a Brokaw interview in Saudi Arabia. H&K also appeared to have convinced the Kuwaitis of their own sincere commitment to the cause. "To them it's not only advice for business," Dr. al-Ebraheem told me. "They really believe in what they're doing."

But noting these prosaic activities does not do justice to the overall H&K effort. The job entailed far more than teaching Americans how to find Kuwait on a map, or putting a gloss on the emirate's troubling history. If the campaign were to be successful, a real horror story would have to be written to arouse the wrath of America, where, as Dr. al-Ebraheem explained, there exists a "popular psychology [of] standing for the underdog and trying to stand for justice."

While public relations professionals must rein in any tendency toward irony, they are free to indulge in exaggeration. Dr. al-Ebraheem did not restrain himself with me: "Kuwait's history in the past two hundred and fifty years has not witnessed a single incident of violence. Unlike any other country in the Gulf peninsula, there is no blood in our history . . . There is a total commitment to democracy and the Constitution." The public relations theory here is that if you say something enough times with sufficient conviction, some people will believe you, regardless of the truth.

In modern wars, exaggerated or manufactured enemy atrocities have frequently played an important part in the cause of boosting war fever at home. There is no more spectacular example of this than the alleged crimes committed by German soldiers against Belgian civilians in World War I. Journalist and historian Phillip Knightley wrote that "the Germans caused the deaths of some 5,000 civilians" when they overran Belgium in August 1914. In truth, Knightley recounted in *The First Casualty*, his indispensable book about war reporting, the Belgian civilians "were shot as guerrilla fighters, as hostages, or simply because they got in the way of a victorious advancing army in which not every soldier was a saint." The French and the British, however, seized upon the killings for propaganda purposes and converted the German army into a barbarian horde that committed all manner of unspeakable crimes against women and children. Crucial to this effort was the British-sponsored Bryce Committee, which "documented" the German "atrocities." "Murder, lust, and pillage prevailed over many parts of Belgium on a scale unparalleled in any war between civilized nations during the last three centuries," charged the distinguished panel of lawyers and historians. Among the most sensational allegations were the public rape of Belgian girls in Liège, the bayoneting of a two-year-old child by eight German soldiers, and the mutilation of a peasant girl's breasts. According to Knightley:

> The committee had not personally interviewed a single witness. The report was based on 1,200 depositions, mostly from Belgian refugees, taken by 22 barristers in Britain. None of the witnesses were placed on oath, their names were omitted (to prevent reprisals against their relatives), and hearsay evidence was accepted at full value . . . a Belgian commission of enquiry in 1922 . . . failed markedly to corroborate a single major allegation in the Bryce report.

The French were no amateurs either in the realm of war public relations, and they may have topped the British with their own counterfeit atrocity accounts, embellished from a London *Times* dispatch in August 1914. *The Times* had reported the story of a man who saw "with his own eyes German soldiery chop off the arms of a baby which clung to its mother's skirts." Knightley relates that the French propaganda bureau "produced a photograph of the handless baby, and on September 18, 1915, *La Rive Rouge* published it, later making the story even more lurid by carrying a drawing showing German soldiers eating the hands . . . After the war a series of investigations failed to find a single case of this nature.''

Slaughtered and mutilated Belgian babies were a tremendous propaganda triumph for the Allies. In retrospect, the success of these manufactured stories possessed ominous implications for future wars, especially the one to liberate Kuwait. For as Knightley noted with unwitting prescience:

> By the time the atrocity story was discredited it had served its role. It had not only rallied opinion on the home front and strengthened the resolution of Britain and France to prosecute the war to the finish, but had also achieved the important task of lowering resistance to the war in the United States.

There would be reports of baby atrocities in Kuwait as well, with parallel results.[4]

Toward the end of our interview, Dr. al-Ebraheem launched into a critique of Saddam Hussein of the variety not generally recommended by the professionals at Hill and Knowlton. Ad hominem attacks can sound less than noble and are best reserved for confidential, off-the-record conversations. However, the war was won and Dr. al-Ebraheem was evidently relaxing after his nation's long trial. Hussein, he explained to me, was a "stupid" and "ignorant" man who simply didn't know better than to attack Iran and invade Kuwait. Dr. al-Ebraheem's English is not perfect and his comedic delivery is unsure, but the joke he told me was clear: "What is in common between Saddam and his father? . . . Very important . . . He did not know when to withdraw at the right time." It is a fact that Hussein was not a genius at molding public opinion. His first mistake after invading Kuwait—sealing off the country to reporters and human rights investigators—turned out to be critical to the success of the Administration's public relations campaign. Hussein could not refute the charges made by Bush's people in part because some were true, but even more so because he wouldn't permit confirmation that some were not true. And of all the accusations made against the dictator, none had more impact on American public opinion than the one about Iraqi soldiers removing 312 babies from their incubators and leaving them to die on the cold hospital floors of Kuwait City.

It is not certain where and when the baby incubator story surfaced. The first reference in the press seems to have been in Britain on September 5. The London *Daily Telegraph* reported the claim by the exiled Kuwaiti housing minister, Yahya al-Sumait, that, in the *Telegraph*'s words, "babies in the premature unit of one hospital had been removed from their incubators so that these, too, could be carried off." Two days later the *Los Angeles Times* published a Reuters story about the atrocity accounts of a San Francisco woman identified only as "Cindy" and her traveling companion "Rudi," who had recently been evacuated from occupied Kuwait in a group of 171 Americans. "Iraqis are beating people . . . taking hospital equipment, babies out of incubators. Life-support systems are turned off . . . They are even removing traffic lights." What "Cindy" lacked in her sense of proportion, she more than made up for in color. "The Iraqis are beating Kuwaitis . . . cutting their ears off if they are caught resisting . . ."

Reporters are often gullible; sometimes they can be ignorant. But even the mediocre ones are usually suspicious of people who won't give their last names. This is because cub reporters—at least on newspapers—have it drilled into them by their city editors that they must never fail to get full names (correctly spelled), ages, and addresses of witnesses and victims in crime, fire, and disaster stories. Photographs of victims are important, too, but full names are sacrosanct. That Reuters and the *Los Angeles Times* allowed "Cindy from San Francisco" to remain essentially anonymous was a serious breach of one of the few ironclad rules that exist in journalism.

Now that the baby atrocity accusation was out, another journalistic axiom was triggered: once bad information burrows into what's traditionally known at newspapers as "the morgue" (the clippings file organized by subject and name in the newspaper library), it gets repeated over and over again. Newspaper reporters are perpetually in a hurry, and their principal historical sources when writing a story on deadline are past stories from their own paper. Like a computer virus, inaccuracy infects a newspaper morgue (the morgues at large newspapers are now mostly computerized), and it can sometimes take years to cleanse the system. But the consequences here were more serious than usual.

Even so, a few anonymous charges in the media do not make a successful atrocity public relations campaign. President Bush needed more to swing the balance in favor of the war option. Fortunately for the Administration, help was on the way from a most unlikely source.

Universal human rights as a popular political concept came into fashion in America during the Carter Administration. After the creation of the United Nations in 1945, and the adoption of the Universal Declaration of Human Rights in 1948, American Presidents had piously invoked the Declaration to condemn Communist depredations while overlooking the crimes of right-wing allies. But Carter was the first to apply human rights doctrine more or less without prejudice—the way it was intended—so that dictatorships and military governments supported by the United States came under official scrutiny alongside the Soviet empire.

Under Reagan and Bush the pendulum swung back toward highly selective application, so that from 1981 to 1985 Elliott Abrams (who in 1991 pleaded guilty to withholding information from Congress) would stain the post of Assistant

Secretary of State for Human Rights and Humanitarian Affairs. President Bush was similarly deaf to the entreaties of human rights representatives when they interfered with Administration objectives. As a former director of the Central Intelligence Agency and former chairman of the Republican National Committee, he was practiced in the art of realpolitik, which cannot exist in harmony with the notion of a universal standard of human rights. In the first half of his maiden term, Bush had distinguished himself as a devotee of the unsentimental game of nations by displaying marked indifference to the Chinese government's slaughter at Tiananmen Square in 1989 and the crimes of none other than Saddam Hussein. Indeed, as late as July 27, Bush was threatening to veto the 1990 farm bill if it carried with it trade sanctions aimed at punishing Hussein. Setting the tone for future pronouncements on the matter, Senator Alfonse D'Amato of New York had denounced the dictator in unequivocal language: "He's no president . . . This guy's a butcher . . . a mad dog and a killer . . . He gasses women and children."

The Administration was unmoved by D'Amato's eloquence. State Department spokesman Richard Boucher, presaging another future debate, disparaged the effectiveness of economic sanctions. "We just don't think it would help . . . in achieving the goals we want to achieve in our relationship with Iraq," he told the *Los Angeles Times*. No one evidently thought to ask what these goals were, but it hardly mattered in a world where symbols counted more than substance. The *Times* dispatch paraphrased an unnamed Administration official, saying the congressional sanctions amounted to a largely symbolic "blunderbuss approach liable to enrage Hussein without causing him to change his behavior." California congressman Wally Herger injected a note of healthy parochialism by remarking that Iraq bought a lot of rice from his state. In arguing successfully for a weaker version of the anti-Iraq amendment, Herger made a revealing statement: "There is no one here who does not abhor the human rights situation in Iraq, but sanctions like these don't work."[5]

In the final analysis, human rights were not much more than a political angle to the Bush Administration. Consequently, the major human rights organizations—Amnesty International, the Human Rights Watch committees, Physicians for Human Rights, and Article 19—were accustomed to being ignored by the Reagan/Bush people. There were exceptions, of course. If they chastised Administration allies, or were too moderate in their criticism of Administration enemies, the rights groups could expect the back of the State Department's hand from time to time.

Thus, one can imagine the astonishment among the staff at London-based Amnesty International, the oldest of the rights groups, when suddenly they found their services much admired and quoted by the Bush Administration and Hill and Knowlton. The work of Amnesty is, indeed, quite admirable. By dint of experience, independence, and good research, it enjoys a reputation for accuracy and credibility unmatched by almost any other entity, including the United Nations and the U.S. State Department. Among those in the know in international law and refugee work, Amnesty's reports were among the most authoritative available. The Amnesty imprimatur mattered also because of its international reach and its "urgent action network," which was capable of marshaling hundreds of telegrams from members to protest the torture or impending execution of political prisoners anywhere in the world at a moment's notice. Amnesty had evinced a lively interest in Saddam Hussein for years, so when he converted Kuwait into the nineteenth province of Iraq, it naturally increased its scrutiny. For once the rights group had the rapt attention of official Washington.

On October 10, the congressional Human Rights Caucus provided the first formal opportunity for Amnesty—and Hill and Knowlton—to present their evidence against Iraq on

Capitol Hill. Conveniently for the Washington war party and its burgeoning Saddam-is-Hitler industry, the caucus provided the appropriately informal setting in which to spread hysteria. The Human Rights Caucus is not a committee of Congress and therefore it is unencumbered by the legal accoutrements that would make a witness hesitate before he or she lied. Generally speaking, affairs concerning Iraq and Kuwait came within the purview of the House Committee on Foreign Affairs and the Senate Foreign Relations Committee. But just then, Congress was strenuously avoiding the Persian Gulf crisis, staying far out of harm's—and the President's—way. So the initial forum for public discussion in Congress was the Human Rights Caucus, which could cloak itself in the pieties of international law without messing around in politics.

Lying under oath in front of a congressional committee is a crime; lying from under the cover of anonymity to a caucus is merely public relations. There were indeed lies floating about that day, but they were not immediately discernible amidst the chorus of atrocity testimony. Amnesty sent Maryam Elahi of its Washington office, a genuine human rights worker with a first name and a last name. H&K sent a fifteen-year-old girl named "Nayirah," allegedly a Kuwaiti with firsthand knowledge of the situation inside her tortured land. Among other things, Nayirah had witnessed some of the same horrors as Cindy from San Francisco. She could not, of course, reveal her last name for fear of inviting reprisals against family and friends in Kuwait. The following is a sample of her tearful testimony, as highlighted in the CFK media kit:

> I volunteered at the al-Addan hospital . . . While I was there, I saw the Iraqi soldiers come into the hospital with guns, and go into the room where 15 babies were in incubators. They took the babies out of the incubators, took the inclubators, and left the babies on the cold floor to die.[6]

As young as she was, Nayirah was probably unaware of the historic significance of her statement. Practically everyone listening to her horror story was also unaware of something significant—that she was the daughter of Saud al-Sabah, Kuwait's ambassador to the United States, and therefore something less than a disinterested witness. Curiously, none of the congressmen present bothered to ask Nayirah, the hospital volunteer, why she hadn't bent down to pick up one of the dying infants, or called for help. But other forces were at work in the remarkably unskeptical minds of Caucus cochairmen Tom Lantos, a California Democrat, and John Edward Porter, an Illinois Republican. Up to that day, what Porter knew about the plight of Kuwait he learned on September 12 in a meeting with H&K vice president Gary Hymel and Dr. al-Ebraheem. Before taking on the Kuwait account, Hymel was best known to Congressman Porter as the hired apologist for Turkey's habitual torture, killing, and unjust imprisonment of its own citizens, as well as for the persecution of its hapless Kurdish minority.* As Turkey's representative, Hymel was also required to defend his client's unchecked "naked aggression" in Cyprus dating back to 1969. In his new capacity as lobbyist for the exiled government of Kuwait, Hymel had graciously agreed to provide witnesses for the Caucus hearing.†

Maryam Elahi told me months later that Nayirah's lurid tale was the first time she had heard the baby incubator story. I imagine that she and the rest of the Amnesty staff profoundly wish that it had been the last, for a short time later, the baby incubator story was bequeathed to Amnesty with tragic consequences for the organization's reputation for accuracy. The hearing, though, was an unqualified success for

* Hymel was also known on the Hill as the former administrative assistant to retired House Speaker Thomas P. (Tip) O'Neill.
† Porter continues to insist that he did not know Nayirah's true identity until he was told in December 1991. His cochairman, Lantos, admitted he knew who she was before the hearing. Ambassador al-Sabah said both congressmen were aware of Nayirah's identity before she made her now celebrated statement.

CFK/H&K. That night, at a White House function, President Bush told Porter that he had watched the hearings on CNN and had been delighted to see the caucus spotlight focused on the rape of Kuwait.

Of the terrifying "testimony," Caucus cochairman Lantos said, "In the eight-year history of the congressional Human Rights Caucus, we have never had the degree of ghoulish and nightmarish horror stories coming from totally credible eyewitnesses that we have had this time."* To anyone who followed atrocities in Africa, Asia, and Central America, this was truly an incredible statement.

One wonders what Representative Lantos was doing while the Guatemalan army was killing tens of thousands of civilians, and more than a million people were dying under brutal government policies in the Horn of Africa. Understanding the Lantos school of human rights may require a lesson in the way influence is bought and sold in the nation's capital. In 1990, besides chairing the Human Rights Caucus, Lantos and Porter were also cochairmen of the Congressional Human Rights Foundation, which they founded in 1985. Legally separate from the Caucus, the Foundation occupies free office space valued at $3,000 a year in Hill and Knowlton's Washington, D.C., headquarters. Messages for the Foundation's executive director, David Phillips, can be left with the H&K switchboard, which in the fall of 1990 was frequently lit up with calls from government representatives of Indonesia, another H&K client. Like H&K client Turkey, Indonesia is a practitioner of naked aggression, having seized (without objection from the U.S.) the former Portuguese colony of East Timor in 1975. Since the annexation of East Timor, the Indonesian government has killed, by conservative estimate, about 100,000 inhabitants of the region. On

---

* In his January 11, 1991, speech to the House advocating the war resolution, Porter concurred with Lantos on the scale of Iraqi atrocities: "the most sadistic, cruel, barbaric, brutal, and vicious program of torture and repression against the people of Kuwait that can be imagined."

November 8, 1990, a grateful Citizens for a Free Kuwait donated $50,000 to the Foundation; it was the second-largest contribution that year after the U.S.-government-funded National Endowment for Democracy grant. During the course of 1990, the Foundation paid Lantos's and Porter's travel and lodging expenses (sometimes covering their wives as well) for trips to New York and Europe. (These trips were said to be human-rights-related.) In October 1991, not long after H&K picked up the China account, Hill and Knowlton vice chairman Frank Mankiewicz joined the board of the Foundation.* Completing the circle, Lantos accepted a $500 campaign contribution from H&K's political action committee in 1988. But in 1990, he rejected the PR firm's political generosity and returned another $500 contribution. Lantos's press secretary, Bob King, told me the congressman didn't "need" H&K's money for his 1990 reelection campaign against a "not terribly tough opponent," and that Lantos did not consider taking political donations from a PR firm that represents egregious human rights violators to be a conflict of interest. "H&K has . . . a wide range of clients," he remarked. King said that Lantos and Mankiewicz are "old friends," and that his boss "has a good relationship with the [H&K] executives."

Middle East Watch, the New York–based human rights group, was also pursuing the baby reports. In a memo to executive director Andrew Whitley, its investigator, Aziz Abu-Hamad, cited a press conference in Jiddah, Saudi Arabia, on October 14, at which a Dr. Ahmed al-Shatti related stories of Iraqi torture and seizures of incubators. Abu-Hamad did what a good reporter is supposed to do and questioned the doctor, who was unable to document his

* In its 1990 report of "activities," the Foundation cited its work "with Citizens for a Free Kuwait to organize a Congressional Hearing in human rights in Kuwait following the Iraqi invasion." Indonesia and Turkey were notably absent from the report.

claims concerning the incubators or the premature babies who supposedly died. Abu-Hamad kept poking around in the region, interviewing refugee doctors who said that Iraqi soldiers had stolen hospital equipment and executed medical staff, but found nothing solid about the incubators. Abu-Hamad said in a memo to Whitley that on November 11 a Kuwaiti physician, Dr. Ali al-Hawil, denounced Iraqi attempts to disprove the baby incubator story by inviting foreign journalists to Kuwait. Al-Hawil, according to Abu-Hamad, said that between sixty and seventy babies had died in the Kuwait City maternity hospital after soldiers dismantled the premature-babies unit. He claimed that he and his colleagues had buried fifty babies, mostly premature, on August 20. But for every supposed eyewitness, Abu-Hamad found another doctor who provided conflicting evidence or outright refuted the incubator story. At last, in a December 19 memo to Whitley, Abu-Hamad warned his organization off babies and incubators. Exhibiting more restraint and maturity than the average journalist, Abu-Hamad wrote of the eyewitnesses to the incubator thefts: "What is . . . possible is that some of these witnesses—Drs. Ali al-Hawil (military hospital), Ibrahim Bahbahani (Red Crescent) and Fawziyya al-Sayegh (pediatrician), in particular—are doing their part in a public relations campaign by the Kuwaiti government, where truth is stretched quite a bit."

Furthermore, Abu-Hamad noted:

While it may be interesting for journalists or political scientists to study this story, I do not think we should go public with the information [contradicting the incubator story] we have.

It may look like we were trying to exonerate the Iraqi occupation from the gross abuses they committed in Kuwait hospitals. It would also detract from our work of documenting actual abuses. Moreover, trying to prove a deliberate disinformation campaign, assuming one exists,

is not an easy matter. In any case, this is not the province
of a human rights organization, especially in the case of
a habitual human rights offender such as Iraq.

In the fall, while Abu-Hamad was trying to find the truth
about the baby incubator story, Hill and Knowlton was busy
selling it to anyone who would listen. Following the success
of the congressional Human Rights Caucus hearing, the eager press agents took their baby atrocity campaign to the
eminently mediagenic locale of the United Nations Security
Council chamber. Nations have been invading one another
for most of the past forty-five years, but rarely in the history
of the U.N. had the Security Council permitted the sort of
dog-and-pony show that H&K presented on November 27
—via the exiled government of Kuwait—to illustrate the depredations of one country upon another. It didn't hurt, of
course, that the revolving presidency of the Council had
landed on the United States, so that U.S. Ambassador
Thomas Pickering was presiding over the meeting of the five
permanent members and the ten rotating ones. Pickering
informed the Council that at the request of Kuwait, "the
Council chamber has been equipped so that they may view
an audiovisual presentation," and that "in keeping with past
practice, I have requested the Secretariat to make the necessary technical arrangements." (Imagine, for a moment, the
response by Pickering if Nicaragua, through the good offices
of a public relations firm, had requested permission to present an audiovisual depiction of U.S.-backed contra killings
of women and children in cross-border raids from their U.S.-
financed bases in Honduras.) Nobody formally objected to
Pickering's invocation of "past practice," but the Cuban representative, Alarcon de Quesada, did raise procedural questions that highlighted a bit of hypocrisy over Council delays
in considering a resolution concerning the Israeli-occupied
West Bank.

In any event, the audiovisual presentation by CFK/H&K

was slick and effective.* It was also loaded with anonymous charges of Iraqi thuggery, mayhem, and murder. One
videotaped "witness" was clearly scripted to sound the
Saddam-is-Hitler theme that proved so useful to the White
House: "What Saddam did points to the Hitlerism of his
character. I was driving in my car when Iraqi troops came
racing up behind me. They mounted my car and gave me
these injuries." It seemed that Saddam was everywhere, personally meting out punishment, torturing Kuwaitis, and bayoneting and raping women. The videotapes were interspersed
with live witnesses, one of whom reiterated the baby incubator story. A Kuwaiti claiming to be a surgeon, and identified in the U.N.'s provisional transcript as "Dr. Issah
Ibrahim," or Witness No. 3, explained that after the Iraqis
took over "the hardest thing was burying the babies. Under
my supervision, 120 newborn babies were buried the second
week of the invasion. I myself buried 40 newborn babies that
had been taken from their incubators by soldiers."

The next day, the major media failed to mention Hill
and Knowlton's involvement with the hearings, and their
news reports converted the claims of the "witnesses" into
"testimony." Evidently no one thought to point out that the
Kuwaiti spokesmen were not under oath. As Victoria Graham, U.N. correspondent for the Associated Press, explained after the war, "There was not a great deal of inquiry
[by] the media."

Had they made inquiries, the U.N. reporters might have
discovered that five of the seven witnesses at the U.N. that
day—coached by the Hill and Knowlton team led by Lauri
Fitz-Pegado—had used false names without saying they were
doing so. Nayirah, in publicly maintaining her anonymity,
had used the cover of trying to protect her family in Kuwait.
"Dr. Issah Ibrahim" made no such pretense. His real name

* Two days later, the Security Council passed Resolution 678 authorizing member states to use military force to evict Iraqi troops from Kuwait.

was Dr. Ibrahim Behbehani (the same person as the Dr. Bahbahani mentioned in Abu-Hamad's memo to Andrew Whitley) and he was a dentist, not a surgeon. In response to my questions in January 1992 about Behbehani's credibility, Hill and Knowlton made much of his status as head of the Kuwaiti Red Crescent, an organization similar to the Red Cross, although government-controlled. But why would a well-known public health official—even one working for the Kuwaiti government—need to hide his identity if not to mislead the media and human rights investigators, and to make follow-up inquiries more difficult?

The other "witnesses" to Iraqi bestiality at the U.N. included Fatima Mutawa, the wife of the man who was then Kuwait's planning minister and formerly the host of a television show in Kuwait. Mrs. Mutawa was identified as "Mrs. Fatima Fahed," or Witness No. 1.[7] Information on the destruction of Kuwait's economy came from Witness No. 7, who was introduced as "Fawzi Badr." Mr. Badr was really Fawzi al-Sultan, a vice president of Citizens for a Free Kuwait and for the preceding six years a vice president of the World Bank, based in Washington. (Hill and Knowlton insisted that a press conference and press release after the Security Council hearing made it clear that the witnesses had used fake names to protect relatives in Kuwait against Iraqi reprisals. I was never shown proof of this.)

Before the Security Council media show, the baby incubator story had already begun to work its way into the national political debate. On October 15, at a fund-raiser for Texas gubernatorial candidate Clayton Williams, President Bush began spinning political gold out of dead babies. "I met with the Emir of Kuwait. And I heard horrible tales: newborn babies thrown out of incubators and the incubators then shipped off to Baghdad." Bush referred to the baby incubator story five more times in the next five weeks. In a speech to the troops near Dhahran he did his best imitation of an H&K press release: "It turns your stomach when you listen to the tales of those that have escaped the brutality of Saddam the invader. Mass hangings. Babies pulled from incubators and scattered like firewood across the floor." Congress and the United Nations had been plied with the story, which left only Amnesty and Middle East Watch to convince. Amnesty was the one to bite, and when it did, Bush would be able to stop calling the baby incubator story a "tale." Amnesty's blockbuster eighty-four-page report on human rights violations in occupied Kuwait appeared on December 19 with some considerable impact. The baby incubator story appeared with slight qualification on page 57 of the report, but was promoted as a fact in the second paragraph of Amnesty's press release: "Amnesty International details how Iraqi forces have . . . left more than 300 premature babies to die after looting incubators from at least three of Kuwait City's main hospitals." Now the tale had the ring of authority because it carried Amnesty's imprimatur. The text of the report read as follows:

> In addition, over 300 premature babies were reported to have died after Iraqi soldiers removed them from incubators, which were then looted. Such deaths were reported at al-Razi and al-Addan hospitals, as well as the Maternity Hospital.

For backup Amnesty cited two unidentified doctors who reported observing the burials of seventy-two and thirty-six premature babies, respectively. One of them said that 312 had died this way. Amnesty also cited Nayirah's testimony to the congressional Human Rights Caucus without mentioning even her first name. Baby incubators had made a quantum leap in public relations terms and helped move the world closer to war. Bush was quick to capitalize on the Amnesty report, and on January 9 he used it to execute a brilliant maneuver: an open letter to college students that was sent to campus newspapers all over the country. It read in part:

> The terror Saddam Hussein has imposed upon Kuwait violates every principle of human decency. Listen to what Amnesty International has documented. "Widespread abuses of human rights have been perpetrated by Iraqi forces . . . arbitrary arrest and detention without trial of thousands . . . widespread torture . . . imposition of the death penalty and the extrajudicial execution of hundreds of unarmed civilians, including children . . .
>
> There's no horror that could make this a more obvious conflict of good vs. evil . . .
>
> Each day that passes means another day for Iraq's forces to dig deeper into their stolen land. Another day Saddam Hussein can work toward building his nuclear arsenal and perfecting his chemical and biological weapons capability.[8] Another day of atrocities for Amnesty International to document . . .

Amnesty's U.S. executive director, John Healey, had compounded the baby incubator error in testimony to the House Committee on Foreign Affairs on January 8, despite Andrew Whitley's urging before the hearing to hold back. By then, the media had bought the baby incubator story lock, stock, and barrel, with only a few minor exceptions. On September 30, two days after the Emir visited Bush in Washington, the *Seattle Times* published an interview with a Palestinian doctor who had visited Kuwait, contradicting the incubator allegations. The story ran on page 13. *USA Today* published a brief story on page 7 of its December 10 edition, quoting an Icelandic doctor who had left Kuwait three weeks earlier. Of the incubator story, Dr. Gisli Sigurdsson said, "That news was not true . . . However, there were lots of babies who died because of lack of staff over the last few weeks." Most pediatric specialists in Kuwait were foreigners and many had fled, he explained. To his credit, ABC's Peter Jennings on December 18 cited Middle East Watch's refusal to confirm the incubator story. But until Alexander Cockburn openly challenged what he called "the incubator myth" in the January 17, 1991, *Los Angeles Times*, no one in the media stood up to the avalanche of propaganda emanating from Hill and Knowlton and the White House. Cockburn's column came too late to make a difference; the bombing of Iraq had begun the night before.

The significance of the baby incubator story in the larger propaganda campaign against Saddam Hussein and for the war option cannot be underestimated. Without it, the comparison of Hussein with Hitler loses its luster; to make the case effectively, one had to prove Hussein's utter depravity. Aziz Abu-Hamad of Middle East Watch summed things up rather well in a January 6 memo to Andrew Whitley dealing with incubators and propaganda in general. First the incubators:

> Because Iraq has refused to allow neutral observers and journalists to monitor the situation in Kuwait, rumours sometimes were the only source of information. The incubator deaths may be one of these stories . . . It is possible, though not very likely, that a number of babies may have died because of some unauthorized action by some over-zealous Iraqi soldiers . . . What is not possible is deaths in the numbers reported by AI, or even close to them. I wonder if AI has the names of any families of the reported 350-plus killed premature babies. They have, as we do, names of people killed in other ways, and names of detainees, but I have yet to come across the name of one family whose premature baby was allegedly thrown out of an incubator.

Then a coda on the effect of propaganda in wartime:

In August, while in Saudi Arabia, I reported to MEW
how the leading Saudi daily, *Al-Riyadh*, published on its
front page photographs of four children who had died of
thirst while trying to cross the border from Kuwait. It
turned out that the story was bogus and so were the
photographs, as the newspaper had to admit a week later.
Saudi, Kuwaiti, and Egyptian newspapers are full of similar stories. So are U.S. papers. Many prominent Kuwaitis had been reported dead before I left for Saudi
Arabia in mid-October, but I was surprised to find them
alive and well in the Kuwaiti Popular Conference. For
example the L.A. *Times* reported [on October 5] that
Dr. Abdul al-Sumait, a senior official of the Red Crescent, had been killed and his mutilated body was thrown
in front of his house. Dr. al-Sumait is also alive and well.
When he is not on public relations tours for the Kuwaiti
cause, he shares offices with the Kuwaiti government-in-
exile. He is also the source of much of AI's information
on incubators.

There is no doubt that Saddam Hussein's troops did terrible things in Kuwait, but given the record of distortion and
propaganda it will require a detailed investigation by an experienced observer to discover what really happened during the
seven-month occupation. The Kuwaitis clearly have no incentive to give such a balanced account, but someone should
attempt it. The perceived degree of violence and terror
committed had everything to do with America's choice of
war, and even with the acceptance of the distortions it was a
narrowly won decision. Who is to say whether minus the
incubator story the Administration would have carried the
day? How many other reported atrocities were false? House
Committee on Foreign Affairs member Stephen Solarz co-
sponsored the congressional war resolution that was ultimately passed by both houses of Congress; at the January 8
hearing on Kuwait, he quoted the Amnesty report verbatim:

"Over 300 babies were reported to have died after Iraqi soldiers removed them from incubators." In the Senate, where the resolution for war authorization passed on January 12 by a five-vote margin, six pro-war senators (five Republicans and one Democrat) specifically cited the baby incubator allegation in their speeches supporting the resolution.* (Four other pro-war senators invoked the Amnesty report in general or the alleged execution of Kuwaiti children by Iraqi forces.)

None of this could have occurred without the media's overwhelming credulity and willingness to repeat again and again the Hitler analogy. Bush had accused Hussein's troops of "outrageous acts of barbarism that even Adolf Hitler never committed," and reporters were unwilling to challenge the obvious speciousness of the comparison.† In the weird world of public relations, such comparisons do spring up from time to time without necessarily causing wars; this year's Hitler can be next year's stabilizing force. In 1979, for example, Manor Books published Ayatollah Khomeini's *Islamic Government* under a different title, *Ayatollah Khomeini's Mein Kampf*. In the accompanying text, George Carpozi, Jr., wrote: "Like Adolf Hitler from another time . . . Khomeini is a tyrant, a hater, a baiter, a threat to world order and peace. The principal difference between the author of 'Mein Kampf' and the compiler of the vapid 'Islamic Government' is that one was an atheist while the other pretends to be a man of God." Thus it was perhaps fitting when the Iranians turned the rhetorical tables on Hussein during the Iran–Iraq war; a Canadian documentary about Iran that aired in Jan-

* Senator Alan Cranston, undergoing chemotherapy in California on the day of the vote, said he would have opposed the war resolution, making the unofficial tally 52–48. He said he would have left the hospital to vote no had Senate Majority Leader George Mitchell told him the outcome was in doubt.
† President Bush never said that Saddam Hussein was "worse than Hitler." This was a newspaper paraphrase of Bush's aforementioned quote from a speech delivered on November 8, 1990. Thereafter, "worse than Hitler" was attributed directly to Bush.

uary 1987 on PBS quoted an Iranian official saying of Hussein, "He has committed crimes that even Hitler didn't commit." But the Hitler comparison remained largely dormant in the mainstream American press until April 5, 1990, when A. M. Rosenthal of *The New York Times* alerted the public to the notion that Hussein "wants to wipe out the Jews of Israel and rule the Middle East. He has made this as clear as *Mein Kampf* . . . Mass murderers like Hitler and Hussein have a deep urge to tell the world of their blood lusts." After the invasion of Kuwait, the *Times*'s William Safire, formerly an accomplished press agent and speech writer in the Nixon Administration, responded with outrage to Hussein's sinister televised display of English-speaking hostages in Kuwait. Writing in the *Times* on August 24 he bolstered the Hitler comparison in prose better suited to a Hill and Knowlton press release:

> If anyone wondered whether the analogy of Saddam Hussein to a predecessor aggressor and mass murderer, Adolf Hitler, might be an exaggeration, all doubt was removed yesterday when the Iraqi dictator forced the world to triage.

The world could be saved, Safire wrote, if

> by moving quickly we can reduce the capacity of this generation's Hitler to put innocent lives at risk. Nearly 10,000 Western civilians, mostly British and American, are holed up in captured Kuwait City. If Saddam gets his hands on them, as he intends to, they are to be designated human targets and doomed.*

A letter writer to *The New York Times* critiqued the comparison this way after the war: "Hitler's aim was the

---

* Saddam Hussein announced the release of all remaining hostages on December 6, 1990.

annihilation of the Jews, no matter where they lived. Saddam Hussein's [stated] aim is the annihilation of Israel. Since Israel and Iraq are still technically in a state of war, it's perfectly natural for each to wish the annihilation of the other. The difference, however, is that Hitler made war on a people." The writer, Dave Goldman, added this: "My father [who lost several family members to the Nazis] must be turning over in his grave . . . If there is a country to evoke on Holocaust memorial day, it is Germany, the third wealthiest country in the world today. But it has nothing to do with Saddam Hussein or Yasir Arafat or any other Arab who ever lived."

Nonetheless, on the day of the invasion of Kuwait, official Washington picked up the Hitler angle instantly. The vaguely liberal chairman of the Senate Foreign Relations Committee, Claiborne Pell, and right-wing representative Newt Gingrich immediately interjected the Hitler theme on August 2, adding simultaneously a domino theory of Nazi aggression against Czechoslovakia and Poland in the 1930s. Likewise, Israeli Defense Minister Moshe Arens banged the Hitler drum; with Hussein's penchant for using chemical weapons the comparison had particular resonance for Jews. (Representative Solarz would later make pointed reference to the large number of Nazi murder-camp survivors living in his district.)

Hardly any reporters were heard challenging the President on his Hitler comparison at press conferences. If they did under other circumstances, I have found no record of it. Washington is, in the words of former *New York Times* bureau chief Bill Kovach, a "court city," and impertinent questions addressed to the king do not generally advance journalism careers. The main thing is not to be different, but rather to be the same as everyone else. So the baby incubator story and the Hitler analogy stood throughout the war. Anxious liberals like Anthony Lewis, presumably comforted by the stories of Iraqi atrocities, could call the massive U.S.

bombardment "just" though not perhaps "wise." On February 15, in a speech at Fort Hood, Texas, Vice President Dan Quayle fanned the flames of American righteousness, declaring, "There are pictures Saddam doesn't want us to see. Pictures of premature babies in Kuwait that were tossed out of their incubators and left to die." Only one congressman, Jimmy Hayes of Louisiana, publicly questioned the propriety of H&K's promotion campaign. Hayes's protests met with indifference among his colleagues.

After the war, John Martin of ABC News tried to straighten out the mess of false information. On March 15, in Kuwait City, he interviewed Dr. Mohammed Matar, director of Kuwait's primary health-care system, and his wife, Dr. Fayeza Youssef, the chief of obstetrics at the maternity hospital. "No, [the Iraqis] didn't take [the babies] away from their incubator . . . to tell the truth . . . No nurses to take care of these babies and that's why they died," said Youssef. Martin then asked the right follow-up question. "But, I mean, this is very specific," he said. " 'Iraqi soldiers took them out of the incubators and put them on the floor to die.' "

"I think this is something just for propaganda," replied Dr. Matar.

People, including babies, did die, Martin reported, "when large numbers of Kuwait's doctors and nurses stopped working or fled the country in terror."

Displaying initiative sorely lacking before the war, Martin caught up with Dr. Ibrahim Behbehani, the dentist claiming to be a surgeon who told the U.N. Security Council— while using the assumed name "Issah Ibrahim"—of personally burying forty babies that had died after being removed from incubators by the Iraqis. Behbehani, the acting director of Kuwait's Red Crescent Society, was unable to provide documentation on what had happened in Kuwait during the occupation—all the medical records of deaths during the period had been destroyed, he said. On the incubator atrocity question, Behbehani admitted, "I can't tell you if they [the babies] were taken from incubators . . . I didn't see it."* Finally, Martin reached al-Addan Hospital, the place where Nayirah said she witnessed the removal of fifteen babies from their incubators. Martin asked Dr. Fahima Khafaji, a pediatrician, for confirmation. "No," she said. "I didn't see."

"Not at your hospital?" Martin asked. "No," she replied. "In the maternity hospital they did, not in my hospital, in maternity hospital."

Amnesty climbed down from the story a month later. In the seventh paragraph of a press release, the organization stated that

> on the highly publicized issue in the December report of the deaths of babies, Amnesty International said that although its team was shown alleged mass graves of babies, it was not established how they had died and the team found no reliable evidence that Iraqi forces had caused the deaths of babies by removing them or ordering their removal from incubators.

John Healey, Amnesty's U.S. executive director, was fuming when asked how his organization had been misled. But he couldn't really explain what had happened. Neither could Sean Stiles of the London office, who nonetheless told me that witnesses interviewed by Amnesty investigators "seemed incredibly sincere. They didn't seem to be acting." What enraged Healey more than being wrong on an absolutely critical question, however, was Bush's hypocritical exploitation of the Amnesty report and his subsequent refusal

* After the war, Middle East Watch said it was shown death certificates for thirty Kuwaiti babies who were all buried on August 24, 1990. Nineteen of the babies died in June and July, before the Iraqi invasion, according to the rights group, and eleven died between August 2 and August 24, during the occupation. None of the thirty were ever shown to have been removed from incubators. (Dr. Behbehani also backed off his story of "supervising" the burials of 120 babies.)

to meet with Amnesty officials on other issues, including atrocities in newly liberated Kuwait.

Despite the Amnesty retraction, the baby incubator story refused to go away. At a June 1991 hearing of the congressional Human Rights Caucus, Cindy McCain (not the "Cindy" from San Francisco), the wife of pro-war Senator John McCain, insisted under questioning that the allegations were true. Later, Mrs. McCain acknowledged that she, like so many others, was relying on hearsay.

It would be neater if the baby incubator story was the only example of successful, and false, propaganda. But Martin found others. Early reports after the invasion had the Iraqis removing forty thousand Kuwaitis from Kuwait City for transfer to Iraq. At the time of Martin's report, twelve hundred had been returned. Andrew Whitley of Middle East Watch said the number of Kuwaitis seized had likely been between fifteen hundred and two thousand. And, in another example, Amnesty, in its December 19 report, had estimated that "the number of extrajudicial killings runs into hundreds, and may well be over 1,000." A senior Kuwaiti public-health official told Martin the number was "a little bit over 300."

Even the very believable image of raping, looting, and pillaging Iraqi soldiers—completely exempt from ordinary military discipline—came into question after the war. *Paris Match* published a photograph in its March 28, 1991, issue which was taken sometime during the Iraqi occupation of Kuwait and which appeared to show an Iraqi firing squad executing six blindfolded men in Kuwait City. In a caption above the picture, the *Paris Match* editors explained that the photo had first arrived at their office on November 30, 1990, and they had assumed that it depicted Iraqis shooting Kuwaiti resisters. The editors learned on December 1 that the firing squad was in fact executing disobedient *Iraqi* soldiers who had been caught looting Kuwait City. They decided not to publish the exclusive pictures in a December 1990 issue for fear of undermining the French role in the anti-Hussein coalition. "It was our obligation," the editors wrote in the March 1991 caption, "to renounce publication so as not, in the name of the scoop, to aid the image of Saddam Hussein."

John Chancellor of NBC was directly on the point when he wrote, albeit after the war, of Operation Desert Storm: "The conflict brought with it a baggage train of myth and misconception, exaggeration and hyperbole . . . Accounts of Iraqi atrocities were accepted without question. There was the tale of premature babies thrown out of incubators in a Kuwait hospital and left to die. It never happened, although other sickening atrocities took place regularly during the Iraqi occupation . . . There were facts misperceived, truth bent out of shape and a fog of myth and misconception."

This is not to say that babies did not perish by removal from their incubators during the Gulf War. In July 1991, Patrick Tyler of *The New York Times* interviewed a certain Dr. Qasm Ismail, director of Baghdad's Saddam Pediatric Hospital, about the first night of the allied bombardment. Dr. Ismail described the panic that ensued from the explosions and loss of electricity:

"Mothers grabbed their children out of incubators, took intravenous tubes out of their arms . . . Others were removed from oxygen tents, and they ran to the basement, where there was no heat. I lost more than 40 prematures in the first 12 hours of the bombing."

The success of the CFK/H&K campaign can be summed up in one sentence from a February 16, 1991, column in the *Spectator* by the right-wing British author Paul Johnson, who was lecturing critics of the war on their dangerous irresponsibility.[9]

> Saddam's murder of thousands of Kurds by chemical weapons, his slaughter of 7,000 Kuwaitis—including babies torn from life-support machines which were then

stolen—and his systematic stripping of this small country of all its valuables, public and private, are well authenticated.

It hardly mattered by then that they had never been authenticated at all.[10]

CHAPTER 3

Designing War

Real war stinks of rotting corpses.
—MALCOLM BROWNE
from a talk at the Foreign Policy Association in
New York City on April 8, 1991

ON JUNE 16, 1991, hundreds of members of the Broadcast Designers' Association (BDA) and its sister organization, the Broadcast Promotion and Marketing Executives (BPME), assembled in Baltimore for their annual awards ceremony and convention. As with other professional or trade associations, this get-together provided the people who make television look the way it does the opportunity to compare notes, explore the job market, marvel at the latest in design technology, and officially congratulate themselves on their hard work over the past year. But the shoptalk was tinged with something special this year as the graphics people milled about the Baltimore Convention Center in anticipation of the naming of the gold and silver award winners. An exciting undercurrent of BPME-BDA Conference & Expo '91 was the subject of designing war.

Unfortunately for some of the professionals in attendance, the award nominations were limited to 1990 achievements, and could not include their artistry during Operation Desert Storm. Still, two of their colleagues, Mitch Friedman and Don Butler of Post Perfect, had garnered a nomination in the Animation/Production House category for their "Showdown in the Gulf" graphics on CBS. And an early-morning seminar on war design entitled "Design on the Frontlines" drew an interested audience; in keeping with the upbeat atmosphere following the Gulf War, the convention brochure had billed the panel discussion in a humorous vein: "The Schwarzkopfs of the nets and cable show how their strategic command centers of technological design warfare operated during the Gulf War crisis."

Antiwar media critics had complained about network television's proclivity to "sanitize" the face of battle with video graphics. But this missed the point of good television design, which is meant to attract viewers as well as hide ugliness. Well-done graphics, in theory, are supposed to help ratings.

"Perhaps broadcast news graphics faced its biggest challenge during the Gulf War," intoned panel moderator Philip Meggs, a professor of graphic design at Virginia Commonwealth University. "I probably should say the most recent Gulf War, since peoples have been fighting over the Persian Gulf area since the time of the ancient Sumerians five thousand years ago. It might be good if you kept those Gulf map files; you might need them again in a few years."

Professor Meggs was nothing if not sensitive to World War II imagery employed by the Bush Administration. The Gulf War, he said, "was about ghosts—[for example] the ghost of Neville Chamberlain . . . Many of you have probably seen that nineteen thirty-eight newsreel where Chamberlain gets off his airplane and they stick all the microphones in his face and he says, 'I think we have achieved peace in our time.' "* He noted that "The Gulf War . . . was about the ability of the mass media to deliver and even shape the news, and also about the ability of governments, both ours and Saddam's, to shape and control the news."

Pentagon censorship, Meggs suggested, had forced TV

---

* The correct quote is "I believe it is peace for our time," and Chamberlain said it at 10 Downing Street, not at the airfield.

graphics departments to innovate under pressure and ultimately achieve their finest hour.

> [Censorship] put tremendous pressure on graphics to con-
> vey information and support news reports. The broadcast
> news graphics departments at all the networks found
> themselves under siege, working in around-the-clock
> combat conditions to keep pace with rapidly changing
> situations. Maps, battlefield models, and informational
> graphics on weapons systems helped anchors and experts
> explain the war. Technical terms and weapons systems
> mentioned in the constant briefings had to be explained
> to viewers with graphics.

In this challenging atmosphere,

> immediate needs for a specific graphic would appear un-
> expectedly. And, of course, each network needed an
> identity for its war coverage. Thus while the Olympics
> or World Series will have one logo, the Gulf War, which
> became a television special event, went on the air with
> five logos . . . Some editorial writers asked if dazzling
> graphics and upbeat soundtracks had given war the am-
> bience of football playoffs and African adventure movies.
> I think the Gulf War might be seen in a sense as the
> coming of age for broadcast graphics.

Indeed it was. Never before had carefully designed electronic imagery so dominated the coverage of a conflict. It
was the first full-fledged video logo war; Vietnam-era film of
actual fighting would look crude and old-fashioned alongside
the slick production values of Operation Desert Graphic.
And since animated slaughter was obviously out of the question, the imagery harmonized perfectly with the Pentagon's
plans to hide the killing.

"What did people expect to see, bloody limbs?" asked
Steve Vardy, the art director of CBS Evening News. "We

have an obligation to represent what happened, but we don't have to do it in a grisly manner." Not that they couldn't make it grisly if they had wanted to. Vardy said in an interview after the panel discussion that animation "has become so good that people sometimes forget that it's a simulation." Vardy, it seems, assumed a great deal about his viewers: that their delicate sensibilities would be offended by brutal combat scenes and that they would simply "know" war is violent without being shown the evidence. "Part of the problem with the criticism of the media is that nobody is giving the viewer responsibility for what they think," he said. "Unless a person watching is completely brain-dead, they should know that people are dying. It's not our obligation to show that. And I am personally disturbed when they do show that."

Ralph Famiglietta, director of news graphics for NBC Network News and a Vietnam veteran, said he had some qualms about the automated image of war presented on the networks: "That bothered me. People didn't know what was happening . . . it was a little too *Top Gun*–y . . . I was concerned about my children and the way it made war look fun." But Famiglietta apparently did not act on his reservations. "No designer came to me during the Gulf conflict over a political reason; they were concerned about aesthetics and layout. We're a service. We work up concepts of machinery to embellish information . . . It's not our job to put on something that will get millions of people upset."

BDA's president, Judi Decker, was similarly squeamish about disturbing the audience with troubling images. In her work as graphics director of KCRA-TV in Sacramento, she wanted to "stand out [but] be pertinent and go with as much emotion as you can do tastefully . . . The audience is inviting you into their living room, so what we do has to be in good taste and get the message across simply . . . With AIDS, for example, you don't want to show victims, because they're very gaunt and horrible-looking. In the news business you don't show bodies being taken away, you don't show a lot of blood, or injections, and in California dead animals get everyone upset." One needed to keep in mind, Decker said, that "there are people at the table, eating."

According to Steve Cheney, a supervisor at the Associated Press's (AP) television graphics service, the Gulf War provided art directors with "a real kick in the butt." Because good photographs were unavailable, "graphics became especially valuable." Indeed, said Cheney, it became acceptable for graphics to tell most of the story (along with Pentagon videotapes) on the evening news. Cheney's rules of television graphic design are basically to keep it simple, fast, and varied. He criticized CNN's "War in the Gulf" presentation because the music and logo became stale and should have been "freshened" from time to time. Logos, he said, ought to convince the audience that they are about to see something really different. "A lot of Americans thought [the Gulf conflict] wasn't as big as it really was," he said. "The opening [of news broadcasts] was like a fanfare. It said: 'Here comes something important. This is special Gulf War coverage; it's time to perk up your ears.' "

Cheney's AP associate, Brad Kalbfeld, explained that television graphics are less effective in imparting news than they are in creating impressions. Research has demonstrated, he said, that news stories illustrated with graphics leave a deeper impression than those that are unadorned, so that viewers may remember the graphic long after they have forgotten the story that went with it. Because emotions create more powerful impressions among viewers than information, Kalbfeld explained, television producers use graphics to create certain moods as well as to provide information. But there is not much time in which to do this—three or four seconds at most—and this forces designers to eliminate complex issues and boil the news story down to its essence. There simply isn't room for lengthy explanations.

The designer Schwarzkopfs had presented the conceptual framework. But what about the nuts and bolts, the Scuds and Patriots, the graphic hardware, as it were? During the panel discussion, Steve Vardy of CBS described his network's "preparation for . . . coverage of human hostility in the Persian Gulf" in terms that neatly summarized his department's role in the war extravaganza:

> From a design point of view the project had four basic components. First, there was the opening title animation; second, there were the informational graphics, the fact sheets which we refer to as baseball cards, which depicted the military equipment and the weaponry which was deployed in the Gulf; [third] a map format, which included both animated and still maps; and finally, the graphic depictions of events in the Gulf. Obviously there were no video or battle re-creations or illustrations of the Iraqi defenses or what have you.

Vardy gave special credit to his freelancers from Post Perfect, who proposed the "most striking storyboard" for "Showdown in the Gulf," CBS's signature graphic heralding the start of the war. The prize-nominated design was lovingly described in the April 1991 issue of "Clips," the newsletter of Quantel, a British graphics company:

> The open features a map, an animated radar sweep [inside a stylized CBS eye], the CBS News title . . . and icons associated with war, atop rotating beveled glass panels which flip over, revealing war footage and flags from countries involved in the conflict.
> To create the map and radar sweep, animator Steve Blakey sent a hi-con of the map and a moving line to 2-D.
> Then, Quantel Paintbox/Harry artist Don Butler painted the map to give it colour and texture, and created a green trail of light to transform the moving line into a radar sweep. The CBS News title was digitized in Wave-

front from flat art. A brushed aluminum texture, created on Paintbox, was mapped in 3-D onto the title.

At [Mitch] Friedman's request CBS News provided icons of war ships, jet fighters and soldiers, which were manipulated in Paintbox and used in a variety of forms throughout this piece. All elements were composited in [2-D] by special effects editor Tim Farrell.

Quantel should have added that the effect was unquestionably that of a video game, with tiny planes and soldiers moving across the radar screen, presumably targeted for zapping by whoever put a quarter in the machine.

Over at NBC, Ralph Famiglietta, the Vietnam veteran, had seen his department "kind of turned into a graphics MASH unit" when faced with demands for large quantities of imagery in no time flat. Famiglietta described the scene: "In the early days of the coverage, the department started to change its aesthetic look; from a nice-looking records department it started to look like a war room. Maps hung up on the walls, plenty of food in the kitchen because people would be working all kinds of crazy hours." Using some of the jargon of the designer's trade, Famiglietta provided his colleagues with numbers and inventory to illustrate the hard work involved:

Title animations, 2-D and 3-D variations, over fifty to sixty produced in-house; 3-D, 2-D military weapons systems; Scud missiles and Patriots, at least thirty or forty of those. Fifteen hundred to eighteen hundred static graphics. Cross-talk boxes. Tom Brokaw is sitting in a box talking to Arthur Kent, that type of format, at least three hundred of those particular backgrounds. Phoners for correspondents who couldn't get any pictures out of the theater of operations, at least a hundred of those. Base maps for the theater of operation, at least 150 to 200 maps. Combinations of animated maps that worked over those bases, at least seventy to one hundred. Numerous cutouts, two hundred cutouts of symbols, tanks, blasts, every possible combination. You can't really get into the flags and all the other pictures that were in our library system.

Of course, no opening network graphic would be complete without music, and during the war it seemed that every television and network radio report was accompanied by catchy synthesized tunes designed to excite and inspire the populace. Kim Thompson, director of broadcast sales for VTS Productions of Asheville, North Carolina, noted that the style of music could vary from completely synthesized music to a full sixty-piece orchestra. (Her orchestrated packages ranged in price from $20,000 to $40,000.) Thompson particularly admired the work of ABC's "Good Morning America," on which, she said, the theme music introducing war coverage made a strong statement: "It said, this is urgent news, pay attention." One needed this sort of urgency, she said, because television, unlike print, stimulates people aurally as well as visually. Because viewers frequently do other things while the television is on (making dinner, eating, ironing, etc.), "they need audio clues to know when to pay closer attention."

(In my own pondering about theme music, I realized that Steve Cheney of the Associated Press was right. The worst thing that could happen was for it to turn stale, as did the synthesized Desert Storm theme on WINS, Westinghouse Broadcasting's all-news radio station in New York. After tolerating several weeks of punishment, I would immediately turn off the radio upon hearing the beginning strains of its horribly ersatz horn music.)

With one exception—Cathe Ishino, from the "MacNeil/Lehrer Newshour," who opposed the war—the news designers insisted on their right to political neutrality while creating the visually pleasing war imagery that was so central to the public's understanding of Desert Storm and so central to enticing people to tune in. They were, they said, merely following instructions, and it wasn't for them to question them. But on the question of war, who can be neutral? While the graphic artists were designing their so-called "baseball cards," the American and Iraqi armies were gearing up to kill one another. At the same time, network executives were preparing to fight their own war: the one for market share. The contention that the news bureaucrats remained noncommittal on the issue of going to war—either before or during the fighting—is preposterous if one considers a design alternative: Bring up the second movement of Beethoven's *Pastoral* Symphony and flash a dove and three-dimensional olive branch floating through the United Nations logo. Have the voice-over say, *"The quest for peace: CBS News brings you continuing coverage of the world community's efforts to avert war in the Persian Gulf."*

This is not to suggest that network news executives are bloodthirsty warmongers, only that they want to keep their jobs. If Steve Vardy had requested storyboards like the one above—on the possibly legitimate grounds that negotiations to prevent a war were as important a story as preparations to start one—he might have been sent to the company doctor, or fired. The truth is that war, or the threat of war, makes a better story than peace, and the five-and-a-half-month buildup to Desert Storm provided a rare opportunity for media war hype on a grand scale. Alas, "Showdown in the Gulf" only placed third in its category, but Post Perfect said it picked up about $90,000 from CBS for the effort.

In theory, newspapers and magazines were at a tremendous technical disadvantage in their competition with television to cover the buildup and the war. With the advent of instant satellite coverage and CNN's round-the-clock news service, there was virtually nothing print could show that television hadn't already had a crack at. But in a censored war, the pictures can't be very interesting. Video footage of correspondents standing in front of their hotel in Dhahran reading the latest military press release; planes taking off and landing; generals with pointers and maps—all of this can become quite dull. And, as we've seen, the broadcast designers were called on more often precisely because government censorship made it difficult for the networks to obtain really interesting footage. Newspaper and magazine photo editors were similarly constrained by the shortage of lively war photographs. Faced with a visual gap, the print medium, too, was forced to rely more heavily on graphic design to describe reality, and they did it with gusto. Moreover, graphic design in print was far ahead of its parvenu electronic competitor simply because it had been around longer. Steve Cheney of the Associated Press credited a newspaper, *USA Today*, with augmenting the importance of television graphics. "*USA Today* helped redefine graphics for print, which rebounded back onto the way they were used on television," he said. "It became acceptable for graphics to tell most of the story."

The result was that while television had an inherent advantage in images, the press was not very far behind TV in using graphics. Across the country, newspaper readers were supplied with special four-color pullout sections, clearly influenced by *USA Today*. But where was the news? For the most part these bright and punchy graphics amounted to nothing more than Defense Department visual press releases, depicting DOD's official estimates of Iraqi and allied troop and weapons strengths. There was something childlike in these enthusiastic and abstract displays of military power, all the more so because of the Pentagon's gross exaggeration of Iraqi technical capabilities and willpower. And at times it seemed as though the civilian "kids" from an old Mickey Rooney movie—who normally worked blithely on the *USA Today* weather map and sports page—had been drafted into the DOD Department of Public Affairs.

In this atmosphere of cheerfully antiseptic war promotion, magazines had a distinct advantage over newspapers because their longer lead time allowed more planning and their glossy paper produced better-quality images. The competition was particularly intense between *Time* and *Newsweek*, and their bruising pullout map war became the talk of the trade. Operation Desert Storm took place in the midst of a deep recession, and the newsweeklies were desperate for newsstand circulation gains that might rouse a frighteningly poor advertising market. *Newsweek* was first with its "Pullout Map of the War Zone" in its February 4 issue. The section was little more than a poster, with five Hammond maps depicting the Middle East and inset maps of smaller areas. One of the four-color maps of the region was titled "Decades of Turmoil," and purported to tell the history of the Middle East since World War II with small copy blocks within the countries. Evidently nothing worth mentioning had happened in the Middle East before the war. (*Newsweek*'s readers might have liked knowing a little bit about how arbitrarily the British drew the borders of Iraq, Kuwait, and Saudi Arabia in 1922. Or about the stimulating historical irony, in 1938, when the Kuwaiti ruler's advisory council passed resolutions recommending union with Iraq and were prevented from doing so by the British.[1]) After World War II, the narrative picked up a bit. *Newsweek* relates that in 1953 a "royalist coup" took place in Iran, but against whom the coup was directed the reader must guess. Nothing is said about its having been a British- and U.S.-instigated overthrow of Iran's nationalist government. Over in Egypt, *Newsweek* historians discovered that the British withdrawal was "completed in 1956," but nothing was noted about their reluctance to leave or about the British–French–Israeli assault on the Suez Canal. The large-type copy block accompanying the map gives some information about Israel's four wars with various Arab countries and refers vaguely to a matter called the "volatile Palestinian issue." The editors did, to their credit, include one historical irony in this strange summary of events: "In 1980 Iran and Iraq began a bitter and bloody war that lasted until 1988. Oil-rich Kuwait poured billions of dollars into the Iraqi war effort."

In the same issue of *Newsweek*, a piece on military censorship by media writer Jonathan Alter warned that "before long . . . more [television] viewers may come to realize that for all the spooky network music, theatrical correspondents and Nintendo military briefings, they have little real information about the progress of the war." The same could have been said of newsweekly readers who were forced to rely on misleading and superficial graphics.

Time was slow to match *Newsweek*'s geographic expertise, but it finally counterpunched three weeks later with an even more spectacular display of graphic journalism. "Special: Pullout Battle Map," the editors announced in light blue type above the *Time* logo, even though it was really only an elaboration of smaller maps published in earlier issues. On one side of the glossy, heavy-stock insert was a map of the war zone with many tiny images representing oil wells, air bases, soldiers, desalination plants, tanks and artillery, bridges, navy ships, "nuclear facilities," and other strategic targets in Iraq. Tiny skull-and-crossbone symbols marked Iraqi "chemical and biological warfare factories." One inset showed a map of the entire world, with the Middle East identified by a black rectangle. The overall effect was rather old-fashioned and static, a Parker Brothers board game that lacked only dice and movable pieces, rather than a snazzy computer action game. One oddity was *Time*'s placement of Saudi Arabian, Kuwaiti, and other Arab troops on the front line ahead of American army and marine units. This was Pentagon propaganda aimed at convincing the public that Arab troops were going to do their fair share of the fighting. (American troops, of course, led the assault into Kuwait and did most of the killing and dying. After the war, *Time* reported that Schwarzkopf considered the Arab ground troops to be the worst among the allied forces.) The map also erroneously indicated a fortified defensive line on the Kuwaiti side of the border, implying a kind of Iraqi Maginot Line, which never existed outside the collective imaginings of military and media war planners. (The fortified line turned out to be sand berms, starving Iraqi conscripts in poorly constructed trenches, largely visible minefields, or nothing at all.) *Time*, too, presented a summary of events called "countdown to war," but its history of the Middle East was even more absurdly compressed than *Newsweek*'s, beginning on August 2, 1990. The major news was described in fairly straightforward language, but omissions often speak louder than words; the imposition of the Pentagon's official censorship policy, for example, failed to qualify for inclusion. *Newsweek* may have assigned a disproportionate weight to things Israeli on its map, but at least it acknowledged the existence of the Palestinians and the Israeli occupation of the West Bank, Gaza Strip, and Golan Heights. *Time* had virtually wiped the Palestinians off the map by coloring the occupied territories in the same pale green as Israel and neglecting to say they were occupied. The flip side of *Time*'s war map carried a dense array of allied and Iraqi weapons facing off against one another with their names and countries of origin identified. Iraqi ground troops were put at 540,000, a significant exaggeration, as it turned out, but the word "estimate" evidently did not occur to *Time*'s editors. Based on the intimidating number of pale-blue allied images, the Iraqi goose was obviously cooked. But *Time*'s pièce de résistance was not a weapon; it was a cartoonish human form clothed in American desert camouflage and gas mask, striding forward with an M16A2 rifle gripped in its vastly oversized hands. Shod in one green combat boot (the other one was merely a tan outline filled in with black space), the machine-like soldier was not of this world, resembling a faceless GI Joe or an American Darth Vader leaping into the void of space. Given the official censorship, the conflict's blurry objectives, and the general unreality of the war as portrayed to Americans, *Time*'s android soldier may well have served as the signature emblem of media coverage during Operation Desert Storm.

After the war, *Newsweek* took out a full-page ad in *The New York Times* to declare victory over *Time* in the map war. *Newsweek* claimed its pullout map issue had doubled the usual newsstand sale to nearly 400,000 copies, leaving *Time* in the dust. Some might have argued that editors had precious little to show in a censored war, but *Newsweek* bragged that its "ahead-of-the-curve journalism" had resulted in a 90 percent jump in newsstand sales for its "war issues" compared with the same period in the previous year. Instead of denouncing the government's cynical control of the news, the *Newsweek* people were celebrating their own sad performance under its strictures.

Maps of the Middle East were all the rage, and no one had a bigger map than Peter Jennings and ABC. The map was roughly the size of two tennis courts and filled an entire studio. Jennings, at his most genial and reassuring, was wont to stride across it while hosting his three major specials before and during the war, stepping with alacrity from Iraq to Kuwait to Saudi Arabia to Jordan to Israel and back again. The map appeared in its first starring role in "A Line in the Sand," Part 1, on September 11, 1990, and ended its run on January 26 in the ABC children's special on the war, entitled "War in the Gulf—Answering Children's Questions."

The children's program was Jennings's most memorable contribution to the media war effort. It was created jointly by Jennings and executive producer Pat Roddy, both of whom were said to be sensitive to youthful concerns about the war—Jennings, in particular, after listening to his children's classmates in the days before the fighting began. Jennings, who seems sincere to a fault, revealed not the slightest embarrassment when asked about the children's special. But it should have been embarrassing to anyone associated with it. During the program, the anchorman unctuously fielded lisped, stuttering questions from the children, aged eight to fifteen, who were gathered around him like campers attending a fireside nature lecture. The map studio suggested a cozy and impermeable theater of operations, as safe from Saddam's missiles as Mister Rogers's neighborhood. Here the relatively gigantic Jennings could control the fate of the world and protect the innocents from slaughter.

Jennings explained the situation in storybook style that a child could understand: "It's almost seven thousand miles from New York to Iraq and almost ten thousand miles from California to Iraq, and [Hussein] doesn't have an airplane and he doesn't have a missile that can get this far." An 800 number allowed children around the country to phone in questions and comments for Jennings and his "friends," other correspondents, and military experts. In some cases the children seemed more alert to distinctions between real war and televised war than the journalists: One of the callers remarked, "We play war. It's fun. It gets our feelings out 'cause we always make Saddam Hussein lose; 'cause we fire Patriot missiles . . . when his planes come. It gets our minds off the real war that's being fought."* Another child asked about the argument between reporters and the military regarding censorship. Jennings answered with pious condescension more appropriate to Pete Williams and Marlin Fitzwater:

> What we do have in times of war between reporters and
> the public are things called censors. When Dean Rey-
> nolds was doing his broadcast from Tel Aviv last night,
> there was a military censor from the Israeli army in the
> office with him who told him there were certain things

---

* Eight months later ABC further blurred the distinction between real war and television. In an introduction to *The Heroes of Desert Storm*, a "docudrama" about the Gulf War, the network issued this disclaimer: "Tonight's film is based on true stories and interweaves news footage and dramatizations with actors and actual participants. To achieve realism, no distinction is made among these elements."

> he could say and there were certain things he couldn't
> say. And in Saudi Arabia, with all the American re-
> porters and reporters from around the world, there are
> military censors, because even while it is the natural in-
> stinct of a reporter to find out what is going on (and by
> the way it is not necessarily the natural instinct of a re-
> porter to tell everything he knows in the course of a war),
> there are military censors set up so that this kind of
> delicate information . . . is not disseminated and thus the
> enemy can't hear it.

So much for the education of the young about press freedom, the First Amendment, and the informed consent of the governed.

In keeping with his role of a cautious Gulliver addressing the Lilliputians, Jennings was careful not to claim omni-science, and turned to his friends when he was unsure about the answer. Retired Admiral William Crowe, former chair-man of the Joint Chiefs of Staff, sat nearby on a stool. In avuncular fashion, he told one boy that the United States would never run out of Patriot missiles, and that Americans were the "best in the world" at organizing for war. He also spoke fondly of his marine son: "I'm sure he is nervous, but he's very positive about what he's doing, he believes in it strongly, he's well trained, and he thinks he ought to be there and I agree with him."

War might be frightening if it weren't for Peter and his friends; they mentioned death just once in the ninety-minute program, and then only in connection with Iraqi chemical weapons, which, after all the months of Administration ad-vertising, were never used. In describing the potential effects, science editor Michael Guillen ended on the first truly pes-simistic note of the show: ". . . and finally you die. It's not very nice." But in case anyone was alarmed, the folks at ABC News produced another friend, this one fully outfitted in a chemical protection suit, which Jennings asserted would leave him "very well protected from all these deadly weapons." Near the end of the show Jennings added another note of reassurance. "Most people who go to war come home from war." He neglected to mention that certain Iraqi children who never went to war would never leave their homes again.

Putting maps and graphics aside, the motivation of the media companies and their star performers must be questioned. Clearly all the visual gimmicks—ABC and CBS both estimated their extra war-design costs at around $500,000— were aimed at drawing more viewers and readers in cynical corporate efforts to gain a competitive advantage over their rivals. But what of the behavior and motives of individual anchors and columnists? Asked about motive, virtually everyone professed to being objective and interested principally in "getting the story."

The three best journalism critics America has produced disagreed on the question of journalistic behavior. H. L. Mencken tended to ascribe the actions of newspaper reporters to sheer stupidity and ignorance. A. J. Liebling granted individual journalists far less responsibility for their work, saying that owners got from their employees exactly what they wanted; he prescribed a journalism school for publishers. Walter Karp wrote that reporters and their employers, with rare exceptions, are handmaidens to political power, merely awaiting instructions from high official sources.

Some critics on the left look for right-wing or militaristic ideology in the words of anchors and the news columns of *The New York Times*. Others blame advertisers who discourage "controversial" programming like the news by refusing to sponsor it. NBC president Robert Wright expressed great frustration about advertiser squeamishness. Wright said his network "lost" $55 million on its war coverage, including $20 million in advertising revenue as a result of sponsors pulling their commercials when war news supplanted regular entertainment programming.

A war—even one as short as the Gulf War—can have a troubling psychological effect on ambitious and self-important journalists. There need be no sinister ideological plan afoot or the presence of avaricious intent to explain the wartime behavior of reporters and editors. Many journalists simply thrill to the excitement of military conflict and are easily swept up by the martial spirit of the moment. Others see war as an opportunity for self-promotion. For the most part, the anchors, editors, bureau chiefs, and reporters who expressed themselves publicly during the Gulf crisis seemed to be apolitical, respectful of power, and careerist to a fault. The functionaries of the White House press office said again and again that Kuwait must be liberated, by force if necessary. Consequently, many media people picked up the drumbeat of war merely to remain in sync with the engine of ambition inside each of them. Otherwise, they might have missed out on a rich opportunity for career advancement, or risked the displeasure of their colleagues and bosses.

Among the higher echelons of the Washington media establishment there exists a certain class of journalists who fancy themselves high-stakes players in the policy deliberations of the government. Not content with their role as court stenographers, they wish to influence the king directly. Sometimes they offer political advice to his ministers. At other times they attempt to clothe the king's decisions in epic poetry or patriotic rhetoric.

Simple careerism can explain the soldierlike behavior of the network graphic designers and the producers who ordered them around. The pressures of commerce can explain the pathetic *Newsweek* and *Time* pullout maps. But neither factor can account entirely for the out-and-out war boosterism and jingoism displayed by the major media as the White House moved the nation toward war.

Among the textbook examples of this overt media war promotion was the November 26 issue of *Newsweek*. The cover photo presented the silhouette of a soldier against the desert sky at dusk, speaking on a radio phone, with a very large weapon strapped to his back. The cover line read: "Should We Fight? Americans Take Sides." Underneath, the editors touted an "exclusive" entitled "Why We Must Break Saddam's 'Stranglehold.' " The author of this exclusive, according to *Newsweek*, was George Bush, a man not generally known for either his writing style or his facility with the English language. The contents page displayed a photo of the President in the Oval Office as he "prepares his essay on the gulf crisis." Like most recent Presidents, George Bush is famously reliant on professional speechwriters, like the cliché-spinning Peggy Noonan. Why then did *Newsweek* publish what was in effect a speech by a President who appeared to be having no trouble getting his point of view across through televised statements, press conferences, and perhaps the most sophisticated public relations operation in the world? Were Bush's views in November really so difficult to discern or worthy of media support that he required free space in a national magazine?

Newsweek's Washington bureau chief, Evan Thomas, told me that the idea to solicit the President came from the newsweekly's White House correspondent, Ann McDaniel, as an accompaniment to the war debate that was to run inside the magazine that week. "At the time there was a lot of complaining that [Bush] had not articulated his message clearly," said Thomas. "It was confusing, and he kept coming up with a different reason every day for going to war . . . This [was] partly a response to that, to give him a chance to clear the air and see if he could come up with a coherent reason as opposed to one that changed every day." Thomas said that McDaniel "just went to the White House and said, 'We're running a debate cover, the pros and cons, and here's a chance for you to have your say if you want to have it;

we'll give you some space.' " A grateful press office "seized [the opportunity] with alacrity," Thomas said. The White House later told *Newsweek* that Bush had written the essay himself. Thomas thought this possible, he said, because the piece "wasn't that well written." But more likely, according to Thomas, "someone wrote him a draft and he fiddled around with it."

The large photograph of Bush that accompanied "Why We Are in the Gulf" revealed a studious President striving like Thomas Mann's von Aschenbach "to liberate from the marble mass of language the slender forms of his art." The photo caption read: "In the Oval Office, President Bush reviews his case for the U.S. presence in the Persian Gulf: stopping Saddam's aggression and defending energy security." To underscore the President's commitment to the essayist's craft and lend the enterprise a patina of authenticity, *Newsweek*'s art department reproduced the first page from the "manuscript" with Bush's large black signature on top. Certainly no one at *Newsweek* expected the President to actually write the article, but the readers of the magazine and the world at large were evidently supposed to believe he'd composed every word. White House chief of communications Dave Demarest confirmed that the first draft was not written by Bush, but he could not recall the names of the authors. "My office and [the National Security Council] sat down and collaborated on a draft," he said. White House speechwriter Dan McGroarty told me he wrote portions of the essay with Richard Haass, Special Assistant to the President for National Security Affairs.

McDaniel said she thought of the idea for a *Newsweek* essay by Bush after hearing a week earlier of a White House lunch for "friends" of the President, which had been organized to help Bush make his case for intervention clearer. "I knew that they would be looking for new formats to make their case," said McDaniel. After checking with the home office in New York, she and deputy bureau chief Thomas

DeFrank wrote a note to Presidential press secretary Marlin Fitzwater, volunteering the pages of *Newsweek*. McDaniel also enlisted the help of Sheila Tate, press secretary to Bush when he was Vice President. Fitzwater accepted the offer upon agreeing to *Newsweek*'s condition of exclusivity. "Guest artist" Bush's work survived remarkably intact through *Newsweek*'s rigorous editing process. "I think we changed one word," said McDaniel, possibly, she thought, about Bush referring to himself as a "columnist or something," but "needless to say we didn't change the substance." Despite the fact that *Newsweek* had thus eagerly invited the President to use the magazine as a platform, McDaniel told me, "We are not interested in being a mouthpiece for the President of the United States."

The timing of *Newsweek*'s request could not have been better for the Administration's public relations strategy. On November 8, the President had in fact hosted a lunch at the White House for a group of trusted advisers and friends, many of whom had worked for Bush in various stages of his political career. The stated purpose of the gathering, according to one who was there, was to advise the President on shoring up what was perceived by the White House to be a "softening" of public support for military intervention in the Gulf. Not everyone at the lunch knew Bush had already decided to double American troop strength and planned to announce it that very afternoon. Among those in attendance were Bush's chief of staff, John Sununu; Vice President Quayle; Hill and Knowlton's Craig Fuller (then a vice president working on the Kuwait account); Fred Malek, who ran Bush's 1988 convention effort and was named the President's 1992 campaign manager;* Vic Gold, onetime press secretary

---

* Malek was forced to resign as deputy chairman of the Republican National Committee in 1988 after it was revealed that in 1971, at the request of President Richard Nixon, he compiled a list of Jewish officials in the Bureau of Labor Statistics. Malek, then White House personnel chief, said Nixon had complained of a "Jewish cabal" out to discredit his performance on economic issues.

to Spiro Agnew and coauthor of Bush's 1987 memoir; political consultant Hayley Barbour; former Bush press aides Pete Teeley and Sheila Tate; and Jenie Austin from the Republican National Committee. Teeley and Tate challenged Bush to clarify his Gulf policy, and the President allowed he "could be doing a better job" of explaining it to the public. The idea of a bylined article by Bush emerged from this exchange.

When I interviewed Thomas and McDaniel, they acknowledged that some might suggest *Newsweek* was "used." They believed, they said, that by helping the President refine his vague position, they were performing a legitimate journalistic function. It is telling, however, that none of their justification for running Bush's views appeared alongside the essay.

The real motive for publishing Bush is revealed in the candid remarks of Evan Thomas and of Stephen Smith, then *Newsweek*'s executive editor. Thomas prefaced his comments by saying that the editors felt protected from criticism because of having published a cover story about Bush's "wimp factor," which supposedly demonstrated *Newsweek*'s independence from the White House: "Now it is true that we were pretty pro-war. We disguised it, but I think the majority view among the top editors was fairly hawkish . . . among the top editors, including me, it would have been to take military action [rather than rely on sanctions]. I think that although we made an effort to be balanced about it . . . the editors were fairly hawkish and the magazine probably reflected that, at least marginally . . . If we were senators we would have voted [for military force]."

Stephen Smith was one of the hawkish editors to whom Thomas was referring, and he agreed with Thomas and McDaniel that press conferences and speeches were insufficient to the task of explaining Bush's vision, and that the President needed some help: "You need a statement . . . You need somebody to make his case." Smith was convinced that giving Bush the space "was news because he hadn't made the case [for war] before. . . . Up to then we were pretty much hearing from people who either opposed [it], or might have been for it but didn't really have a direct say in [the decision] . . . So it was a newsmaking piece; it was not a free advertisement for the President in my mind." Smith explained that commercial considerations were another reason for publishing Bush: "It is a business. You want people to buy and read your product . . . the more [the public] think that you have access to the President of the United States, that he would pick you as the forum to discuss a very serious issue, the better you look . . . If George Bush is taking *Newsweek* seriously, then readers ought to take it seriously . . . Having the bragging rights to George Bush was probably the most important consideration in doing this."

Thus we have the happy marriage of political and commercial ambition, a veritable surfeit of cynicism. As for the text itself, Bush's essay revealed nothing new, and certainly nothing that could be called coherent. Evan Thomas was right about the poor style. At best it was a slight elaboration on dozens of earlier ominous pronunciations aimed at justifying the huge commitment of troops and the option to use them: "The history of this century shows clearly that rewarding aggression encourages more aggression. . . . Can the world afford to allow Saddam Hussein a stranglehold around the world's economic lifeline? . . . Innocent lives are at stake." And because no pronouncement by George Bush on the Gulf crisis would be complete without the baby incubator canard, thanks to *Newsweek* he succeeded in spreading it once again—in the second paragraph: "Babies have been torn from incubators . . ."

The *Newsweek*–Bush collaboration deserves special attention as one of the most shameless examples of media war promotion disguised as journalism that occurred during the Gulf crisis. But plenty of other publications and broadcasters participated in the White House/Hill and Knowlton–sponsored anti-Saddam frenzy, and the individuals involved were often less candid about their motives than the *Newsweek* team. Everyone from Jann Wenner, the owner of *Rolling Stone*, to Dan Rather did his bit to promote the war effort. In Wenner's case, the motive for weaving a yellow ribbon through his magazine's logo in the March 21 special college issue was undoubtedly commercial. With hundreds of thousands of target readers digging through the sand on behalf of demographically correct college students back home, *Rolling Stone*'s February 20 press release caught the spirit of the times:

> The decision to include the ribbon on the magazine's cover is unprecedented in *Rolling Stone*'s 24-year history, announced Jann Wenner, editor and publisher. "No matter what one's feelings about America's involvement in the Gulf, or war in general, it's in the spirit of humanity to show compassion and support for the men and women over there . . ."

No matter what one's feelings, there were plenty of chances to cash in on war fever. In the case of Dan Rather, it was the opportunity to revive a flagging career, for CBS trailed ABC and NBC in the ratings throughout the war. Rather's prestige was also reportedly suffering within the network hierarchy. According to *The Wall Street Journal*'s Kevin Goldman, the mercurial anchor had been left out of much of the network's planning for war coverage, and CBS executives had even discussed the possibility of replacing him. So perhaps Rather was simply feeling desperate when, in a broadcast coanchored by Connie Chung, he said: "Connie, I'm told that this program is being seen [by the troops] in Saudi Arabia . . . And I know you would join me in giving our young men and women out there a salute." Rather then proceeded to salute.

The breathless excitement in Washington before and

during the war extended even to the usually sober newspaper
of record, *The New York Times*. At the beginning of the
buildup, on August 19, the *Times*'s chief Washington correspondent, R. W. Apple, joined the overheated mood of
official Washington and its media mob; America, but more
importantly its capital city, had been restored to pre-
eminence:

> Washington is not the backwater that it seemed to some
> when the action was in the streets of Prague or at the
> Berlin Wall . . . even in a hot, humid month when much
> of Washington is on vacation, there is a rush of excite-
> ment in the air here. In news bureaus and Pentagon
> offices, dining rooms and lobbyists' hangouts, the fever
> is back—the heavy speculation, the avid gossip, the gung-
> ho, here's-where-it's-happening spirit, that marks the city
> when it grapples with great events.

During the fighting, Charles Krauthammer echoed Apple's theme of American renewal, in an essay published in
Time:

> A month ago, conventional wisdom had the U.S. being
> overtaken as a great power by Japan. Perhaps. But is
> making a superior Walkman a better index of techno-
> logical sophistication than making laser bombs that enter
> through the front door? Is a nation's ability to make
> VCRs a better index of power than the ability to defeat
> aggression?

Such reportage typified the larger, more general process
of media war hype and justification. In a rational world, the
wooden jingoism of an R. W. Apple or a Charles Krauthammer could be explained in the context of excitement and
adrenaline overload, but these are journalists who aspire to
the status of the thoughtful. How else to characterize their
pretentious and overwrought prose than as cheerleading for

the government? Time Warner provided a forum for another thoughtful sort, Roger Rosenblatt, with its nostalgia-soaked special weekly edition of *Life*; his "Letter to a Child in Baghdad" was perhaps the outstanding example of big-media rationalizations for the slaughter of innocent civilians. While Rosenblatt was writing, the largest aerial bombardment since the Vietnam War was falling on Kuwait and Iraq, and hundreds, maybe thousands, of women and children were being maimed and killed. Rosenblatt, it seems, wished them well.

> It is the duty of adults to try to protect their children from the nightmares we manufacture. It is also our duty to try to explain how the world got to be where it is.

> I must tell you right off, so that we do not misunderstand each other, that I believe this war was brought on by the leader of your country. *By him and only him*. He is a taker; he takes what he wants. And he kills what impedes him . . . [Author's italics]

> You may still ask: Was it necessary in January to go to war against Saddam?

Rosenblatt was evidently uncertain about the requirement of two sides to make a war, so he never answered his own question. But, like Peter Jennings, he loved children and wanted to reassure them that in spite of all the explosions, the world viewed from the fourth floor of the Time-Life Building in New York City still made sense:

> Countries in a war do not really like themselves very much . . . they know they are engaged in a contemptible exercise. The best they may make of the worst circumstance is to be on the side of justice, to win as cleanly as possible and to leave the vanquished with their honor and humanity intact.

> I trust that my country will behave that way toward yours.

In short, I would like to be able to rescue you from this war, from all wars, and from the blatant, pathetic shortcomings of grown-ups everywhere . . . I could tell you that the world is in your hands, entrust you to see that this war is the last. Yet you will have your wars and your children theirs.

Look at the antiquities of your country, the statues and reliefs, and see how many celebrate men killing men.

But, continues Rosenblatt, throughout the history of battle, we're all in it together—or something like that.

We, you and I, are Thermopylae, Troy, Waterloo, Antietam, Heartbreak Ridge, and Baghdad.

And we are responsible for Baghdad, you and I, as everyone is in some way responsible for all that ever happens, including the horrors. You cannot know this yet. I mean only to prepare you for the day you discover how remarkably close you are to waging war.

There's still hope, however. Let's look on the bright side, Time Warner style:

I mean to tell you something else. The world that must seem to you as a heap of broken parts is not always a heap of broken parts. There are times—you have caught them in your eyes—when a guillotine of light descends on a summer wall or a flower petal is scooped up by the wind and hovers in midair or a hand slips into yours and holds it warm, where the world is so overwhelmingly beautiful it takes your breath away.

This world is as real and true as the dangerous one. It exists inside you and out, and strives with all its energy to make life good. It lives in Christian, Jew and Arab, in Africa and China, in the plazas and the outposts, in all the places of which you have read and to which you

will travel, I hope, when the noise has stopped and the
dust has cleared.

And it lives in America, which you may feel has brought
you only pain and confusion, but from which I send you
love.

Someone on the copy desk at *Life* may have questioned
Rosenblatt's nearly incoherent efforts to achieve a properly
epic pitch. But the reference to Troy and Thermopylae suggests that the author had been lifted beyond the realm of
mortal editors.

Rosenblatt need have looked no further than the weekly
editions of *Life* to see that this country at war very much
liked itself, at least in the texts and images of the media. Not
since World War I had the country seemed so in love with
the military and its weaponry. Commentators everywhere
extolled the tonic effect of war.

"The war is over everywhere and we feel together," said
Andy Rooney to nineteen million viewers of "60 Minutes."
"There are some good things about war sometimes. Everyone accomplishes more in times of war. Our hearts beat
faster. Our senses are sharper . . . This war in the Gulf has
been, by all odds, the best war in modern history, not only
for America, but for the whole world, including Iraq,
probably."

Patriotism—ersatz or genuine—blared out from magazine covers and television sets. The cover photographs of the
four weekly issues of *Life* depicted in succession a smiling
young boy clutching a small American flag while standing in
front of a massive but unidentified machine; a solitary marine
trudging across the sand holding aloft a large American flag;
a beaming and victorious General Schwarzkopf surrounded
by grinning soldiers; and Schwarzkopf again, this time em-
bracing a returning POW named Melissa Rathbun Nealy.

A memo issued during the war from Telephoto, a New

York City photo agency, to freelance photographers nicely summarizes the sudden demand for patriotic pictures in the advertising market as well:

> One result of [the war] that affects us all professionally is that it is clear that the direction of the advertising marketplace in America will, in the weeks and months ahead, undergo a significant change . . .

> This direction is: Patriotic images of all kinds will be embraced by American businesses to demonstrate what it is that is worth standing for and living for. Values such as Freedom, Friendship, Strength, Justice, Fearlessness, Heroism will be glorified. In addition, traditional values of Home, Family, Community, The Heartland, The American Way, God and Apple Pie will be evident everywhere.

> We want to be ready for this change, and we need your help!

> We'd like you to explore, with your eye, your camera, the *idea* of America: What makes us strong . . . What makes us unique . . . from an advertising point of view. If you were doing a patriotic ad, or Annual Report, or Magazine cover, with what kind of visual would you wish to associate your company image, your company name, your company product?

> Symbols that would be appropriate for this are: The American Flag, Statue of Liberty, Bill of Rights, The Constitution, Lincoln and Jefferson Memorials, Yellow Ribbons, etc.

> We want images that include the traditional flag-waving views of patriotism . . . as well as pictures that wave an idea, not just a flag.

> We want you to describe visually those ideals of which we're most proud . . . those American values we'll sacrifice to keep and protect.

Perhaps the greatest beneficiary of the new patriotic fervor reflected in the media was not President Bush, who had been milking the flag since his 1988 campaign, but General H. Norman Schwarzkopf. Many hands were needed to achieve his deification, and it is illuminating to track the portly commander's media career both in drama and reality. Schwarzkopf's first major television exposure had come in April 1979, when C.D.B. Bryan's book, *Friendly Fire*, was brought to a mass audience in a television movie of the same name. The story concerned the accidental killing by American fire of a soldier under Schwarzkopf's command in Vietnam. However, the sympathetically portrayed Schwarzkopf was given another name (Lieutenant Colonel Byron Schindler) in the film, so it was mostly readers of Bryan's book who had heard of him when he stepped into the limelight in Saudi Arabia in August. "Stormin' Norman," as he was dubbed by the media, fortunately had escaped notice as deputy commander of the botched U.S. invasion of Grenada in 1983. In a 1984 article in the *Boston Globe*, former army intelligence officers Richard Gabriel and Paul Savage wrote, "What really happened in Grenada was a case study in military incompetence and poor execution." The real cause of American casualties, according to the writers, had been covered up by the Pentagon: of the 18 American servicemen killed during the operation, 14 died in friendly fire or in accidents. This is not to say that Schwarzkopf was directly responsible for mistakes made in the Grenada operation, only that reporters might have done a bit of homework before anointing him a hero.

The Schwarzkopf buildup in the Gulf began with an admiring "60 Minutes" profile in early September. Correspondent David Martin described the general's humble lifestyle:

Schwarzkopf settled into a routine of seventeen-hour days, working out of an office in the Saudi defense min-

istry. Rank definitely has its privileges . . . but Schwarzkopf is too old a warhorse to let the general live in luxury
while the troops swelter in foxholes . . . The Saudis
offered Schwarzkopf a villa, but he chose a small room
tucked away behind his office.

Schwarzkopf was shown in his bedroom, smiling, and
saying: "This is home, and I drag my body out at seven in
the morning and go back in there and start work again."
Martin asked Schwarzkopf if he worried that "we're going
to make you a hero and then if it doesn't go right you're
going to become a scapegoat?" The general said he didn't
worry about such things, and he was right not to bother. By
the beginning of the war he had become "a certifiable genius
with an IQ of 170" who spoke fluent German and French,
according to the Associated Press. The *Washington Post* television critic Tom Shales, describing a briefing in Riyadh, said
the general "gave a performance as spellbinding as the toniest
of Hamlets." *Newsday* feature writer Michele Ingrassia asked
how Schwarzkopf "has gone from mere general to genuine
sex symbol faster than a speeding smart bomb," and speculated that the bearlike hero of the desert might qualify as
People magazine's "Sexiest Man Alive" for 1991. And Ran-
dom House's commemorative postwar volume, *Triumph in
the Desert*, explained that "the victor of the Gulf war is a
fighting man because he is an idealist. He believes freedom
is worth dying for."

The general was so famous by the end of the war that
he finally threw off the yoke of humility, signed a $5 million
book contract, and announced his retirement from the army.
Schwarzkopf's homecoming to his wife, Brenda, was featured
on the cover of *People*, and his speaking fees hit $60,000 per
appearance. Thanks in large measure to the media, New
York public relations woman Peggy Siegal could proclaim
him "the biggest celebrity in the world."

It can certainly be argued that "Stormin' Norman"

earned what he got and that there's nothing wrong with cashing in on a job well done. But it is worth recalling that General George Marshall, a somewhat more substantial hero of World War II, declined on principle the opportunity to write a memoir.[2]

The media's love of the military mind and demeanor personified by Schwarzkopf was such that network television could not get enough of retired generals and admirals and former Pentagon analysts to explicate the Pentagon's press releases and videotapes of "surgical" bombing. Suddenly, every anchor had to have a sidekick, who tended to be a hawk in civilian clothing. Ratings leader ABC provides a good example for study. Of all the national security pundits, Anthony Cordesman received the greatest exposure on television, appearing on ABC eleven times in the fourteen days surveyed by Fairness and Accuracy in Reporting, a left-leaning media watchdog group. The grim-faced Cordesman is a former Pentagon official, and until the start of the war on January 16, he was national security adviser to Republican Senator John McCain, a proponent of military action against Iraq. At one point Peter Jennings asked his analyst on camera if the Pentagon was telling the truth. Cordesman replied, "I think the Pentagon is giving it to you straight." Cordesman went back to work for McCain a month after the war ended.

CBS was more overtly hawkish, relying on the presence of Retired General Michael Dugan, the former Air Force chief of staff, for its own military expertise. Dugan had been fired in September for publicly advocating a direct attack on Saddam Hussein's family and the bombing of important Iraqi cultural sites.

Given the general enthusiasm exhibited on the networks for the invigorating effects of war coverage, it is difficult to understand how anyone could make political distinctions between the anchors. After watching the ABC children's special and later hearing Anthony Cordesman refer to civilian casualties as "collateral damage," it is even more confusing to learn that Jennings maintains the reputation as being the most "liberal" of the three network anchors. Jennings himself seems mystified by that perception, as well as by the accusation leveled by many pro-Israeli groups that he is anti-Jewish or anti-Israel.[2] Yet a right-wing Washington group calling itself the Center for Media and Public Affairs rated ABC's war coverage as the most "antiwar" of the three networks and the one "most likely to air criticisms of U.S. leadership and policy and to quote Iraqi sources."

In the case of Israel, it was NBC's Martin Fletcher, not an ABC reporter, who was taken off the air by Israeli censors on January 22 for reporting what were said to be too many details about a Scud attack on Tel Aviv. And the Israel lobby might take heart from the fact that Jennings's war map, like *Time*'s, did not explicitly identify the Israeli-occupied territories as occupied. When interviewed in his New York City office in June, Jennings wondered out loud what was at the root of his "liberal" problem. Perhaps, he agreed, it is his Canadian origin, which gives him a slightly distant manner and makes him seem less jingoistic than the other anchors. It also may be that Jennings, following the example set by the British Broadcasting Corporation, instructed correspondents to avoid using the word "we" when describing actions by the U.S. or allied military forces in the Gulf. (Dan Rather and Tom Brokaw could not resist employing the royal "we" in describing the crushing of Iraq; even the paragon of objectivity, Walter Cronkite, announced on CBS: "We knocked one of their Scuds out of the sky." Brokaw, in fact, seemed frightened that the war might end too soon, calling a negotiated settlement "a nightmare . . . the worst possible scenario.")

In contrast with his colleagues, whatever restraint was occasionally exhibited by Jennings becomes meaningless when one listens to his actual language. On a January 21 ABC News Special Report, Jennings remarked with apparent wonder at the "brilliance of laser-guided bombs" then pulverizing Iraq. The next day Anthony Cordesman described the Iraqi Scud to Jennings as "a horrifying killing mechanism."

At a March 15, 1991, Gannett Foundation Media Center discussion on coverage of the Gulf War, the talk was supposed to center on government censorship. But *Los Angeles Times* Washington bureau chief Jack Nelson, perhaps unwittingly, pointed the finger at the government's collaborator: "If you look at it from the outset, the press was reflecting the views of the government, and it never really changed."

CHAPTER 4

Vietnam Syndrome

What *about* withdrawal? Few Americans who have
served in Vietnam can stomach this idea . . . Withdrawal
. . . means that the United States' prestige will be lowered
throughout the world, and it means that the pressure of
Communism on the rest of Southeast Asia will intensify.
Lastly, withdrawal means that throughout the world the
enemies of the West will be encouraged to try insurgen-
cies like the one in Vietnam.

∎

So it becomes a matter of national self-interest to discover
what we can offer [Vietnam] in the future. Bombers and
helicopters and napalm are a help, but they are not
enough.

∎

I believe that Vietnam is a legitimate part of . . . [Amer-
ica's] global commitment. A strategic country in a key
area, it is perhaps one of only five or six nations in the
world that is truly vital to U.S. interests.

—DAVID HALBERSTAM
The Making of a Quagmire, 1965

IN THE FALL of 1990, as Pete Williams and Captain Ron
Wildermuth refined their plans for controlling media coverage of the coming conflict, they were said to be propelled
by the notion that an uncensored American press had "lost"
the Vietnam War by demoralizing the public with unpleasant
news. Whether either man believed this fairy tale is less
important than the reality that many military officers and a

good portion of the American right had adopted it as an article of faith. Implied in the analysis of the "We could have won in 'Nam" lobby was the equally preposterous contention that the media had been specifically opposed to the Vietnam War, and were hostile toward the American military in general. Since unfettered reporters had undermined the anti-Communist crusade in Southeast Asia by sapping the will of the American people, went the argument, they could not be trusted to fall in with the Administration's crusade in the Persian Gulf. During his stay in the Persian Gulf, for example, NBC correspondent Gary Matsumoto found a "spirit of confrontation" among the U.S. officer corps there, stemming from America's defeat in Indochina: "Several officers . . . charged the Press with negativity, sensationalism, and questionable loyalty in Vietnam."

Unfortunately, such nonsense must be treated seriously, for it not only formed a basis for successful government censorship during the Gulf War but perpetuates a myth that has now significantly eroded, in practice, the protection guaranteed the press by the First Amendment. Obviously, it is armies which win and lose wars; obviously, it is politicians who start and end them. In the history of the United States there is perhaps one example—the Spanish–American War —in which the press has had a significant effect on military policy, and in that case it was in favor of making war. The typical behavior of the press—exemplified again in the Gulf War—has been to follow the lead of politicians, and then to rally round the flag when the shooting starts. There have been exceptions to this rule, of course, but events such as *Newsweek*'s collaboration with President Bush are emblematic of the press's behavior in wartime, not aberrant. Put another way, the press has never prevented a war from starting and has never forced the government to terminate one.

For serious journalists, the notion of the media acting as handmaidens to politicians is difficult to accept. It is far more gratifying for former newspaper reporters like Gay

Talese and David Halberstam to exaggerate the power and willfulness of the large national news organizations. In this distorted world, godlike publishers and network executives stride across the stage of world events and intrepid reporters can become the instigators of history.

Some left-wing media critics also resist the concept of a passive press because the image of a forceful and ideological media suits their theory of a powerful political conspiracy against the left. The pitiful reality of most journalists' relationship with power is found in the slavish letter that the "liberal" Theodore White wrote to Richard Nixon upon the publication of his *The Making of the President: 1968*:

> Dear Mr. President:
>
> Herewith the first run off the press of a book called *The Making of the President: 1968*, whose hero is Richard M. Nixon . . . The book goes to you with my great thanks for your help. I have had few somersaults of emotion greater than in the years 1967–1968. My previous reporting of Richard Nixon must, I know, have hurt. I felt that way then. If I feel differently now it is not that there is a new Richard Nixon or a new Teddy White, but that slowly truths force their way on all of us. The campaign that this book tries to describe was the campaign of a man of courage and of conscience; and the respect it wrung from me—which I hope is evident—surprised me week by week as I went along . . .

White sets up his next book, *The Making of the President: 1972*, by expressing his intention to "describe a campaign in a country which the President has brought to peace and in which he has stilled hates." He closes in a hail of sycophancy:

> There's so much difference between being a reporter and being a citizen. A reporter owes a duty to the "public"

and tells it as he sees it, which sometimes hurts. But a citizen owes a duty to the country; and the President describes the duty. I am both a reporter and a citizen. And this President can also call on me as a friend.

While it may be shocking to learn that White viewed the venal Nixon as a "man of conscience," it is even more instructive, for the purpose of understanding censorship in the Gulf War, to consider the curious case of another famous journalist, David Halberstam, and his relationship to power. For it is paradoxical in the extreme that Halberstam has achieved the status of both journalistic subversive (from his Vietnam reporting) and respected chronicler of the supposedly great and powerful media barons (from his book about media executives). Neither image is either merited or based on fact.

In a 1979 review in *Esquire* of Halberstam's media book, *The Powers That Be*, Walter Karp noted the author's "inability to distinguish between kings and courtiers . . ." In "Halberstamia," Karp wrote, "It appears soon enough . . . that nothing in that curious country is quite what Halberstam says it is." On one hand, Karp noted, Halberstam builds his media barons—the Sulzbergers of *The New York Times*; Henry Luce of Time Inc.; William Paley of CBS; the *Washington Post* family of Eugene Meyer and Katharine Graham; and Otis Chandler of the *Los Angeles Times*—into mythic figures, while, on the other hand, he relates how time and again they caved in or toadied to politicians.

When Halberstam wrote *The Making of a Quagmire* in the years just prior to the huge American military escalation in Vietnam, he was, strangely enough, the most visible symbol of what in some quarters of American society was viewed as a subversive press. In the minds of cold warriors from the Kennedy and Johnson Administrations, and their journalistic acolytes, Halberstam's sin had been to report the failure of the South Vietnamese army (ARVN) and its U.S. advisers to halt the insurgent, mostly Communist (partly nationalist) guerrilla army commonly known as the Vietcong (officially the National Liberation Front). By his own account, the *Times*'s man in Saigon wasn't reporting anything that colleagues Peter Arnett and Malcolm Browne of the Associated Press and Neil Sheehan of United Press International weren't also saying. But the *Times* occupies a privileged place in American society, and Halberstam, as a consequence, had become the most prominent target for White House displeasure.

The Kennedy White House was so disturbed by Halberstam's dispatches that in late 1963 the CIA prepared an analysis of Halberstam's "lugubrious and pessimistic" work for CIA director John McCone and Presidential assistant McGeorge Bundy. "A review of all the articles written by Mr. Halberstam since June indicates that he is by and large accurate in terms of the facts that he includes in his articles," the CIA analyst wrote. "The conclusions he draws from his facts, plus the emphasis of his reporting, however, tend to call his objectivity into question."

But it shouldn't have called into question his loyalty to the war effort. Halberstam's own words, and his own account of his two years covering the war in 1962–63, *The Making of a Quagmire*, prove that the accusations against him are red herrings. While his reporting was generally accurate—based as it was on firsthand observations of combat and information supplied by junior American military and CIA officers—there is nothing in the book that suggests he was anything other than a patriotic and ambitious journalist. Halberstam subscribed to chauvinistic Cold War assumptions of the most tedious variety:

> We do not demand servitude, and in comparison with our enemies, we are not doctrinaire. We want stability for these people, whereas the Communists actively provoke inconstancy. So, we cannot abandon our efforts to

help these people, no matter how ungrateful they may seem, or how frustrating the task is for the giver, or how often we are accused of being soft or liberal.

How could someone who wrote "Bombers and helicopters and napalm are a help, but they are not enough" come to be thought of as a liberal, let alone an antiwar subversive? In part, the reason rests in the degradation of American political language since World War II. In the 1950s and 1960s, during the apogee of the national security state, if one seemed insufficiently anti-Communist, then one was "not on the team" and thus was liable to be classified as "liberal" or even as an enemy dupe. In Halberstam's Vietnam there appear to have been two competing teams. One team was made up of older military officers and diplomats, representing the interests of Secretary of Defense Robert McNamara and Secretary of State Dean Rusk, and it insisted that things were going fine and that the Vietcong was losing. These people tended to support the U.S.-installed government of Ngo Dinh Diem. Another team was made up of younger army officers, like the somewhat deluded Lieutenant Colonel John Paul Vann, and junior CIA agents who knew the Vietcong was actually winning and wanted the autocratic Diem removed. (In his memoir, former ambassador William Sullivan recounts how Kennedy's CIA director, John McCone, had in 1962 become "a dove on Vietnam" after playing on the losing side of a war game in which the Vietcong had essentially defeated the South Vietnamese and American armies.) Halberstam threw in his lot with the latter group of young Turks. This probably can be attributed to their proximity in age, and because the government men were feeding the young reporter solid information about failed military operations. But Halberstam was no lone wolf, merely the most visible one. His colleagues in the Saigon press corps were reporting much the same news. In his Vietnam book, *A Bright Shining Lie*, Neil Sheehan termed "ludicrous" the charge that the Saigon reporters were manufacturing bad news. "By the late summer of 1963 . . . the majority of the established correspondents in Asia who regularly visited Vietnam saw the war in essentially the same terms that we did." And Halberstam was certainly no enemy of the army, or anything approaching a pacifist. Sheehan describes his colleague as the "most prominent graduate of the Vann school on the war and the reporter with whom Vann formed his closest relationship" in those early days of Vietnam. In his book, Halberstam clearly likes his army-officer sources:

> On the whole they were a remarkable group; of course they had all been to college or West Point, and with the Army's help many of them were working toward additional degrees. Far more than most of their contemporaries, they had a sense of America's responsibilities and problems, and they were committed to one of the most pressing problems of our time. In general they were more alert, better motivated and more sophisticated than the average American of their generation . . .

Halberstam also maintained warm social relationships with his military friends:

> Many of the officers we knew in the field had no base or friends in Saigon, so they always came to our house. Gradually the villa became something of a hotel . . .
> Our huge villa with endless space had everything we could possibly want save hot water. But one day some of our friends in the military quietly showed up, installed a hot-water heater in the bathroom and disappeared.

When describing a battle, Halberstam generally refers, without irony, to South Vietnamese and American military as "we." He clearly thrills to the action, as exhibited in the following account of a helicopter attack, worth quoting at length both for its enthusiasm and as an example (for Halberstam was, it seems, a perfectly good reporter of what he saw) of what censorship caused us to miss in the Gulf War.

> Shortly before noon we hit pay dirt. Out of one village came a flock of Vietcong, running across the paddies, and there was intense fire from the treeline. While five of our ships emptied their troops, the rest of the choppers strafed the area. Soon the guerrillas broke from their positions . . . We bore down on one fleeing Vietcong. The paddy's surface was rough and his run was staggered, like that of a good but drunken broken-field runner against imaginary tacklers . . . The copilot fired his machine guns but missed, and the man kept going. Then there was a flash of orange and a blast of heat inside the ship, and the helicopter heaved from the recoil of its rockers. When they exploded the man fell. He lay still as we went over him, but when we turned he scrambled to his feet, still making for the canal, now only about fifty yards away. While we circled and swept toward him again he was straining for the bank, like a runner nearing the finish line. We had one last shot at him. Our copilot fired one last burst of the machine gun as the guerrilla made a desperate surge. The bullets cut him down as he reached the canal, and his body skidded on the hard bank as he collapsed.

Later on, after returning to Bac Lieu, Halberstam concluded:

> It had been a good day. There had been few Government losses, and there was a chance that from all those prisoners we might learn something important. Everyone was tired and relaxed and happy . . .

Here we see Halberstam clearly, not as a subversive, but as an excited young cold warrior, very much on the U.S. government team.

Nevertheless, Halberstam was already in evil repute with the government; in October 1963 President Kennedy had

even asked *New York Times* publisher Arthur O. Sulzberger
if he was planning to transfer him. Other journalists were
also on his case. Hearst columnist Frank Conniff and the
New York Journal-American had accused him, in Halberstam's words, of being "soft on Communism" and "paving
the way for a bearded Vietnamese Fidel Castro." The well-
known *New York Herald Tribune* columnist Marguerite Hig-
gins had written that "reporters here would like to see us
lose the war to prove they're right." And Washington's
preeminent establishment columnist, Joseph Alsop, had attacked the "reportorial crusade against the [Diem] government" by the Saigon press corps.

If there was a crusade going on in Saigon, it was pro-
mulgated by officers like Vann and the young CIA men, who,
Halberstam said, "were brutally frank about the Government's unpopularity and its inability to fight a war." In this
1963 atmosphere of infighting within the U.S. mission, *Time*
published in its September 20 issue a critique of the Saigon
correspondents, which outraged the reporters, who included
Time's own Charles Mohr and Mert Perry.

"The printed piece was truly staggering," Halberstam
recalled, "for it was an indictment not only of us, but of two
of *Time*'s own reporters as well. It read as if written by a
high Pentagon PIO, and it set off a minor furor in the newspaper world."

In retrospect, the piece itself is less than "staggering,"
although it was clearly an Administration-inspired hatchet
job aimed at shoring up Diem. It actually made a couple of
good points about the failings of foreign correspondents,
which *Time*'s editors might have heeded: "Foreign correspondents, wherever they are stationed, are tempted to band
together into an unofficial club . . . None of them speak the
language with any fluency . . . [Their] reporting is prone to
distortions. The complicated greys of a complicated country
fade into oversimplified blacks and whites." (Regarding Halberstam, Neil Sheehan agreed in part with the *Time* analysis:

"He was a man who saw the world in light and dark colors with little shading in between.") *Time*'s Mohr was properly humiliated by the piece and resigned. But the article contributed to Halberstam's enduring reputation as a subversive, because it singled out *The New York Times*'s ambivalent coverage of the war and, ironically, its unwillingness to back wholeheartedly Halberstam's reporting.

"Freedom of the press is guaranteed only to those who own one," wrote A. J. Liebling, and Halberstam served at the pleasure of the owners of *The New York Times*. This was never more evident than in August 1963, when the *Times*, according to the author of the *Time* press critique (said to be managing editor Otto Feurbringer), "threw up its hands helplessly and, beneath an editorial apology, printed two widely divergent accounts of events; one presented the picture as viewed from Washington, the other as viewed from Saigon." The event in question was the suppression by Diem of rebellious Buddhists, but the *Times* had equivocated, not apologized. Halberstam's front-page story reported that Diem's chief adviser and brother-in-law, Ngo Dinh Nhu, had acted without the knowledge of the South Vietnamese army. An adjacent story by Tad Szulc in Washington aired the Administration's contrary contention that Diem had moved against the Buddhists at the urging of his army commanders. The view from Saigon as usual implied pessimism about the war against the Communists. The view from Washington suggested a more optimistic scenario. The *Times* had never gone in for adversarial reporting, and its cautiousness in the face of Administration pressure caused the paper to run the stories side by side on the front page beneath a brief introduction by the editors that referred to "the confused situation in South Vietnam." According to Sheehan, the way the two stories were played was unprecedented at the *Times*, and a less determinedly ambitious reporter than Halberstam might well have resigned over this timid vote of half-confidence. (The editors had wanted to run Halberstam's story inside the paper, but James Reston persuaded them to place it on the front page.) The government admitted three days later that the Washington version was wrong. While Halberstam was not alone in filing negative dispatches, the incident, as Sheehan said, was "a measure of how low Halberstam's credibility was with his New York editors—and how high they held the credibility of government in 1963."

Thus, while cold warrior Halberstam was reporting the truth according to Vann, his paper actively undermined his work—hardly a treasonous combination.

Halberstam and his confreres deserve their due for at least opening up to Vann, whose calculated strategy was to go over the heads of his superiors by sending messages to Washington via the Saigon press corps. Whatever his political opinions, Halberstam, in *The Making of a Quagmire*, at least told Americans in 1965 that something was amiss in Vietnam. But the Vann view relayed to the American public was, in its way, as misguided and self-delusional as the original Administration belief that U.S. advisers could turn the South Vietnamese army into an effective force against the Vietcong. Halberstam's mentor believed that the war could be won by facing the facts of guerrilla warfare and adopting some of the enemies' tactics. The good guys needed to learn how to fight the bad guys on the bad guys' terms, up close and eye to eye. And no one in the Saigon press corps in those days, including Halberstam or the Associated Press's Peter Arnett, questioned Kennedy's, Vann's, or Lyndon Johnson's belief that America needed to kill Vietnamese rebels.

Another implausibility in the press-lost-Vietnam theory becomes evident when one notes the events that followed Halberstam's and Sheehan's reporting in 1962–63. Before *The Making of a Quagmire* was published in 1965, Halberstam wrote a profile of John Vann that appeared in the November 1964 issue of *Esquire*, which, Sheehan said, created "Vann's public legend." When the Halberstam book came out, President Johnson was in the midst of his first large-scale escalation of the war using U.S. combat troops. If the press had undermined the country's commitment to the war, then why was Johnson able to step up the war effort so successfully? One reason is the Gulf of Tonkin incident, in which North Vietnamese gunboats were said by the Johnson Administration to have fired without provocation on American ships off the coast of Vietnam. The Pentagon Papers later revealed the official version of events to be false, but almost everyone believed it at the time. The Senate subsequently passed a resolution by a vote of 88–2, following a 416–0 House vote of approval, granting Johnson broad powers to wage a wider war against the North Vietnamese. If the antipress theorists were right, surely a number of members of Congress would have questioned the Administration's story. But perhaps the Vietnam revisionists failed to realize that in 1964, American newspapers (as well as the Saigon reporters) were pro-war, or equivocal in their editorials about the war.

Indeed, the press in the mid-1960s often employed the same sort of flag-waving rhetoric and jingoism exhibited by the media more than two decades later in the Persian Gulf War. "Congress is responding with commendable promptness," said *The Washington Post* in an editorial praising the Gulf of Tonkin resolution. President Johnson, it said, "wished to demonstrate before the world the unity of the American people in resisting Communist aggression. That unity has been demonstrated despite the reckless and querulous dissent of Senator [Wayne] Morse."

The New York Times was more cautious in its assessment and expressed the hope that "the administration can and should now demonstrate that it is as resolute in seeking a peaceful settlement as it is in prosecuting the war." But the tone of the *Times* editorial was upbeat: "[Johnson] now has proof of a united Congress and a united nation; he has demonstrated his own capacity for toughness. And the Communists have been left with no doubt about American determination."

Over at *The Wall Street Journal*, Communists were still known as "Reds." However, the *Journal's* editorial writer was downright skeptical of the Pentagon's progress against them to date, remarking that "the history of [U.S.] involvement has been marked by indecisiveness and confusion. The U.S. has drifted deeper and deeper into war, without ever appearing to know how to achieve its aims or always knowing what the aims were." But there was no question of giving up: "We have gone so far that there appears no acceptable alternative. And if the President's order means the Government is at last on the road to firmness and decisiveness, it may be the best hope the circumstances offer."

The *Los Angeles Times* seemed relieved that the Gulf of Tonkin crisis had clarified the nation's obligations, and lauded Johnson's military response as "warning enough to the Communists not to try such foolishness again." The answer to "unprovoked attacks" had been "fitting in selectivity, proper in application and . . . inevitable in delivery . . . At least now the cause is clear and we know what we are doing and why we do it."

The editorial page of the rabidly anti-Communist *Chicago Tribune* ridiculed U.S. allies reluctant to back Johnson's actions in the United Nations, and criticized United Nations Secretary General U Thant, "himself an Asiatic," for "loftily informing the world that we cannot win [in Vietnam] and should negotiate ourselves out of the sticky mess on Communist terms."

While highly sophisticated readers in those days did conclude from the work of Halberstam and his colleagues that Vietnam was a disaster in the making, they were in a minority, partly because of the overwhelming support for the war pouring forth from the nation's largest newspapers. There were few well-known critics of the Administration's

Vietnam policy in the press, or of the Cold War assumptions which underlay the policy. Halberstam himself was speaking for the frustrated Vann, who wanted to fight harder and better to defeat the Communist menace. Halberstam, of course, was not the only symbolic subversive who covered the war in Vietnam. Peter Arnett, then of the Associated Press, was another cause of Administration unhappiness. In a memo to Lyndon Johnson in August 1965, the President's devoted thirty-one-year-old press secretary, Bill Moyers, criticized the "irresponsible and prejudiced coverage" of Arnett and of Morley Safer of CBS. Moyers pointed out that the two reporters might be especially undependable in their war coverage because they were foreign-born, Arnett in New Zealand and Safer in Canada. They "are not Americans and do not have the basic American interests at heart," Moyers wrote. He promised to "try to tighten things up," and Johnson handwrote an enthusiastic "Good!" at the bottom of the memo.[1] In a May 12, 1965, memo to Johnson in preparation for a meeting between the President and Associated Press executives, Presidential assistant Jack Valenti advised his boss: "You may want to bring up the problem of Peter Arnett who has been more damaging to the U.S. cause than a whole division of Vietcong. His stories on: defective ammunition, antiquated aircraft, use of 'poison gas.' "

But Arnett, the fifth columnist, effected no change in the American resolve to win the war, or in the media's determination to promote it. For example, the July 2, 1965, issue of *Life* is filled with top-notch war photographs by Horst Faas (again contrasting starkly with the Gulf War): wounded American troops grimacing in pain; wounded Vietnamese children and their anguished families; mutilated Vietcong corpses; refugees; a tearful soldier—in short, the real, uncensored face of war. None of these images appear to have frightened Henry Luce, the owner of *Life*, or the magazine's editors into abdicating their global responsibility to fight the spread of Communism. In the same issue they published an essay defending American military intervention by Eugene V. Rostow, former dean of the Yale Law School and brother of LBJ's arch anti-Communist adviser, Walt Whitman Rostow. Sounding a bit like the young David Halberstam, Rostow wrote: "If North Vietnam were allowed to annex South Vietnam without a fight, where could the flow be held? How would the political orientation of Japan be affected? That of Europe? . . . President Johnson's firm, controlled move in Vietnam is a major step toward world stability, and therefore toward world peace. The president has cut the Lilliputian cords which have bound the Western allies since the war and which have denied them political influence commensurate with their power."

Such was the self-confidence of the United States during Luce's American Century. Horrifying pictures of war could be published, but the Johnson Administration kept sending more troop ships. Uncensored reporting seemed to shock virtually no one's conscience, and certainly not the editors at Time Inc.

In the gallery of alleged anti-Vietnam heresies, one series of dispatches from Hanoi by Harrison Salisbury—the first published in *The New York Times* on Christmas Day, 1966—stand out. Salisbury's reporting from enemy territory has particular historic resonance because it mirrors the controversy surrounding Peter Arnett's reporting from Baghdad. Again, the premise of the pro–Vietnam War revisionists is patently false, but it must nonetheless be held up to the light.

Salisbury was no Communist sympathizer when he turned up in North Vietnam; he was one of the most celebrated foreign correspondents of his era and a *Times* assistant managing editor. The idea for him to go, Salisbury said in June 1991, was that of managing editor Clifton Daniel, the son-in-law of former President Harry Truman, whose Truman Doctrine sent the United States into Korea, and ultimately into Vietnam.

"This was not a sudden whim or anything of that kind," Salisbury told me. "It was a project initiated by Clifton Daniel and the management of the *Times* . . . nine months ahead of when it actually happened." The plan was for Salisbury to make "a grand trip around the periphery of China, and report on China from the outside. Simultaneously [I was] to attempt three things: actually get into China by making contact with Chinese on the periphery, and to get into Hanoi by making contact with Vietnamese on the periphery, and to get into North Korea." Salisbury obtained permission from the State Department to travel to these three off-limits Communist countries, but he failed to get into any of them from his base in Cambodia. At Daniel's insistence, he kept trying other channels after returning to New York. Then, in December 1966, "out of the blue we got a message from the *Times* bureau in Paris that the North Vietnamese representative there wanted to see me. We pretty well knew what that meant."

Traveling to North Vietnam via Paris and Phnom Penh, Salisbury arrived in the capital just before Christmas, and his first story—"a very leisurely dispatch about conditions in Hanoi on Christmas Eve and all that"—created a sensation back home. "Down about six paragraphs, I went into the meat of the situation, which was that I walked down a couple of streets in Hanoi, and they'd been hit by American bombs. This was at the time when Lyndon Johnson was saying that we were only hitting steel and concrete."

Salisbury had happened on a story that undermined one of the major euphemisms of the day, "precision" bombing, much later to go by the name of "surgical" bombing. "Lyndon [Johnson] said . . . we are striking at freight yards and a trucking center outside of Hanoi," Salisbury recalled. "But as I walked down the street, here were these houses down there bombed. So I threw that into the story, naturally."

What Salisbury saw, in his opinion, was "extremely trivial as far as anyone, who, like myself, had been through the blitz in London and seen the bombing in Germany, Poland, and the Soviet Union." But more than thirty civilians had been killed, and it gave the lie to what James William Gibson has called the "technowar" fantasies of Defense Secretary Robert McNamara, in which American technology killed according to the rules of a computer-simulated production model: the results would be profitable and clean, with U.S. warplanes virtually never missing their targets. The news of the fallibility of what Gibson termed the "managerial" approach to war, appearing in the nation's paper of record, meant far more than earlier reports from foreign journalists revealing the same information. In fact, one of the earlier civilian casualty stories by a British correspondent, Salisbury said, had even been published in the *Times*—on an inside page. The tremendous impact of Salisbury's story was a result of timing and the famous LBJ "credibility gap," then in its adolescence:

> This bomb damage was so small by the standards of what happens in actual bombing it would never have been reported there or anyplace else if Johnson hadn't set himself up by saying we're not killing any people. Any correspondent who'd been through bombing knew perfectly well that no matter how accurate your bombing is, there always are strays off your target and . . . you kill some people . . . This was, as I say, a trivial example of that. I could even tell exactly what they were [aiming] at, because straight ahead about a mile and a half from this area in downtown Hanoi was the Red River and a very important bridge across that river; American bombers had been trying for weeks and months to knock this Goddamn bridge out . . . They hadn't figured on heavy antiaircraft fire or something . . . but they had not hit the bridge; it was still operating, but you could just see he dropped his bombs a little early. At least that's what I presume.

The actual story as published in the newspaper was a bit more dramatic than Salisbury's recollection twenty-four years later. But not until well into the story did the correspondent challenge the Administration line, and even then his prose seemed mildly sarcastic, not adversarial.

> This correspondent is no ballistics expert, but inspection of several damaged sites and talks with witnesses make it clear that Hanoi residents certainly believe they were bombed by United States planes, that they certainly observed United States planes overhead and that damage certainly occurred right in the center of town.

Because of the Christmas holiday, the White House was slow to respond. Then it did so with venom. Salisbury was dubbed "Harrison Appallsbury of the *New Hanoi Times*" by Pentagon spokesman Arthur Sylvester. Reliable pro-war columnists Joseph Alsop and William Randolph Hearst, Jr., weighed in with attacks that suggested Salisbury had gone over to the enemy side. Alsop questioned "whether a United States reporter ought to go to an enemy capital to give the authority of his by-line to enemy propaganda figures . . ." *The Washington Post*, perhaps borrowing from Jack Valenti, said Salisbury had become Ho Chi Minh's latest weapon of war. For his treason, Salisbury was denied a Pulitzer Prize by a one-vote margin in 1967. As Phillip Knightley put it in *The First Casualty*: "Being a war correspondent on the enemy side was clearly not the easiest way to advance one's career."

Looking back, it all begins to sound like Senator Alan Simpson and Arabic scholar Bernard Lewis attacking Peter Arnett when they appeared on a televised discussion of censorship during the Gulf War. Simpson fired away with innuendo:

> I said how come the Vietnamese would allow him to stay there after the government had slain fifty-seven thousand

of our human beings, and he stayed there and he had
free access to the country. How come he's the only man
they allowed to stay in Baghdad for three weeks while
nobody else was allowed to be there unless he has some
feeling for the cause?

Lewis attacked with sly sophistry: "Does one really take
the position that the media should adopt complete impar-
tiality between their country and its enemies?"

Salisbury found the entire matter all too familiar. "Essentially the identical arguments which are used against Peter
Arnett's reporting from Baghdad were the ones which had
been voiced when I went to Hanoi. I was called Hanoi Harry
and the *Times* was called the *Hanoi Times*. I was called a
Commie . . . There was the denunciation of the *Times* for
sending a man to the enemy side, and reporting the enemy
side. Of course, that's exactly what Peter encountered."

Both Arnett and Salisbury found their loyalty questioned on the grounds that they had spent too much time
covering Communists. "Quite a few picked up this line about
my having been a Moscow correspondent," Salisbury said.
" 'What do you expect from this guy? Is he [still] reporting
from Moscow?' It's somewhat parallel to the claim that Peter
Arnett's correspondence from Vietnam had been distorted
because his ex-wife's brother was in the Vietcong or something like that."

Salisbury's final act of treason, upon his return home,
was to attempt to meet with President Johnson. Dean Rusk
had urgently requested a conversation with the correspondent when his dispatches from Hanoi appeared in the paper,
and Salisbury was willing to comply. He did not intend either
to apologize or to protest, but he thought he might be helpful,
for before leaving Hanoi he had been granted a lengthy interview with North Vietnamese Premier Pham Van Dong.
Although this was second best to Ho Chi Minh himself, Pham
Van Dong had hinted at some interesting matters that could

not be put in a news story. Despite Salisbury's assertions to the contrary, Ho Chi Minh's deputy had insisted on treating him as an emissary of the U.S. government and had strongly implied a willingness to begin direct negotiations with the United States.

"I had told them again and again that I was not the government," Salisbury said. "I not only didn't support the government's policy but my paper was very critical of it . . . No matter how I attempted to divest myself of responsibility of being a spokesman," he recalled, "they continued to believe that I must be, otherwise I wouldn't be there." Out of a sense of "patriotic duty, if you want to call it that, a moral duty to pass the information on to my government," Salisbury decided to violate his "deep conviction that reporters shouldn't muck around in diplomacy," and requested the meeting with LBJ via *Times* Washington bureau chief James Reston. Word came back from Presidential aide Bill Moyers that Johnson "wouldn't under any circumstances" see him, and Salisbury agreed to see Rusk instead, so "that at least somebody would have this information." The request was granted and the meeting took place on January 13, 1967, at the State Department with Rusk and Assistant Secretary of State William Bundy. Salisbury recalled:

> I might say I'd known Dean for many years, so I was not terribly surprised that he began to lecture me about the reality of the situation and the propaganda these people were making and so on. He kept asking me, "Did they say this, did they say that?"—things which had never gotten into the conversation [with Pham Van Dong]. Fortunately, Bundy . . . listened to what I had to say and asked some intelligent questions . . . although I don't think Dean ever listened to anything I had to say.

Not surprisingly, the American buildup continued despite Salisbury's diplomatic initiative. In 1966 American military personnel in Vietnam stood at 389,000. In 1967 it rose to 463,000, and in 1968 to 495,000; it peaked in 1969 at 541,000.

There was some satisfaction for the reporters who tried to tell the truth in Vietnam, at the time and years later. The Administration eventually admitted, for example, that Salisbury's Christmas Eve dispatch was accurate. Some good came of this, for a young press officer in the White House named Tom Johnson was paying close attention to the Salisbury and Arnett controversies and noting the truthfulness of reports his office had been required to deny. Twenty-four years later, as president of CNN, a much wiser Johnson found himself defending the presence of Peter Arnett in Baghdad.

Much has been written about Vietnam as the first television war, and many, on the left and right, have argued that violent televised images swung public opinion against the war, particularly around the time of the Tet offensive in early 1968. Certainly the Pentagon of Desert Storm feared a recurrence of weak-kneed irresolution if Americans witnessed body bags and wounded soldiers on their screens at dinnertime. But like most pro-war revisionist theories about Vietnam, this one also appears to be false.

Lawrence W. Lichty, Daniel Hallin, and Michael Mandelbaum, among others, have studied the anti-television arguments of the Vietnam revisionists. Lichty quotes the noted media critic General William Westmoreland, who said that "television's unique requirements contributed to a distorted view of the war . . . The news had to be compressed and visually dramatic." Thus, "the war Americans saw was almost exclusively violent, miserable, or controversial." He also cites Robert Elegant's assertion that "for the first time in modern history, the outcome of a war was determined not on the battlefield, but . . . on the television screen." Writing in *Dædalus* in 1982, Michael Mandelbaum recalled President Johnson's like-minded remarks to the National Association of Broadcasters delivered on April 1, 1968, the day after he announced he would not seek reelection:

> As I sat in my office last evening, waiting to speak, I thought of the many times each week when television brings the war into the American home. No one can say exactly what effect those vivid scenes have on American opinion. Historians must only guess at the effect that television would have had during earlier conflicts on the future of this nation: during the Korean war, for example, at that time when our forces were pushed back there to Pusan; or World War II, the Battle of the Bulge, or when our men were slugging it out in Europe or when most of our Air Force was shot down that day in June 1942 off Australia.

Johnson was implying that horrifying televised images had caused Americans to lose heart over Vietnam and would have lost the other wars as well, but Lichty found that even though "about half of all the TV reports filed from Vietnam were about battles and military action, most showed very little actual fighting." He determined that from August 1965 to August 1970 "only about three percent of all the evening news film reports from Vietnam showed 'heavy battle' (defined as 'heavy fighting, incoming, with dead or wounded seen')." That came to seventy-six serious combat stories out of twenty-three hundred. Furthermore, says Lichty, a sample of evening-news stories from 1968 to 1973 found just 3 percent with combat footage and only 2 percent depicting any dead or wounded. Hallin employed a broader definition of combat, but came to the same conclusion as Lichty: "In fact, about 22 percent of all film reports from Southeast Asia in the period before the Tet offensive showed actual combat, and often this was minimal—a few incoming mortar rounds or a crackle of sniper fire (perhaps followed by distant film of air strikes called in to 'take out' the unseen enemy)."

Hallin found that 24 percent of the TV war stories showed dead or wounded, "and again this might be no more than a brief shot of a wounded soldier being lifted onto a helicopter." Out of 167 stories before Tet, Hallin noted "only 16 had more than one video shot of the dead or wounded."

Lichty quotes Michael Arlen of *The New Yorker* for a more accurate assessment of television's presentation of the war:

> A nightly stylized, generally distanced overview of a disjointed conflict which was composed mainly of scenes of helicopters landing, tall grasses blowing in the helicopter wind, American soldiers fanning out across a hillside on foot, rifles at the ready, with now and then (on the soundtrack) a far-off ping or two, and now and then (as the visual grand finale) a column of dark, billowing smoke a half mile away, invariably described as a burning Vietcong ammo dump.

As for the points of view aired on television, the hawks vastly outnumbered the doves during the years of greatest military escalation. Prior to Tet, according to Hallin, "Editorial comments by television journalists ran nearly four to one in favor of Administration policy." Lichty states that before 1966, TV talk shows and documentaries featured prowar voices nine to one over antiwar voices. From 1966 to 1970, he says, "About two-thirds of those discussing Vietnam policy on such programs were 'hawks.' "

Phillip Knightley also downplays the impact of television on the war, citing a *Newsweek* poll in 1967 that found 64 percent of viewers surveyed stating that television coverage had increased their inclination toward "backing up the boys in Vietnam," while only 26 percent asserted it moved them to oppose the war. In 1972, *Newsweek* found that the public may have become inured to the war from watching too many newscasts. According to Knightley:

For many Americans in Vietnam, there emerged a strange side to the war that became directly related to television—the fact that the war seemed so unreal that sometimes it became almost possible to believe that everything was taking place on some giant Hollywood set and all the participants were extras playing a remake of *Back to Bataan*.

In considering the proclivities of the network bosses, one need only recall the actions of William S. Paley, chairman of CBS, after Vice President Spiro Agnew attacked the media in a 1969 speech in Des Moines. In response, Mandelbaum says, Paley "ordered the network to discontinue its commentaries immediately following televised presidential speeches. (They were subsequently resumed.)" Mandelbaum dubs television "the most timid of the media," and observes that even before the Agnew speech, "the networks had begun to avoid reporting on the war in ways that they thought might court unpopularity. Stories about the peace talks in Paris replaced combat footage from Vietnam on the evening news. The negotiations and the withdrawal of American forces, not the fighting, came to be defined as the newsworthy aspects of the war." Knightley arrives at the same conclusion.[2]

Much has been written about the effect of media coverage of the 1968 Tet offensive on American public opinion. Hawkish revisionists can cite former *New York Times* reporter Peter Braestrup's finding that the battle was inaccurately reported to be a Communist victory, when in fact both the Vietcong and the North Vietnamese army suffered heavy casualties and can be said to have "lost" their holiday surprise attack. In this scenario the media dealt another body blow to the war effort. But the argument has more to do with ideology than reality.

By January 1968, even the Johnson Administration's premier whiz kid, Robert McNamara, had turned against the war, convinced at last that it could not be won. Opposition against the war had begun to solidify within the President's own party in the form of Senator Eugene McCarthy's insurgent Presidential candidacy. Tet intensified an antiwar movement that was already well developed. A Gallup poll taken in October 1967 had already found that 47 percent of Americans believed it was a mistake to send troops to Vietnam. With U.S. dead reaching more than 150 per week, the American public hardly needed the media to tell it that something was wrong.

Lichty found that directly following Tet, the three networks presented about an equal number of pro- and antiwar guests, and that after 1970 the number of war critics on television surpassed war defenders. "This opinion trend," he writes, "paralleled the trend in the publicly expressed opinions of many senators and congressmen, perhaps because senators and congressmen were so often those interviewed."

Daniel Hallin noted that editorial commentaries on television shifted after Tet from nearly four to one for the war policy to two to one against. However, he found that while television became less likely to report "victories" for the United States, America was still portrayed as winning more often than losing.

As Max Frankel, the current executive editor of *The New York Times*, explained to Todd Gitlin:

> As protest moved from the left groups, the antiwar groups, into the pulpits, into the Senate—with Fulbright, Gruening, and others—as it became majority opinion, it naturally picked up coverage. And then naturally the tone of the coverage changed. Because we're an establishment institution, and whenever your natural constituency changes, then naturally you will too.

In terms of gauging media impact later in the war, we must certainly consider *My Lai*, Seymour Hersh's great exposé of the classic American atrocity against Vietnam civilians. In the popular view, this story—of the unprovoked massacre of between 90 and 130 men, women, and children by U.S. soldiers on March 16, 1968—changed the course of the war. Credit for originating the story must go to an ex-GI named Ronald Ridenhour, who doggedly wrote letters to politicians, including Congressman Morris Udall, who forced the investigation that led to the court-martial of Lieutenant William L. Calley, Jr. Hersh has become so renowned as an investigative reporter that it is easy to forget how modest were his beginnings and his difficulty in selling the My Lai story. He was a relatively obscure freelancer in Washington when in October 1969 he began to explore the virtually unnoticed army proceedings against Calley. *Life* turned down the story, but Hersh managed to distribute it through the Dispatch News Service, a small press syndicate that had been founded by one of his neighbors. On November 13, a good many newspapers published the account, which was based on Hersh's interview with Calley at Fort Benning, Georgia, and eventually pictures of the slaughter taken by an army photographer made their way into the mainstream press. A more detailed version of Hersh's story was subsequently published by *Harper's Magazine*, and a spate of atrocity stories followed from other correspondents.

Thus, Phillip Knightley asks, "If there were atrocities before My Lai, why did not correspondents write about them at the time? My Lai . . . was an unusually pure example of the nature of the war in Vietnam and departed little—if at all—from common American practice." The answer, in 1971, from Peter Arnett, cannot be reassuring to proponents of the press-lost-Vietnam theory:

> I accompanied Neil Sheehan on some of those military operations he wrote about; I watched hooches burning down; I saw the civilian dead. I did not write about war crimes either. We took pictures of those burning buildings, we told of the civilian dead and how they died, but

we didn't make judgments because we were witnesses, and, like witnesses to robbery, accident, or murder, surely it was not for us to be judge and jury.

Notwithstanding the speciousness of the press-lost-Vietnam argument, or the relative docility of most of the press during the Vietnam War, America's future war planners decided not to risk uncensored press coverage of their own conflicts. They determined—evidently beginning in the Reagan Administration—that reporters would never again have the opportunity to confuse the American public about the government's war aims, whether deliberately or by accident. For every independent soul like Harrison Salisbury or Michael Herr, the author of *Dispatches*, the acclaimed and harrowing book about Vietnam combat, the government knows that there are dozens of reporters who will repeat what they are told by the authorities. Thus, the government's goal became to reduce the chances of wild cards turning up and making trouble.

For inspiration, the U.S. military could turn to the British. In the Falklands War of 1982, twenty-nine correspondents, photographers, and technicians were placed by the Thatcher government in various pools on Royal Navy ships steaming toward the Argentine enemy in the South Atlantic. Then, and later, they were subjected to strict censorship of their dispatches. Lieutenant Commander Arthur A. Humphries, in a lively article in the May–June 1983 issue of *Naval War College Review*, placed Falklands War news management in useful perspective for his military colleagues, noting that "in spite of a perception of choice in a democratic society, the Falklands War shows us how to make certain that government policy is not undermined by the way a war is reported."

U.S. Navy "public affairs specialist" Humphries saw a valuable comparison between the Falklands and Vietnam because of "the capability for immediate mass communication," and he presented some basic recommendations for military public relations that may well have served as a partial blueprint for Operation Desert Storm. Not surprisingly, Humphries was operating under the standard military assumption that Vietnam television images had seriously dampened enthusiasm for the war effort:

> There was the potential in the South Atlantic to show the folks back home a vivid, real-life, real-time picture of men from two opposing nations on two ordinary and theretofore unimportant islands doing some very permanent, ugly things to each other. After the Vietnam Tet Offensive of 1968, the American public, and for that matter the whole world, saw a sample of South Vietnamese–style capital punishment—a real execution of an enemy soldier, via their television sets in their own homes. That is not the sort of thing that would engender support at home for a war. If you want to maintain popular support for a war, your side must not be seen as ruthless barbarians . . .
>
> When relatives of servicemen see their boy, or someone who could be their boy, wounded or maimed, in living color, through imagery right in front of them, that tends to erode their support for their government's war aims. That happened during the Vietnam war. We know what happened to public opinion as a result of repeated doses of blood and guts given to a public that wasn't prepared to cope with it. The issue remains, then: What can a government do about that sort of problem, given the factors of high-tech communications capabilities and a worldwide public attuned to freedom of information?

The answer? From Humphries: "Control access to the fighting, invoke censorship, and rally aid in the form of patriotism at home and in the battle zone. Both Argentina and

Great Britain showed us how to make that wisdom work."
In addition, "to effect or help assure 'favorable objectivity,'
you must be able to exclude certain correspondents from the
battle zone."

Playing off of Mao Zedong's famous aphorism, "Political
power grows out of the barrel of a gun," the astute Lieutenant Commander Humphries wrote that "power also
bounces down a beam from a communications satellite and
goes to the side which tells the story first." He admired in
particular the Israelis, calling them "masters" at news management, and observed that in contrast the British were
"heavy-handed" and inconsistent in their censorship, or "vet-
ting" system. He even chided the British Ministry of Defence
for ceasing background briefings for too long a period. "It
is essential that a government and its military branch give
regular briefings to representatives of all news organizations,
as practicable, in order to sustain a relationship of trust, to
foster the flow of correct information, and to halt faulty
speculation."

Humphries's 1983 observations also criticized the British
for failing "to appreciate that news management is more than
just information security censorship. It also means providing
pictures," a view that would be taken to heart in the Pentagon's management of Desert Storm.

Noting that advances in technology were making it more
difficult to control information, Humphries suggested what
to an adversarial press would seem a sinister prescription:
"Plans should include criteria for incorporating the news media into the organization for war." On another point, however, he was wrong:

> Probably never again will the Ministry of Defence, or
> the defense department of any other democratic nation,
> be able to control all means of transportation to the scene
> of the fighting and the sole means of communications
> both for copy and pictures.

The first field test for the post-Vietnam military information order was the U.S. invasion of Grenada in October 1983. By Humphries's standards it was not handled very efficiently, but in terms of news management Grenada was a resounding success. There simply *wasn't* any news; the invasion was kept secret even from the press offices at the White House and the Pentagon until an hour after it began. We have, thanks to Mark Hertsgaard's *On Bended Knee*, an account of how ABC News missed its chance, through its excessive cautiousness, to report the invasion as it began and to therefore scoop the world. It was the last opportunity for any significant journalism during the entire action. Over the next four days the Reagan Administration did everything in its power to keep reporters off the island. One who managed to get to Grenada on a hired boat, Edward Cody of *The Washington Post*, wound up confined on a U.S. Navy vessel far from the fighting. When reporters finally were allowed on the island, they were able to refute one of the rationales for the invasion—that Grenada had become a supply dump for Soviet and Cuban weapons, a veritable staging ground for subversion. But by then so many newspeople had repeated the Reagan Administration's lie about warehouses stacked to the ceiling with sophisticated Soviet weapons, and hordes of Cuban military advisers roaming the island, that the truth had little impact.

As for the number of American, Grenadian, or Cuban casualties, no one could say for sure. Michael Kaufman, now deputy foreign editor of *The New York Times*, was part of the makeshift pool thrown together by the Pentagon after the fighting had ended. "We still don't know how many Americans were killed in Grenada," he said in February 1991. *Time* initially reported the number of American dead at eleven, with sixty-seven wounded. No one in the government even ventured a public guess at the number of dead Cubans and Grenadians, and no one in the press seemed very eager to find out.

The Grenada invasion news blackout did elicit protests from the major media, as well as a resignation within the ranks of the government public relations apparatus—that of White House communications director David Gergen—who felt compromised by the lies of his superiors. As a result, the government established a commission that was allegedly to study the question of war reporting, under the direction of Major General Winant Sidle. The Sidle commission recommended the creation of the National Media Pool, which was still functioning as of February 1992. In principle, this rotating group of trusted and knowledgeable military reporters—all regular Pentagon correspondents—was now on call to depart at a moment's notice for American surprise attacks in parts unknown. In theory, the Pentagon would be honor-bound to bring them along in a timely fashion.

Major General Sidle and his twelve-member panel of former journalists, journalism professors, and military public affairs officers did not, however, address censorship of pictures and articles; the commission merely argued for the presence of some reporters near the scene of the fighting. The Sidle panel naively assumed that reporters' material would somehow make its way back to the home office without interference.

A few freelance photographers had managed to sneak into Grenada, and one of them, Claude Urraca of Sygma, captured on film a dead American helicopter pilot sprawled spread-eagle on his back on a beach. Blood was visible near his body; his face was not. It was routine war photography, made exceptional by the near-total absence of nongovernment pictures. It told the American public, better than any article, that Reagan's calculated little political maneuver had gotten some Americans killed. To its credit, *Time* published the picture and received a great many complaints from readers for what was fairly tame stuff compared with what had appeared in the weekly issues of *Life* fifteen years earlier. The Pentagon flaks must have noticed, because they made certain it didn't happen again. Eight years later, Retired Vice Admiral Joseph Metcalf III put the Grenada military and news management operations in historical perspective. Asked by Fred Friendly why reporters weren't allowed to tag along, Metcalf replied:

> Because they get in the way . . . We were given specific objectives: we were told to install a friendly government, we were told to do this with a minimum loss of life of Americans, Cubans, Grenadians, and press people. I didn't have this prejudice [against media] until after the operation . . . It was going to be a marvelous sterile operation. I had directives to do the kind of thing that's going on right now in Desert Storm.

The next serious test of the new rules for war coverage came on December 20, 1989, when U.S. troops invaded Panama to oust General Manuel Noriega. Now Dick Cheney and Pete Williams were in charge and the official censorship was only a bit less heavy-handed than during Grenada. This time the Pentagon simply delayed the departure of the National Media Pool until just two hours before the fighting started, and then upon its arrival in Panama the government held the reporters captive on a U.S. base for another five hours. During this time, the media missed the heaviest action of the operation. Outside of Pentagon pictures spoon-fed to journalists, little real information reached the American public, and some reporters finally started to get wise. One of them was Jon Meyersohn, a CBS News producer held hostage for three days by Noriega loyalists. After returning to New York, he wrote a letter to *Harper's Magazine* editor Lewis Lapham summing up the post-Vietnam reality of war reporting:

> In watching U.S. television coverage [with his captors] of Operation Just Cause, we noticed constant updating

of U.S. casualty figures without mention of Panamanian dead or injured; the playing and replaying of stock scenes of heroic American soldiers in helicopter gunships or parachuting onto the beaches but no scenes of hospitals with civilian casualties; the upbeat news conference by President Bush while bodies of dead U.S. troops arrived home; the constant descriptions of Manuel Noriega as a voodoo-practicing pervert and drug runner, never as a longtime U.S. ally.

Since returning home, I've seen that the President's approval ratings for the invasion have been high. The invasion troops have headed home, and . . . Panama is yesterday's news . . .

It's comforting to know that a few people out there are taking notice of this public-relations guided invasion and putting it in its proper place . . .

I certainly saw more as a hostage than I could have as a journalist. It's a little depressing to think that you did a better job reporting the story from your desk than we all did from the field.

The number of Panamanian civilians killed during the invasion remains murky—ranging from 202, the official Pentagon figure, to an estimated 4,000. The best estimate seems to be one thousand, and comes from an Army source cited in Kevin Buckley's *Panama: The Whole Story*. But the Pentagon has stuck to its much lower number as well as to an unlikely total of fifty Panamanian military dead.

As for U.S. casualties, the military said twenty-three Americans died in the Panama invasion and 312 were wounded. Unlike Grenada, no pictures of corpses appeared in the mainstream media. Next time there wouldn't even be pictures of coffins.

In the wake of Operation Just Cause, still another commission was appointed to study problems between the military and the press, this time headed by former Pentagon spokesman Fred Hoffman. Everyone agreed mistakes had been made by the military commanders, and Pete Williams promised things would go better next time.

One further point, which the "public affairs specialist" Lieutenant Commander Arthur A. Humphries made in his 1983 *Naval War College Review* article, would prove prophetic. One must never be "neglectful of the needs of the news correspondents," Humphries exhorted. "The news media can be a useful tool, or even a weapon, in prosecuting a war psychologically, so that the operators don't have to use their more severe weapons."

CHAPTER 5

Operation Desert Muzzle

Now I know why I haven't had children. It's because
later in my life, I don't want some innocent child saying,
"Daddy, what did you do in the Gulf War?" Because I
would have to reply, "Child, I watched it on CNN, from
an armchair in a big hotel in Dhahran, Saudi Arabia."
                    —TONY CLIFTON
                    Newsweek, February 11, 1991[1]

PERHAPS THE ONLY appropriate citation for Gulf War
media coverage was suggested by Walter Goodman of *The
New York Times* for Tom Brokaw of NBC: the "Don't Leave
Home Without Your Tailor" award. The dashingly costumed
Brokaw, Goodman observed, seemed to his viewers to be
fresh from a "daily pre-engagement inspection for hang and
flair by a high official of Hunting World."

The conceit of television aside, the obstacles to producing good journalism during the Gulf War were considerable.
At the top of the list was military censorship—the twelve
hundred U.S. journalists covering the mostly American side
in Saudi Arabia (the media had little choice but to cooperate
with the Administration's evocation of World War II in calling it the "allied" or "coalition" side despite the hugely disproportionate share of U.S. troops) simply weren't permitted
to file much that was worth either reading or watching. Another obstacle may have been the briefness of the fighting,
and that it was conducted mostly from the air. As Benjamin
Bradlee, retired executive editor of *The Washington Post*,

put it: "The trouble with this war was it was so fucking fast." Still another impediment was fear. Most reporters want to survive to tell the story, or just survive, and only a small minority have a taste for battle (Malcolm Browne calls it a "sickness").

There is also the essential randomness of good war correspondence to consider in judging the work done during the Gulf War. Edwin Lawrence Godkin of the London *Daily News* and William Howard Russell of *The Times* of London made a spectacular inauguration of modern-war reporting by exposing the incompetence of British officers in the Crimean War. But the quality of war journalism since 1853 has been spotty, and some of the most successful reporters and photographers have simply been lucky—they found themselves in the right place at the right time and rose to the occasion. Freedom of movement increases the chances of good reporting, but it is no guarantee. And the odds don't improve on a vast desert battlefield.

More often than not, the job of describing what really happened in war falls to the former soldier and to the historian. Paul Fussell is both, and his *Wartime* delineates the wide gap between the sentimental journalism and histories of World War II (Studs Terkel ironically dubbed it "The Good War") and its horrid reality. Seriously wounded as an army lieutenant in Europe in 1945, Fussell has no patience for pseudo-historical accounts of war such as the series issued by Time-Life Books. He notes, for example, the complete failure of Time-Life to record some of the fatal blunders (now euphemized as "friendly fire") of battle caused by simple fear, panic, and ignorance. In one uncelebrated incident during the Allied invasion of Sicily in July 1943, Fussell recounts how U.S. Navy and ground gunners shot down twenty-three planes carrying 229 men of the U.S. 82nd Airborne Division. The green and frightened gunners "had been told that transports and gliders carrying the airborne troops would be flying over them, but at the crucial moment they seemed to forget and blasted away, some of them shouting 'German attack! Fire!' " Time-Life's 1978 volume *The Italian Campaign* omits the incident entirely. Fussell observes that the famous chronicler of the grunt, Ernie Pyle, was on hand for "the Sicilian debacle but either chose not to mention it in his dispatches or, more likely, was forbidden to." Time-Life's egregious omission is, according to Fussell,

> typical behavior for the series, which has done more than perhaps any other popular account of the war to ascribe clear, and usually noble, cause and purpose to accidental or demeaning events. It has thus conveyed to the credulous a satisfying, orderly, and even optimistic and wholesome view of catastrophic occurrences—a fine way to encourage a moralistic, nationalistic, and bellicose politics.

The words describe almost precisely the aim of the White House in Operation Desert Storm.

Fussell doubts that veterans of his war were surprised by the accidental downing of an Iranian airliner by a U.S. Navy ship in July 1988 in which 290 innocent people were killed. Neither, then, would they be shocked by the extraordinarily high percentage of Americans hit by their own side during the Gulf War—23 percent of the dead and 15 percent of the wounded.*

Another question in considering Gulf War reportage is whether what took place should be called a war at all, since a war presumes two sides and the Iraqis barely fought back. Was it a war or a police action that turned into a slaughter? Are the requirements for covering a massacre the same as those for covering a "war"?

Some critics of traditional war correspondence argue that being at the front is greatly overrated as a means of

---

* Of the 148 U.S. troops killed in action, 35 were killed by friendly fire. Out of 467 wounded in action, 72 were injured by their own side.

conveying the heart of the story to the people back home. Writing in the *Columbia Journalism Review* after the liberation of Kuwait, Michael Massing contended that "to get the real story in the gulf, reporters did not have to travel to the front. They did not even have to travel to Saudi Arabia. Most of the information they needed was available in Washington. All that was required was an independent mind willing to dig into it. In short, this war needed fewer David Halberstams and more I. F. Stones."

Massing is probably right. During the 1960s and early 1970s, *I. F. Stone's Weekly*, Mary McCarthy's and Theodore Draper's critical articles in *The New York Review of Books*, and Robert Scheer's writing in *Ramparts* undoubtedly did convey a better understanding of America's doomed Vietnam policy than was available to readers of *The New York Times*, and certainly to viewers of the CBS Evening News. None of the excellent work by these writers required that they witness combat. Stone specialized in mining the bureaucratic alleys of Washington, realizing that most of what he needed could be found on a piece of paper somewhere in the federal government's vast information-production machine, or in the mind of a neglected civil servant. McCarthy, Draper, and Scheer read widely and thought and saw clearly.

Among the prominent examples of war stories broken at home that one might have expected to find broken at the scene was the secret bombing of Cambodia. William Beecher, then Pentagon correspondent for *The New York Times*, revealed for the first time, on May 9, 1969, that U.S. warplanes had struck targets inside neutral Cambodia in an effort to root out Vietcong and North Vietnamese sanctuaries. Another example is the story of the My Lai massacre. Indeed, when I pressed the Pentagon's Pete Williams on the need for unrestricted battlefield reporting to expose the mistakes and corruption of field officers or their commanders, he retorted, "The sainted arrangements in Vietnam did not lead to coverage of My Lai. That was written in Washington."

It was a clever rejoinder, but it hardly spoke to the point. Williams seemed to be arguing that freely roaming reporters were unnecessary because the truth eventually comes out.

The truth, of course, does not always come out, and if the military had been able to sustain its initial lie, the truth about My Lai would never have been known. Williams had no doubt forgotten that the U.S. command in Saigon announced My Lai as a military victory. The day after the massacre, March 17, 1968, *The New York Times* reported on its front page that American units had killed 128 North Vietnamese soldiers as part of an "offensive to clear enemy pockets still threatening the cities." No civilian casualties were reported by the military, and General William C. Westmoreland sent a note congratulating the men who did the killing on their "outstanding action." Obviously, it would have been far better if a reporter had been at My Lai; such a presence might have prevented the killing, or at least the killing might have been reported sooner. As Benjamin Bradlee of *The Washington Post* told me:

> What if [My Lai] had come out the day it happened? . . . The war would have been over two years earlier— not a bad goal for the United States Army; not a bad result for the world or the good guys; certainly not bad for the army. My Lai had a terrible effect [once it was made public] because everyone knew they were covering it up.

If we take seriously the concept of informed consent in a democracy, then ideally we want I. F. Stone, Seymour Hersh, Harrison Salisbury, Michael Herr, and Neil Sheehan all working on the war story, both in Washington and overseas. We want enough information from these journalists so that in theory, at least, we can change our minds in the middle of a war and end it. To a limited extent this is what happened in Korea, a war that concluded in a stalemate, and Vietnam, where a significant minority of voters and members of Congress became convinced that the war was immoral and should be stopped, thus raising the political cost to an unacceptable level for the majority that supported the war. In the Gulf War, unfortunately, we had neither I. F. Stone in Washington nor Michael Herr in Dhahran. And in any case, it is doubtful that even the highly skilled combat correspondents could have reported anything worthwhile had they been there, except the breadth and depth of the censorship.

The temptation to minimize the efforts of the Desert Storm correspondents is made stronger both by the fact that most of them acceded passively to the Pentagon management program (some would argue they had no choice) and because they were made to appear so bumbling and informationless in the televised press briefings, contrasted as they were with the purposeful and self-assured military briefers. Such was their vulnerability to ridicule that on February 9, 1991, "Saturday Night Live" performed a parody of a Gulf War briefing in which reporters repeatedly asked idiotic questions, which, if answered, would have compromised battlefield security. At least some of the program's viewers hoped the target would be the Pentagon censors, and their disappointment signified a public relations triumph for the White House. According to *The New York Times*'s Jason DeParle, this little bit of satire convinced the White House that it had won the day over the media and need no longer be defensive about its censorship policy—an outcome that can hardly have pleased the program's officially antiauthoritarian producers.

But the war was not a farce. Nor was the censorship, which had a deeply serious purpose. And although most of the media in Saudi Arabia collaborated with the government, there were a few who resisted honorably, with no particular encouragement from their home offices.

The most formidable obstacle to reconstructing what happened among the Gulf press corps is that reporters and their bosses, in describing their work during the six-week conflict, tend to speak in two distinct idioms: the honest journalistic and what A. Bartlett Giamatti dubbed "the higher institutional." In general, the honest journalistic voice admitted that censorship was highly effective and that few reporters saw anything of real significance. The institutional voice, on the other hand, insisted that *this* institution was different; *this* institution broke away from the escorted pools and saw the real action, or heard the real voices of the troops. If one believed all the institutional voices claiming important scoops during the war, one might come to the conclusion that Pete Williams was right when he praised the Gulf War coverage as the best ever. At the same time, the big media organizations were required, in part for institutional reasons, to be officially unhappy about censorship.

Thus we have weirdly contradictory assessments of the coverage from such media corporations as Time Warner. *Time*'s Washington bureau chief, Stanley Cloud, was bluntly critical of his magazine's coverage. He was so annoyed by the censorship policy that he suggested a *Time* boycott of the pools. John Stacks, *Time*'s chief of correspondents, rejected the idea when Cloud informed him that no other news organizations were willing to go along with *Time*. After the war, Cloud considered himself the "radical" among the group of news executives protesting Pentagon censorship because he advocated abolition of the Department of Defense National Media Pool. But Time Warner was corporately ambivalent about censorship. Back in the early fall of 1990, after American soldiers and correspondents had been in Saudi Arabia for two months or so, *Time Insider*, a special supplement for certain subscribers to *Time*, published a chatty article entitled "Inside the Pentagon Press Pool." The accompanying photograph showed a smiling Jay Peterzell and photographer Dennis Brack posed in front of a group of determined-looking soldiers dressed in full combat gear, automatic rifles at the ready. The *Time* men had arrived in the desert in August courtesy of the National Media Pool and were evidently glad to be there, censored or not.

Although there was as yet no war and the American presence at this point was being presented as strictly defensive, censorship was already in effect. During this early period, according to *Time Insider*, "Dispatches were cleared by the Pentagon and released to the news media in Washington." But as both Cloud and Pete Williams have noted, Peterzell was not particularly bothered by the first official wartime censorship since Korea. (Censorship of reports was relaxed somewhat when non–National Media Pool reporters began arriving in Saudi Arabia, and became much stricter in January when the combat pools were instituted.)

"We found there were ways of getting away from our 'escorts' and that you could actually move pretty freely around Saudi Arabia," Peterzell told *Time Insider*.

> The pool concept has received a lot of criticism, and much of it is justified, but it misses an important point. The pool did give U.S. journalists a way of getting into Saudi Arabia and seeing at least part of what was going on at a time when there was no other way of doing either of those things. Also, in the first two weeks after the wave of TV, newspaper and magazine correspondents flooded into the country, they did not produce any story that was essentially different from what we in the pool had filed.

Peterzell is observing the maxim of not biting the hand that feeds you. Moreover, he evidently preferred it when there were fewer reporters and things were thus better organized: "When non-pool correspondents were first let in, the Saudis were immediately overwhelmed and their solutions ranged from throwing everyone out to going back to the pool. The Pentagon people worked hard to keep the press in the country. Finally, King Fahd himself decided to open it up to everyone and within several days there were 300 reporters. It was chaotic." (In an interview after the war, Peterzell seemed to realize he could have been bolder: "We were sort of like dogs; the doors had been open the whole time, but we didn't think we could go through. Once we went through and we weren't prisoners, that raised the issue that maybe we could go other places, too.")

From apologizing for the pool system in October, *Time* progressed to the point in March where its parent company bragged about reporters escaping the pool. In *FYI*, an in-house newsletter, corporate press agents celebrated the "short" but "glorious" history of the special weekly edition of *Life: In Time of War* by touting its "big scoops." These astonishing feats of journalism had been accomplished by reporter Ed Barnes and contract photographer Tony O'Brien. I suspect O'Brien was embarrassed by the promotion of what was at best ordinary and unrevealing war photography. A good and courageous photojournalist, he surely recognized the difference between his pictures for the weekly *Life* of Desert Storm and the work of great combat photographers like Larry Burrows, Horst Faas, Robert Capa, and Carl Mydans for the pre-1972 *Life*. Barnes's and O'Brien's "scoops," according to *FYI*, were as follows:

> The first week, wandering far from the Pentagon press pool, the *Life* team helped "capture" four surrendering Iraqi soldiers. Next they found 50,000 graves freshly dug for potential allied victims of the ground offensive.* For the third issue, they beat the allies into Kuwait City—in spite of a cautionary injunction from the managing editor . . . And in the last issue, the team showed what life was like in a rebel-held Iraqi town—the first public proof in the West that the rebels controlled any territory at all.

---

* In fact, Barnes reported in the March issue of *Life* the discovery of ninety-six graves. A "source" told him the plan was to dig fifty thousand graves. This undoubtedly never happened.

The first feat is an amusing stunt, not a scoop. The second is interesting, but pales given the lack of actual combat pictures or photos of wounded or dead soldiers and civilians; it is as if to say that photographing an empty military cemetery is a scoop. Getting to Kuwait City before the troops is fun, but what about witnessing some fighting before you arrive? The fourth "scoop" occurred after the war ended. As Jeff Z. Klein of *The Village Voice* put it after the war: "But where are the corpses?" In fact, the most gruesome pictures in the four special issues of *Life* were of corpses from the Iran–Iraq war, and were taken by freelance photographers. Just one dead Iraqi appeared in the glorious resurrection of the weekly *Life*. (Some of the better pictures in the war were taken by a roving band of French photographers who called themselves the "Fuck the Pool" pool. But despite the best efforts of these mavericks, Robert Schnitzlein, a Reuters picture editor, was correct when he told *American Photo*, "There is really no photographic document of actual fighting in the Gulf."*)

Time Warner's postwar corporate cheerleading was both pathetic and dangerous. The institutional voice smothered the honest voice in an immodest effort to create success out of the terrible failure of the press to record what happened in the Gulf. And yet the honest journalistic voice appeared in the same issue of *FYI* that promoted the false achievements of Barnes and O'Brien. In an article headlined "We Won't Get Pooled Again," Stanley Cloud was quoted saying:

> They [the Pentagon] figured out a way to control every facet of our coverage. They restricted our access to a point where we couldn't do any of our own reporting.

* The most horrifying photograph of a corpse in the Gulf War—depicting the ghoulish and charred head of a dead Iraqi soldier still seated upright in his disabled vehicle—appeared well after the war in a special Time Warner book. But the picture, by Kenneth Jarecke, appeared in *The Observer* of London on March 3, when it was still timely.

> They fed us a steady diet of press conferences in which
> they decided what the news would be. And if somehow,
> after all that, we managed to report on something they
> didn't like, they could censor it out . . . It amounted to
> recruiting the press into the military.

Of course, the corporation's middle management had been all too happy to be recruited the previous fall when they passively accepted the Pentagon restrictions. So were the correspondents like Peterzell. Yet for institutional reasons, we must be told that Time Warner resisted the pools. As *Time* picture editor Michele Stephenson told *FYI*: "We fought this tooth and nail but wound up doing what they wanted us to do . . . The defense department designed this system to give the government strict control over the public's perception of the war, and for the government it worked perfectly." So why were photographers Tony O'Brien, Dennis Brack, and Cynthia Johnson shown smiling so broadly in their *après guerre* photographs?

FYI's postwar wrap-up correspondent, Cory Johnson, deserves credit for getting the real scoop: the contradictions of Time Warner's position vis-à-vis the government. The only problem with his story was the limited circulation it received. Time Warner employees, it seems, got much more revealing coverage of the censorship issue and the war than did readers of *Time* or *Life* magazines. For example, *Life* reporter Ed Barnes criticized his allegedly more timid colleagues in a most uncollegial way: "I'm embarrassed at how the American press went along with the restrictions. The British and the French media got away from the pool. Why couldn't the Americans? They weren't trying."

On the supposed military perfection of Desert Storm, Barnes was even more candid:

> All this praise of American bombing accuracy is crazy.
> That wasn't even the American bombing strategy. It was

about B-52's and carpet bombing. There were stories never told about the strained relations between the coalition forces, about U.S. troops who didn't get supplies for months and months, about troops who were killed by friendly fire. A lot of journalists over there, after they had their stories axed by the military, thought they would just tell them after the war was over, but that's naive. Once the war is over, no one cares.

Barnes, through *Time*'s house organ, begins to sound like Seymour Hersh and Harrison Salisbury rolled into one. Asked by the intrepid Johnson if, "as long as the government wins its wars, the press will fight losing battles," Barnes replies simply and profoundly: "The people who own the media are the ones who have pull in Washington and they're going to have to raise a stink about this to keep it from happening again." He is echoed by Cloud, who says ominously:

> We can never accept this pool system again. We need to use the leverage we have. We can't worry about the public's support. Mark my words: This is no longer limited to war or the Defense Department. This was an object lesson for bureaucrats everywhere. They can control the press . . .

It's unlikely that anything approaching what Barnes told *FYI* turned up in a Time Warner publication before or during the war. Thus *Time*'s in-house hero becomes institutional journalism's severest critic, but only after saving his best stuff for the company newsletter, which comes out when the war is over.

Not all of Time Warner's editorial workers were as honest and outspoken as Barnes and Cloud, and after the war, far more people got to read senior correspondent Bruce van Voorst's fawning "Insights on Desert Storm" in *Time Insider*. Among van Voorst's pearls of inside information were that Secretary of Defense Cheney and Joint Chiefs Chairman Colin Powell are not close personal friends, but that they meet daily at 5 p.m. in Washington, after which Powell "retires to repair Volvos and Cheney reads about flyfishing."

"Volvos?" asks the unnamed questioner for *Time Insider*.

"Yes," replies van Voorst. "Powell loves Volvos."

From his "perch" as *Time*'s "national security" correspondent, van Voorst was in an excellent position to observe Pentagon censorship policy. Asked how he felt about the news blackout during the first twelve hours of the American-led ground invasion of Kuwait, van Voorst said, "I couldn't fight it, to be honest. As much as it runs counter to my professional interest, I think the refusal to give briefings in the first phase was perfectly reasonable." Van Voorst said he objected to the pool system and that it "didn't work very well." Nonetheless, he wanted *Time* insiders to know, "I will say a lot of nice things about [Pete Williams]"—even though he was one of the architects of the censorship policy. But the policy, according to van Voorst, didn't "hurt" *Time*'s coverage. In his opinion: "Our problem was not really too little information. I think what our readers wanted were judgments that made use of the information we had to put the action in some perspective."

Time Warner was not alone in its corporate ambivalence toward censorship. Efforts to save face were everywhere in the media after the war. At *The Washington Post*, for example, foreign-news editor Michael Getler was at pains in an interview to express his displeasure with the censorship, but both he and Pentagon correspondent Molly Moore simultaneously insisted that the *Post* had done a good job covering the war anyway. Here is Getler, who stayed in Washington during the war, speaking in the honest journalistic voice:

The war had the largest armored movement in history, and essentially no one saw it . . . There are no pictures of it. There's nothing. I guess it was all dust-covered anyway, but there's nothing to record this.

Moreover, Getler said:

We don't know what we missed. It is possible, I hope not . . . that some commander may have made a really bad battlefield flaw . . . we don't know that. We don't know if the M1 tank and the Bradley Fighting Vehicle performed as well as [they] seemed to. We just don't know. There were large [military] units that there were no reporters with. If there were big breakdowns, we don't know that.

Moore, who worked within the pool structure, initially seconded Getler's assessment:

I learned more in the two weeks after the war than I learned during the entire war . . . Most of what's in [my follow-up stories] I had no idea what was going on, and I was right in the middle of the war. I mean, I think we're going to keep finding out things . . . nobody knew about at the time, in the ongoing reporting process . . . The American public got only the military view of this war for the most part. There was not the access to get independent information . . .

Despite these views, Getler and Moore reverted easily to the higher institutional voice, with no hint that they heard a contradiction in what they were saying. Getler told me in the same interview that the *Washington Post* "coverage was good, essentially, despite the Pentagon restrictions." What's more, the public "thought the press coverage was really very good, in the sense that ultimately they got pretty thorough reports, or at least they thought they got pretty thorough reports on what happened. Whether they got it a day or two or three or four days later doesn't seem to matter."

Moore's remarks were even more disconcerting. "In my view," she said, "censorship was not the problem; access was the problem . . . censorship in my mind is them telling me you can't report the outcome . . . I think it's semantics in the way we look at censorship and the way we look at access." Getler also declined to describe what the Pentagon was doing as censorship, accepting instead the government's euphemism, "security review." The transcript of this interview reveals still more contradictory language:

MACARTHUR: So you think you had freedom to report?

MOORE: Yes, I think I had plenty of freedom to report.

MACARTHUR: Even when you were escorted?

MOORE: Oh yes, absolutely.

MACARTHUR: Then that brings back the question of what did we miss and why is it such a big issue?

GETLER: You weren't able to get to where she wanted to go.

MOORE: You could only go to certain places.

GETLER: Where she had the freedom to report.

MACARTHUR: Do you feel you were being managed at those places that you got to go?

MOORE: You just figured out ways to get around them . . . If you talk to the Pentagon reporters who were out there, they found ways [around the restrictions] . . . I knew the commanding officer [of a unit] and he gave me access that he hadn't given a reporter who had been with him for six weeks. That's how the system works . . .

This is the same Moore who said she "had no idea [what] was going on, and I was right in the middle of the war."

In the end, we have the outsider Barnes, of *Life*, who broke the rules and then reported none of the interesting information he knew (except in *FYI*), and the insider Moore, who followed the rules and found out virtually nothing beyond what the military wanted her to know.

The *Post*'s Getler contradicts Barnes in his assessment of the war's major news: "The story of the war, in fact, was the smart munitions and the fact that they worked very well." So well that twenty-five hundred to thirty-five hundred Iraqi civilians were accidentally killed by allied bombs, according to William M. Arkin, military research director of the environmental organization Greenpeace. Barnes rightly, it appears, decried the "smart bomb" hype as "crazy." After the war the Air Force announced that laser- and radar-guided bombs and missiles made up just 7 percent of all U.S. explosives dropped on Iraq and Kuwait. The other 93 percent were conventional "dumb" bombs, dropped primarily by high-flying B-52s from the Vietnam era. Ten percent of the "smart" bombs missed their targets, the Air Force said, while 75 percent of the dumb bombs were off-target. In all, about sixty-two thousand tons of explosives—or 70 percent— missed their targets. The story of the smart/dumb ratio, one of the biggest untold stories of the Gulf War, would have been difficult to pin down precisely, but a few unsupervised interviews at air bases, or a little digging in Washington, might have yielded some of the information.

Getler and Moore were trying to be honest within institutional limits. It isn't a very good advertisement for *The Washington Post* if the foreign-news editor and the Pentagon correspondent both admit they were completely shut out. And with her high-level Pentagon sources, Moore has as good a chance as anyone to reconstruct something that resembles the definitive battlefield story in her own book. To her credit, she told me that "in retrospect, I thought they were lying to me about the bomb damage assessment." The word "lie" does not escape readily from the mouths of reporters these days, even when it is obvious the government is lying.

Other U.S. news organizations were probably worse when it came to inflating the myth of complete bombing accuracy and the wonders of the Patriot missile. ABC's Peter Jennings, for example, spoke of the "astonishing precision" of the U.S. attack on the Iraqi defense ministry, as shown in a Pentagon video; *Time*, describing the same attack, said: "The pinpoint accuracy of the attacks was spectacular." And ABC correspondent Sam Donaldson displayed even greater enthusiasm when describing a Patriot in action, exclaiming: "Bulls-eye! No more Scud." After the war, the Patriots and the laser-guided cruise missiles lost a considerable part of their glamour. An MIT scientist, Theodore Postol, told a subcommittee of the House Armed Services Committee: "When the Patriot defense was used, it appears that the damage per Scud attack was actually higher than when there had been no defense." In his analysis, Postol found that the number of Israeli apartments damaged by Scuds tripled and the number of injuries increased by half after Patriots were deployed. Apparently, debris from the smashed-up Scuds caused broader (but lighter) damage than a direct hit. Later, the army said a computer failure had temporarily paralyzed the Patriot system in Dhahran, allowing a Scud to strike a U.S. Army barracks and kill twenty-eight reservists and wound ninety-seven others.

The accuracy of the vaunted Tomahawk cruise missile has been called into question as well. In a test after the war, an unarmed navy Tomahawk fired from the Gulf of Mexico missed its target at Eglin Air Force Base in the Florida panhandle by nearly one hundred miles, landing instead in southern Alabama. It was the fourth such miss since testing began in 1985, according to the navy.

Of course, some of America's sophisticated weaponry

was highly effective against an Iraqi army with no air cover, minimal night vision, demoralized and poorly trained ground troops, and inferior Soviet-made tanks that provided excellent stationary targets. In what can only be termed a postmodern moment in journalism, John Balzar of the *Los Angeles Times* was accidentally permitted to view an army videotape shot from the gun camera of an Apache helicopter as it destroyed Iraqi bunkers and mowed down panicked soldiers during a night attack. Ironically, his subsequent once-removed account of combat revealed a true picture of Gulf War violence:

> One by one [Iraqi soldiers] were cut down by attackers they could not see or understand. Some were blown to bits by bursts of 30-millimeter exploding cannon shells. One man dropped, writhed on the ground, then struggled to his feet; another burst of fire tore him apart.

The story survived the censor's scissors, but Balzar found the military far less cooperative after the story was published on February 24. The army video was never shown on television and Balzar suspects it was destroyed. If it had been broadcast, he said in a postwar interview, it would have horrified the American public: "The war would have ended right then."

The mixing of the honest journalistic and institutional idioms confuses the postwar debate about censorship and makes one wonder whether the media really cared very much at all about being censored.

Too late in the game, *The Washington Post* did try to catch up with the truth about the bombing—a June 23, 1991, story by Barton Gellman revealed that the aims of the bombing campaign were a good deal broader than the Pentagon had previously said. Citing air force sources, Gellman concluded that the American-led forces "sought to achieve some of their military objectives by disabling Iraqi society at large." This was probably a nice way of saying that the campaign was aimed at terrorizing Iraq's civilian population, which Gellman only hints at: "Because of these goals, damage to civilian structures and interests, invariably described by briefers during the war as 'collateral' and unintended, were sometimes neither."

Despite prewar Administration posturing that Saddam was a cruel totalitarian with complete control over his people, in the postwar environment Iraqi civilians were required by the U.S. military to share some of the blame with their dictator. The most telling quote of the war came from a senior air force official in Gellman's report: "The definition of innocents gets to be a little bit unclear . . . They do live there, and ultimately the people have some control over what goes on in their country." Gellman quoted another officer, who noted that "strategic" bombing is aimed at "all those things that allow a nation to sustain itself."

When I suggested that life in Saudi Arabia at the 191-room Dhahran International Hotel sounded a bit like camp, CBS producer Lucy Spiegel replied: "It was camp." However, it was camp for hundreds of adults—reporters, photographers, and technicians—in a country that does not allow alcoholic beverages, even in hotels for foreigners. For journalists, this prohibition is more onerous than it may seem to the ordinary citizen. "Colorful media types who could work all day and booze all night in Saigon or Beirut would find Saudi Arabia a bit confining," wrote Andrew Glass of Cox Newspapers. "So far as I can tell, there isn't a single bottle of beer, to say nothing of the stronger stuff, in the whole kingdom." To make matters worse, Spiegel explained, the absence of alcohol-induced conviviality reduced the usual number of affairs that might normally occur between bored and restless reporters on assignment in a foreign country.

The job at hand, particularly before the outbreak of war,

was rather tedious by most accounts. To be admitted to the press corps in Saudi Arabia, the applicants had to sign a lengthy document promising to abide by the military rules, greatly restricting their movements away from the hotel. Back in late summer and fall, the rules were fairly simple. Off-the-record and "ambush" interviews were outlawed, for example. It would have been difficult to do either, in any case, since the rules clearly dictated constant military escorts.

With so much supervision and so little real news to report during the U.S. troop buildup, journalists turned their attention to personal appearance. Extending the camp metaphor, Spiegel said that the press corps "all got extra camp supplies" and competed over the quality of their respective equipment, like "who had the better canteen." As if directly from a "Doonesbury" comic strip, "there were some bozos that came over there . . . outfitted head to toe in matching little outfits." Because of the threat of chemical warfare, special chemical protection suits were de rigueur, and, asked Spiegel, "Who would you imagine would have the most elegant chem suits?" Why, the French, of course. "Theirs were cut beautifully," Spiegel said. "You could wear those jackets and not think twice about them out in the street. The rest of us were struggling with chem suits that you had to pull over your head. [The French suits] were stylish and gorgeous. They had vents and zippers and snaps, and they had the perfect drawstrings which, of course, are the great rage this year. The French journalists were *très élégants*." Some media companies, including CBS, had bought their chemical suits from British Aerospace, which had a salesman stationed at the Dhahran International Hotel.

Having one of the 150 military public affairs officers (PAOs) on hand at every moment could be annoying indeed, as it tended, naturally, to intimidate soldiers and officers who were being interviewed. Some PAOs were more intrusive than others. But many reporters were happy to comply with the rules because it made life easier in the early days of the intervention. Lucy Spiegel described the routine of the Desert Shield phase of the U.S. intervention, when "Hollywood" Mike Sherman was in charge of the Pentagon's Joint Information Bureau (JIB) in Dhahran. Captain Sherman's normal post was liaison to the film industry in the navy's West Los Angeles offices. But from early August 1990 to December 1990, he organized activities for the journalists in Saudi Arabia, "which, of course, was perfect," according to Spiegel, since "he deals in films."

In those days,

> they would do sign-up sheets . . . They would say, "We're giving a trip out to the carriers," and we'd all dash to sign up; or "We're going to go out and see the 24th Mechanized," or the . . . "7th Infantry" . . . If you were lucky enough to be on a tour, you obviously would get up early—everything ran on military time. If you were a TV crew you hoped that you did not have to get on a military bus, that you could take your own vehicle, because then you could break off and come back if you wanted to. You got escorted wherever it was, and you hoped they had a map, you hoped they had gas in the car, you hoped they knew where they were going, because they didn't [always]. There was nothing and the road signs were not good there . . . Of course, it's all sand dunes. Nobody had ever seen anything like it. So you frequently got lost . . . with the military.

The military left little to chance:

> They would have already called ahead and everything was set up. You never really surprised anybody . . . Like everything in the military, you had a mission to accomplish and that was to see, let's say, an air force base. You'd watch them take off and you'd watch them come down. You'd interview the crew and you'd go and watch them eat a meal and you'd talk to the CO [commanding

officer], and you'd come home . . . There will never be
any journalist award given for that stretch [of time].
There were no great investigative stories. There couldn't
be. You were too controlled. If you did go off the road
and they found out about it, or you ran into somebody
who reported you, you were brought in and your hands
were slapped . . . They'd yell at you: "You had no business being up there without an escort. You know better
than that."

The result, Spiegel said, was ten or so basic stories repeated again and again:

Arrival of troops; not enough mail; the weather: it's too
hot, it's too cold; fill in the blank: the helicopter doesn't
work, the gun won't work, too much sand, too much dirt,
too much whatever; women are going to war; husbands
and wives are going to war; should women be going to
war?; making a reunion between the husbands and the
wives or the wives and the husbands—there are one or
two more.

One story Spiegel didn't mention was soldiers questioning their mission; with the nearly constant eavesdropping by
PAOs, it is easy to understand why. As one outspoken soldier
discovered, the censorship policy was aimed as much at gag-
ging the troops as at shutting down the reporters. Acutely
conscious of breakdowns in discipline in the latter years
of the Vietnam War, the military command would not tolerate
the rank and file sounding off about politics, or questioning
the competence of their officers. One who did was air force
reservist Dick Runels, who wrote a series of descriptive letters home to his local newspaper, *The Voice*, of New Baltimore, Michigan. After the second letter was published,
Runels was ordered to submit all future letters to his base
commander for approval; he defied the order. A few excerpts

from his reports provide a picture of what the Pentagon wanted to avoid during Desert Shield.

OCTOBER 11—We at Mirage [air base] do have it better than probably 90 percent of the troops on the peninsula, but that's only because our airplanes require a lot of space . . . That being said, this is a sand-covered, flea-infested, hot, smelly, congested—did I mention hot?—very basic tent/hooch city that has been force-grown in a hurry to deal with a situation nobody really knows about or knows how it will turn out.

Regardless of the interviews given, we are not all happy to be here, nor did we expect to be here. And we can't wait to get home.

So let everyone at home know that we of the 927th are here, but we can't tell you where; will be coming home, but can't tell you when; are doing our jobs well, but can't tell you why . . .

OCTOBER 27—Tell your readers that the letters they get, filled with despair and crying, are our way of venting frustration at a system that has us *completely* under its control. We need them to handle those complaints and cries with compassion. We're not being tortured, starved, beaten, or abused; we're just part of a machine that is grinding toward some vague goal. If it was clearer why we're here, it would be easier to take what is given.

NOVEMBER 4—Apparently, at briefings for dependents, they're being told we're having a holiday camp-out, or field day, or some other neato adventure. That is pure baloney . . .

This is not, I repeat *not*, a picnic . . .

NOVEMBER 22—Morale at Mirage is practically non-existent. Having been extended ninety days has *everyone* terminally bummed . . .

This base is a caldron of unrest. The fact that I was censored has many people upset; the extension has every-one upset; there is a small rebellion by the mechanics

because we are being *ordered* to fly without compensation
or adequate survival equipment even when it says right
on our orders that flying activities are *not* included in our
jobs.

. . . The unrest, unhappiness, misery, and military
BS here *is* the story. The mission is secondary to what
is going on.

My censoring is a tempest in a teapot. All I did was
write about our people, what they've experienced here
and how they are dealing with being treated like children
and betrayed by their own government, while at the same
time being told they are here to "protect democracy"—
protect democracy in countries that have sheikhdoms and
absolute despots ruling them. These are countries where
women are being condemned because they are protesting
for the right to *drive*! . . .

. . . With all the crap we put up with they want
stories about our Thanksgiving dinner (which *was* nice)
and planting flowers. I can't do that . . .

The kind of cheerleading that Runels couldn't do was
just the thing for the Pentagon publicity machine, of course.
To get more of it, Williams's office invented the Hometown
Media Program, in which small-town newspaper and television reporters—especially ones located near military
bases—were provided free round-trip transportation on military aircraft to Saudi Arabia. Reporters like David Garcia
of KTSM-TV in El Paso were given the opportunity (otherwise prohibitively expensive) to visit their local military
heroes over a period of two to four days, and were encouraged to file upbeat stories for the folks back home.

In World War II, which was heavily censored, Ernie
Pyle might have told part of Runels's story (not the political
part), but in this conflict the Pentagon made certain that no
really thorough chroniclers of the Gulf grunt were allowed
to pierce its war management. A modern-day Pyle might also
have learned an important detail about the soldier's life in

the desert that Andy Glass and the *Los Angeles Times*, said to have recorded the gripes of soldiers and their real-life problems, did not. "You read about the lack of alcohol," Runels said after the war. "Well, we saw a whole different picture. There was some to be had, and almost everyone got it." Alas, servicemen do not qualify for journalism awards.

Spiegel said the PAOs varied in temperament from service branch to service branch. Least helpful, she said, were "the army guys, who were refighting Vietnam." The air force PAOs "were all slick, smiling-Jack kind of characters, you know. The navy guys couldn't get anything done because whoever was up above them . . . said no. And the marines, God bless them, were the best, and the reason they were best was not because of great training but because these were people who most recently had to deal with tragedy [the Beirut barracks bombing in 1983]."

But the marines could get nasty, too. Before the fighting began, Susan Sachs of *Newsday* and Carol Rosenberg of the *Miami Herald* were banned from covering the First Marine Division because they asked questions that a marine commander characterized as "rude." The reporters said they were simply being persistent.

NBC correspondent Gary Matsumoto had a bad time of it with a variety of army PAOs. In January, when the First Infantry Division from Fort Riley, Kansas, arrived in Saudi Arabia, he asked a chaplain about the mood of the troops. Nothing in the ground rules prevented the press from interviewing a chaplain. But while Matsumoto and the chaplain spoke on camera, a PAO, Captain Becky Kolaw, abruptly ended the interview by lunging in front of the camera. According to Matsumoto: "She insisted General Schwarzkopf himself had prohibited interviews with chaplains." In the same month, Matsumoto was interviewing soldiers from a Patriot missile regiment out of Fort Bliss, Texas. He recalled:

Whenever I began interviewing a soldier, this PAO would stand right behind me, stare right into the eyes of the [soldier], stretch out a hand holding a cassette recorder, and click it on in the soldier's face. This was patent intimidation . . . which was clear from the soldiers' reactions. After virtually every interview, the soldier would let out a deep breath, turn to the PAO, and ask [something like], "Can I keep my job?"

PAOs could also be very helpful, depending on what sort of news they wanted delivered. Reporter Bob Simon of CBS, destined for his famous imprisonment by the Iraqis for his boldness in breaking away from the pools during the war, explained the PAO system during the early days of Desert Shield to me this way:

You could never, from the beginning, come across a marine unit in the desert and go say "Hi." I mean, maybe you could have, but it was clear that the way to do it was to organize it through the PR guys at the hotel. That was perfectly acceptable to us . . . We wouldn't have known where to look in the desert.

Simon concluded later that the military was fairly cooperative in August and September because "they felt very vulnerable and they wanted our stories to indicate or imply that there were more Americans on the ground than there really were . . . they were using us to send a message to Hussein that it wouldn't be that easy if he decided to come across [the border]." At the same time, however, the Pentagon evidently wanted the American people to think there were more Iraqis in Kuwait than there really were: "They didn't tell us a whole hell of a lot," Simon reported, regarding Administration information on Iraqi troop strength. Estimates were coming out of Washington, and it became clear after the war that they had been greatly exaggerated, possibly from ignorance, but possibly for public relations purposes as well. Next to the smart-bomb/dumb-bomb ratio, the unseen enemy ranks as the biggest uncovered story of the Gulf War.

The U.S. government claimed that by mid-September there were 250,000 Iraqi troops in Kuwait poised to invade Saudi Arabia. By early January, the number had allegedly grown to 540,000 in and around Kuwait, all formidably armed and eager to slaughter invading American troops. From Administration press releases one could imagine a sophisticated Iraqi Maginot Line on the southern border of Kuwait, backed by the always "elite" or "crack" Republican Guard. Although the precise strength of Iraqi troops in the war zone may never be known, the real number turned out to be far lower. (After the war, the Pentagon stuck to its claim of 540,000 eager, battle-ready Iraqi troops, and said the dearth of opposition in the ground war resulted from desertions and deaths caused by allied bombing.)

The focus by the government—and the docile media—on sheer numbers of Iraqi troops obscured the pathetic quality of the conscripted foot soldiers who made up the better part of the enemy forces. Chuck Akers of the 503 MP Company, Third Armored Division, told me that many of the enemy prisoners of war (EPWs) taken in the first day of the ground invasion were ill-equipped, starving, and demoralized—in short, poor specimens of fighting men. Among their number was an eleven-year-old boy, several soldiers with feet so swollen they had to have their boots cut off, and many who were carrying only blank ammunition.*

As with the baby incubator story, there was virtual unanimous acceptance by the media of the allegedly enormous manpower behind Saddam's territorial ambition. Only the *St. Petersburg Times*, a well-respected Florida daily under independent ownership, challenged the government line. In

---

* In all, according to the Defense Department, the allies took seventy-two thousand Iraqi prisoners of war. The bulk were captured in the three days of the ground war.

a top-of-front-page story published on Sunday, January 6, Washington bureau reporter Jean Heller reported that satellite photos of the border between southern Kuwait and Saudi Arabia taken on September 11 and 13, 1990, by a Soviet company revealed "no evidence of a massive Iraqi presence in Kuwait in September." In the story, Peter Zimmerman, a George Washington University satellite imagery expert, went further than the relatively cautious Heller, noting: "The Pentagon kept saying the bad guys were there, but we don't see anything to indicate an Iraqi force in Kuwait of even 20 percent the size the administration claimed." At the time, the Pentagon was estimating up to 250,000 Iraqi troops and fifteen hundred tanks inside Kuwait. "While Iraqi troops cannot be seen," the story continued, "it is easy to spot the extensive American military presence at the Dhahran Airport . . ."

Zimmerman, a Fellow attached to the Reagan-era U.S. Arms Control and Disarmament Agency, had been on to the story since August 1990, when a Japanese newspaper came to him with a request to analyze "moderate resolution" pictures of the region taken on or around August 8 from Soyuz-Karta, a commercial Soviet satellite company. In retrospect, Zimmerman said in an interview, the pictures were good enough to draw conclusions about the weakness of Iraq's military position. "A number" of American news organizations had bought the same pictures and shown them to various experts, Zimmerman said, and "all of us agreed that we couldn't see anything in the way of military activity in the pictures."

But again cautiousness overcame curiosity among the media. "There was a great fight with a number of news organizations," Zimmerman recalled. "Some people decided the Soviets had cheated and that these pictures were not from the date and time they said." Nothing was reported in the media. Then, in October, Mark Brender of ABC News came to Zimmerman with new satellite pictures taken on September 13, which were "astounding in their quality," according to Zimmerman, and again revealed no Iraqi installations on the border. "Once again we didn't see anything—yet we were at the level of being able to see any grouping of several vehicles," he said. As for the possibility of faked dates, Zimmerman noted the authenticating evidence of the absence of boats in marinas along the coast of Kuwait.

"It became known around town within a matter of two weeks that people had examined a good satellite image of Kuwait and didn't find anything," said Zimmerman. But over the next two months, no news organization published or aired the pictures. *Newsweek* ran an item about the photos in its December 3 "Periscope" section, but the magazine itself declined to pursue the story any further. ABC, it turned out, had failed to obtain one picture showing a thirty-kilometer strip of land in Kuwait, where the bulk of Iraqi troops could conceivably have been stationed. Strangely, the network did not follow up and buy the missing image. Brender's explanation for dropping the story typifies the hybrid voice of the honest journalistic idiom buried within the falseness of the institutional voice:

> We were not absolutely sure that the imagery they sent us was really 13 September 1990 . . . They [the pictures] didn't tell us what we could see . . . the imagery would really raise more questions than it would ever answer . . . There [was] also a sense that you would be bucking the trend. If you were going to buck the trend, you better be right. If you're going to stick your neck out and say that the number of Iraqi forces may not be as high as the Administration is saying, then you better be able to say how many there are.

Mindful of not bucking the trend, ABC then accepted the government line from the Pentagon's ever helpful Pete Williams. Said Brender, "He came back to me and said,

'Mark, they're there, believe me.' " Williams's word actually took precedence over the photographs, and together with Sam Donaldson (the expensively advertised iconoclast), Brender decided to drop the story. After the war, a huffy Donaldson defended his decision in terms suggesting that good journalism is dictated by the safety of majority rule. "You keep citing the *St. Petersburg Times*," he said to me with annoyance. "I think it's a pretty good paper, but how many newspapers and magazines are there in the country? You summon as your witness the *St. Petersburg Times*, as against my judgment and the judgment of my colleagues at ABC. Where are the others? All of them are on my side."

Zimmerman urged other reporters from inquiring news organizations to buy the missing photograph, but out of friendship he refused to reveal who they were:*

These are people that got beaten on a major story because of their own stupidity or their own reluctance to spend the money [about $1,500 for the missing satellite picture] . . . major magazines, major newspapers . . .

Only the *St. Petersburg Times* found the story sufficiently compelling to purchase the missing photo from Soyuz-Karta. The new image, like the others, revealed no Iraqi troops.

Zimmerman and another expert hired by the paper suggested two possible explanations for the unseen enemy:

One was that the troops were [widely dispersed and] not in bivouac or fixed fortifications and therefore finding them would be extremely difficult. Or two, that there weren't as many in-country as being claimed, or some combination of the above.

* Pete Williams told the *Washington Journalism Review* that he discouraged ABC, CBS, and the *Chicago Tribune* from pursuing the satellite story.

"We're willing to concede," Zimmerman told Heller, "at least for the purposes of argument, that it is not impossible that all Iraqi activity is below the level of resolution. But if there were tent cities, if there were bunkers, if there were staging, supply and maintenance areas, we find it really hard to believe that we missed them." Zimmerman said after the war that there were "about half or a quarter" as many Iraqi troops in Kuwait as were claimed by the Pentagon, and "we now know that the Pentagon has admitted it overestimated the strength of the divisions."

As for the *St. Petersburg Times* story, it "sank like a stone." Zimmerman said he received a number of calls about the story but then never saw another mention of it. The Associated Press and United Press International did not report on it, nor did the Scripps Howard News Service. (I read it only when it was reprinted in March 1991 by *In These Times*, a left-leaning newsmagazine.)

There might not be a more important story in the Desert Shield period than the unseen enemy. In Bob Woodward's book *The Commanders*, we are told that President Bush wanted to go to war against Saddam Hussein as early as August 1990, so it seems urgently important to know whether he exaggerated the Iraqi threat to Saudi Arabia in order to justify American intervention. Since the United States intervened in the Persian Gulf, it was said, to prevent Iraq from invading Saudi Arabia, then obviously it mattered greatly in a democratic debate whether a deployment in such huge numbers was necessary, and indeed if such action was defensive at all. We might have asked as well whether the Administration was justified in sending so many troops even if Bush's military strategy was ultimately offensive.

Didn't anyone wonder, as Zimmerman asked Jean Heller, if "there were 250,000 [Iraqi] troops or 10,000 [in September]?" It was left to Zimmerman to express the informed skepticism one expects from journalists:

The Kuwaiti border with Saudi Arabia isn't very long. It wouldn't take more than 10,000 Iraqi soldiers to cover the border area to the point that people fleeing would run into them all over the place. In Kuwait City, 2,000 nasty MPs would have been enough to terrorize the city. Everything we've seen and heard about could have been done by a small enough Iraqi contingent that two Marine divisions might have driven back into Iraq relatively quickly with relatively little bloodshed.

In his book *From the House of War*, the BBC's respected foreign-affairs editor, John Simpson, reported that at its maximum strength in early January 1991 the Iraqi army numbered about 260,000 troops in the war zone. "Once the bombing began," he wrote, "the desertions began in earnest. Tens of thousands simply headed home. In the front line among the conscripted men the desertion rate was sometimes more than 30 percent, according to General Schwarzkopf." By the time of the ground offensive, Simpson said, the number of Iraqi defenders may have fallen below 200,000. The allied invasion, he wrote, "was a mopping up of illusions."[2]

In the immediate aftermath of the war, *Newsday*'s "rude" Susan Sachs succinctly confirmed the essential truth of the Soviet satellite photos. On March 1, she wrote the best and most straightforward summary of the "war" and its attendant Administration disinformation campaign in a daily newspaper. Undeniably front-page news, it appeared on page 21:

> The eager allied troops who descended to the battlefield by helicopter, barrelled through sand in cannon-toting tanks and dropped bombs from sophisticated warplanes, fought, in the end, a phantom enemy.
>
> The bulk of the mighty Iraqi army, said to number more than 500,000 in Kuwait and southern Iraq, couldn't be found. Saddam Hussein's supposed chemical-warfare

capability didn't materialize. No artillery equipped with chemical warheads has been discovered.

Iraq's defensive trenches and bunkers, described by military experts as heavily fortified, turned out to be reinforced with little more than crumbling bricks and were abandoned days, perhaps weeks, before the allied ground assault began.

And after months of hearing the Iraqi lines in southern Kuwait described as belts of 12-foot-high sand berms, miles of deadly minefields and treacherous oil-filled gullies, U.S. marines found themselves faced by a flat landscape laced with above-ground mines that they passed [by] virtually unscathed . . .

. . . Until the land assault began, information . . . from American and allied officials . . . created the impression of superb enemy defenses and warned repeatedly throughout the massive military buildup in Saudi Arabia that allied troops faced heavy losses in a head-on conflict.

But advancing soldiers and marines found little in their path to back up the early claims. And one senior commander agreed that the information about Iraqi defenses, put out before the war, was highly exaggerated.

"There was a great disinformation campaign surrounding this war," he said with some satisfaction, this week.

So it was that the major media—perhaps unwittingly— collaborated in George Bush's political and military strategy. There were honorable exceptions. With the agreement of his bosses, Bob Simon of CBS and his crew had officially withdrawn from a pool that would have placed them on an air force base when the shooting started. Simon had covered Vietnam in the latter stages of the war and was chafing under the restrictions. So on the Friday morning after the bombing began, disguised in army camouflage fatigues to help get past checkpoints, the CBS crew sneaked off in their Land Rover and scored what appears to have been the first exclusive of the war: near Khafji, they filmed a burning Saudi oil refinery that Simon believed had been hit by Iraqi fire, and encountered a marine reconnaissance unit, looking for Iraqi artillery spotters, that said it had come under attack. The lieutenant colonel in charge of the company agreed to be interviewed, and the crew—which included cameraman David Green, who had gotten to Khafji earlier—managed to get footage of abandoned Saudi positions as well. The result was a good, uncensored exclusive for the CBS Evening News that night, although Simon respected security and did not report specifically on the marine unit's mission. This bit of initiative engendered "hostile cracks" from the PAOs back in Dhahran, and "Hollywood" Mike Sherman's replacement at the JIB, Colonel William Mulvey, politely asked Simon to join him for a cup of coffee at Simon's convenience. They never got together. The following Sunday, the crew tried something more ambitious and traveled about three hundred miles up the superhighway toward Hafar al-Batin, "to case out a different area." On Monday, reassured by a Saudi customs officer at the border with Kuwait that there were no Iraqi troops on the other side, they wandered over and encountered a solitary Iraqi jeep carrying three soldiers. Simon, producer Peter Bluff, cameraman Roberto Alvarez, and soundman Juan Caldera spent the next forty days imprisoned in Baghdad on suspicion of spying, and more than half that time in solitary confinement. During interrogations, they were blindfolded, beaten, and verbally abused—Simon, in part, for being Jewish. The fate of the executed reporter Farzad Bazoft was never far from their minds.

Ironically, the CBS crew's bravery and imprisonment led to their further firsthand observation of something few journalists experienced during the war—the allied bombing of Baghdad. (In a "60 Minutes" interview after their release, correspondent Ed Bradley took the opportunity once again to praise American bombing accuracy: "But for the four men, more terrifying was the precision allied bombing, which hit the military intelligence headquarters where they were being held." How in the world would Bradley know which of these bombs had hit their targets and which had missed?)

Alvarez called the bombing the "scariest moment I went through," which left him in "shock." Caldera described the attack this way:

> I heard the plane, then I heard the bomb coming. I said—God, the sounds were incredible and I knew it was coming to me. I mean, so I just crouched into a corner and there was a big door and rubble fell . . . rubble fell on my arm and all over me . . . half the room is just absolutely gone. When I went back to the room I could see the sky . . . It was dark, dark, and the whole building, rubble all over and half my room completely gone.

The fate of Simon and his colleagues had inadvertently set a bad example for the rest of the press corps in Saudi Arabia; it was a godsend for the PAOs at the JIB. As Simon put it, the "kindest interpretation" of the passive behavior of other reporters was their fear of suffering the same fate. Tom Brokaw told me that one of NBC's Persian Gulf correspondents was "spooked" by the Simon disappearance.

But some pool reporters declined to follow Simon's lead for less honorable reasons than fear. Among them were "Scud Stud" Arthur Kent of NBC, whom Brokaw characterized as highly enthusiastic about the pool system: "[Kent and others] said, 'We really think we can make this pool thing work for us, and we'll get good pool assignments and we'll be all right.' " Brokaw acknowledged in retrospect that NBC had "drowned" in the pool.

The Washington Post's Molly Moore had a different problem with Simon's maverick behavior; she told me that she and others were bothered by Simon having disguised himself as a soldier because it made reporters vulnerable to accusations of spying. In Moore's tone, however, I detected the resentment of a team player who obeys the rules while others are cheating to gain an unfair advantage. Such sniping between unilaterals and poolers no doubt pleased Pete Williams and his public relations minions.

In the most publicized incident of media infighting, a unilateral, Robert Fisk of the London *Independent*, was reported to a marine PAO by a pool member, Brad Willis of NBC, when both reporters were trying to cover the battle of Khafji on January 31. Iraqi troops had briefly captured the abandoned Saudi border town, and Willis, assigned to marine task force "Taro," was having difficulty getting his crew past Saudi checkpoints to witness the action. According to Fisk's account in *The Independent*, pool reporters had been kept away from the fighting and misled into prematurely reporting the recapture of the town:

> But when *The Independent* travelled to the scene to investigate, an American NBC television reporter [Willis]—a member of the military pool—responded as follows: "You asshole; you'll prevent us from working. You're not allowed here. Get out. Go back to Dhahran." He then called over an American marine public affairs officer who announced: "You're not allowed to talk to U.S. marines and they're not allowed to talk to you."

Willis bitterly disputed Fisk's version of the event. The night before he headed for Khafji, he told me, he had made an agreement with the commander of a TOW missile unit to travel with the unit to the scene of the fighting. The next day, the marines arrived at the appointed time, but the commander announced that Willis couldn't come along because a pool reporter was already accompanying the unit. The "pool" member, it turned out, was Fisk, hiding in the back of a Humvee, the military's latest version of the World War II jeep. Willis said he became angry because Fisk was trying to sneak into Khafji at his expense and the expense of the reporters back in Dhahran. (In the Persian Gulf, the video footage and written reports of the pool reporters were by definition common property and shared—after censorship review by the military—with the rest of the press corps in Dhahran.) Willis said he then exposed Fisk, who was "sent packing" by the marines, while Willis went on to Khafji.

It was a textbook example of the probably deliberate divide-and-conquer strategy of the U.S. military. Fisk, of course, wanted an uncensored exclusive and would do whatever it took to get it; he didn't want to share. Willis, playing by the Pentagon rules, was angry at the prospect of getting beaten by another reporter who was breaking the rules. While I find Fisk's initiative more admirable than Willis's efforts to play ball with the system, Willis was no worse than the other pool reporters who followed the program. And in any case, he had little choice but to fight to retain his pool slot. Even a kept reporter has got to defend his turf.

Infighting among the reporters stuck in Dhahran was institutionalized by a clever maneuver performed by the U.S. military. Journalists were placed in charge of selecting who would travel in which pool, a situation akin to a prison system of inmates guarding inmates. At different times during the Gulf crisis Laurence Jolidon of *USA Today*, John Fialka of *The Wall Street Journal*, Joe Albright of Cox Newspapers, and Nicholas Horrock of the *Chicago Tribune* assumed the mantle of "leadership" and managed to engender the hostility of certain reporters, including Carl Nolte of the *San Francisco Chronicle*. Nolte, who went unilateral, echoed Fisk's complaint:

> These pool coordinators . . . administered the system by favoritism, innuendo, by whispering in your ear like a grand vizier in the court of the Ottoman Empire . . . by taking care of their pals and phasing out the ones they didn't like, and particularly the ones who showed any enterprise . . . You went out on your own, they fixed

you. You didn't have to wait for the military to fix you, the media fixed themselves.

Nolte's last sentence might serve as an epigraph for most of the U.S. media's performance during the Gulf War.

Whether Willis likes it or not, we have Robert Fisk to thank for exposing and condemning some of the most heavy-handed censorship of the war. It was Fisk who reported that while Willis was working in Khafji, a crew of French unilaterals trying to shoot the same action was stripped of its videotape by the military. It was also Fisk who revealed some of the more mindless censorship of pool dispatches, such as the deletion of curse words from the quotes of navy pilots on the carrier *Saratoga*. Similarly, on the USS *Kennedy*, reporters who wrote that fighter-bomber pilots watched pornographic videotapes to relax before missions found this un-American detail stricken from their dispatches.

But Fisk's most significant contribution to exposing the censorship issue was his open contempt for the collaborationist spirit among his American colleagues: "At one American airbase," he wrote, "a vast banner . . . depicts an American 'Superman' holding in his arms a limp, terrified Arab with a hooked nose. The existence of this banner, with its racist overtones, went unreported by the pool journalists at the base." Fisk ridiculed the superpatriotic and syrupy reporting of some of the pool reporters, referring to their "undertone of righteousness, even romanticism." He cited one egregious effort at prose by a *Philadelphia Inquirer* reporter, whose pooled dispatch included the following: "Thursday morning was one of the moments suspended in time . . . paving the way for a dawn of hope."

As Fisk put it:

Journalists are now talking of Iraq as "the enemy" as if they themselves have gone to war—which in a sense they have.

The language is of the early Forties, when Hitler's armies had reached the Pas de Calais and were poised to invade England. Journalists in uniforms and helmets are trying to adopt the *gravitas* of Edward R. Murrow and Richard Dimbleby. We are being prepared for "the biggest tank battle since World War II" and "the largest amphibious operation [which was a fake] since D-Day."

The comparisons with World War II—a comparison eagerly promoted by the White House—were as preposterous as the self-important poses of the pool reporters. "If Ed Murrow were alive today," Fisk wrote, "he would probably be among the reporters in Baghdad describing the effect of allied air raids."

But American Ed Murrows were hard to come by in late winter 1991. Television, it is true, tried harder to cover the war from the other side. NBC and CNN kept a correspondent in Baghdad as long as they could after the bombing commenced on January 17 (Baghdad time); all foreign correspondents except the CNN crew and a reporter for the Spanish newspaper *El Mundo*, Alfonso Rojo, were ordered to leave two days later. However, the four most important American newspapers distinguished themselves by *pulling their correspondents out* of Baghdad before the bombing started. The *Los Angeles Times* correspondent Dan Williams, for example, intended to stay in the capital past the United Nations deadline of January 15 for Iraqi withdrawal from Kuwait. Williams was prepared, for reasons of journalistic integrity, to take the risk and cover the war from the Iraqi side. He had an extra incentive for remaining in place—his wife, Lucia Annunziata, wanted to stay in Baghdad for her own employer, *La Repubblica*, of Rome. Williams's editors, however, wanted him out. Citing concern for his safety, they insisted that he leave the Iraqi capital. In the days before the bombing began, Presidential press secretary

Marlin Fitzwater had been urging the correspondents to leave Baghdad. In a phone conversation with Tom Johnson of CNN, Bush himself had implied that an attack was imminent by expressing the hope that anchor Bernard Shaw "would get in and out of there quickly." In Baghdad, U.S. chargé d'affaires Joseph Wilson was particularly aggressive in urging reporters to leave. According to the BBC's John Simpson:

> [Wilson] went round the al-Rasheed the day before [leaving], trying out an electronic gadget that insulted people in a squeaky voice: "Fuck you! You're an asshole!" . . . He also told those who planned to stay on in Baghdad that they were going to die.

Whether the White House was genuinely concerned about the reporters is certainly open to question. The PR-savvy war managers might have just as fervently desired a news blackout in Iraq to prevent any ugly images of dead civilians from competing with their own ready-made pictures of always-accurate cruise missiles. In any event, the decision to remove Williams was made by *Los Angeles Times* editor Shelby Coffey and foreign-news editor Alvin Shuster. Shuster told me that he and Coffey feared for Williams not only because of the bombing but also because of possible reprisals against reporters by enraged Iraqis. But the presence of Williams's wife made things awkward; he couldn't very well leave her behind to face the allied bombardment. So, Shuster told me, he called the foreign-news editor of *La Repubblica* to find out what their "policy" was and learned, he said, that they were planning to pull Annunziata out; he denied applying any pressure. Nor, he said, did he receive pressure from U.S. government officials to withdraw his man in Baghdad. Shuster, a former *New York Times* Saigon bureau chief, said his judgment had been influenced by the deaths of two previous *Los Angeles Times* correspondents, Joe Alex Morris in Tehran during the Iranian revolution and Dial Torgerson on the Honduran–Nicaraguan border in 1983.

Shuster and Coffey were not alone in their caution. Patrick Tyler of *The New York Times* was also withdrawn, as were Tod Robberson of *The Washington Post* and Geraldine Brooks of *The Wall Street Journal*. But the withdrawal of the *Los Angeles Times* from Baghdad, and its abandonment of its time-honored responsibility for covering war—over the strong objections of its own experienced correspondent—symbolizes powerfully the abdication of the American press in the Gulf War.

Here was an opportunity to cover something outside the purview of Pete Williams's security apparatus, and the big four American papers passed. Certainly Saddam Hussein's censorship was also self-serving and pernicious, and the odds of getting a good story out of bombed-out Baghdad must have seemed poor to the foreign-news editors. But this was a chance that Don Kirk of *USA Today*, American photographer Jana Schneider, and several British correspondents, including Patrick Cockburn of *The Independent* and John Simpson of the BBC—not to mention two American TV networks—were willing to take. Simpson estimated that altogether thirty-three newspeople stayed. Moreover, in a heavily censored war, print reporters enjoy a distinct advantage over their television competitors; they are far more mobile because they do not need to carry equipment that makes their whereabouts so obvious to the authorities.

"I was amazed by the exodus of these correspondents from these leading U.S. papers," *USA Today*'s Kirk recalled in a postwar interview. "It seems shocking to me that people would listen to the White House propaganda, especially after . . . what the United States went through in Vietnam and many other experiences since then. I thought these papers would have had a more skeptical view." Tony Horwitz, a

Wall Street Journal reporter, who is married to Geraldine Brooks, was led to believe that the four papers acted in concert: "What we heard later on was that there was something of a gentleman's agreement between the [New York] *Times*, the [Washington] *Post*, the L.A. *Times*, and the *Journal*, to pull their correspondents out so that no one would feel pressured by competition to stick around. So we all left, reluctantly." Shuster of the *Los Angeles Times* denied making such an agreement.

Ben Bradlee tells a somewhat different version of the story. While admitting that the *Post* ordered Robberson out because "it's not worth" dying for "two minutes of glory," he said that Robberson wanted to leave, too. But Bradlee displayed an unusual double standard, saying: "I think if I was twenty-eight years old and single, I would have stayed. No question." He sympathized with *Times* reporter Patrick Tyler's predicament as the father of two children. (Robberson, who was thirty-four and single, told me he wanted to stay.)

Ironically, *Wall Street Journal* editors later made inquiries as to the best British correspondent remaining in Baghdad, so they could choose their copy accordingly. "That kind of pissed us off," one reporter later confided. "If [they] thought that way, [they] should have let us stick around."

Not long after the major U.S. newspaper correspondents withdrew from Baghdad, John Simpson of the BBC, who had stayed on, found himself literally fighting for stories with Iraqi officials. The contrast with his American competitors is stark:

> We were arrested as we were filming the fire which the [cruise] missile [that hit a conference center] had started and, after a fight in which they outnumbered us, the security people got the tape with the cruise going past the window during my report to camera.

Simpson didn't get the tape back, but soon after he did manage to report some of the action.

Kirk of *USA Today* traveled through the streets of downtown Baghdad during the bombing, was interviewed live by CNN about what he saw, and subsequently filed three stories for his paper before he was told to leave on January 19. "Obviously," he said, "there were incidents in which people were killed, but nothing ever hit the al-Rasheed Hotel."

Those reporters who stayed were able to cover the bombing of Baghdad for two days before being thrown out of the country. Some returned beginning on January 31 after Iraq started issuing new visas.

In the words of *Los Angeles Times* foreign-news editor Alvin Shuster, I once again encountered the institutional voice: "We're proud of all of our coverage; I think we did a terrific job on it." But for the most part Shuster's correspondents simply worked within the pools. And it was *Los Angeles Times* Washington bureau chief Jack Nelson who told a Gannett Foundation forum that "basically speaking, the press was a captive in this war." Yet, following the rout of Iraq, his paper had the gall to publish a compilation of its own front pages from the period, immodestly entitled "Witness to War."

Of the major news organizations, only CNN made something of a public stand in defiance of government wishes; interestingly, its news division president, Tom Johnson, was president of the *Los Angeles Times* when Morris was killed, and publisher when Torgerson died. He said that he and Ted Turner had left it to Peter Arnett and producer Robert Weiner to make the decision on whether to stay. (Anchor Bernard Shaw had planned to leave Baghdad immediately after the U.N. deadline, but he was trapped by the sudden commencement of the U.S.-led attack.) Can Turner and Johnson be said to have behaved irresponsibly for allowing their correspondent to cover the war? Or—remembering the impor-

tance and veracity of Harrison Salisbury's reporting from
Hanoi—was their behavior very, very responsible?

Once the ground invasion was announced in Washington
on the evening of February 23, the Pentagon imposed a news
blackout that lasted for twelve hours. To this day, Pentagon
spokesman Pete Williams refuses to call it a blackout, insisting that it was merely a delay. Reporters may have been
expecting the long-awaited "Phase III" (unilateral coverage)
to kick in as the armor started rolling into Kuwait. But as I
have noted, this Phase III turned out to be only another
variation on the same old theme of Pentagon obfuscation.
There *were* reporters with some of the forward units, but
most of their dispatches and film took so long to get back to
Dhahran that they were too dated to use. The Pentagon's
real Phase III was censorship by delay.

In a postwar memo to Washington bureau chief Tim
Russert, NBC News correspondent Gary Matsumoto characterized the military's courier system this way: "Rube Gold-
berg couldn't have done a better job designing it."

Matsumoto was assigned to Pool #5, ironically designated a "quick reaction" pool, from January 1 to March 2.
In the first seven weeks, he recalled, "I was handed 'hit and
run' assignments from the J.I.B." The usual censorship ap-
plied, but delays were not a problem because his crew could
generally shoot their story in a day and hand-deliver the tape
to the hotel in Dhahran without any involvement by the
military. Then things changed:

> Weeks eight and nine were a different story. The J.I.B.
> reassigned Pool #5 to "Army Ground Combat." Our
> unit [was] the 24th Infantry Division, Mechanized. Here,
> it wasn't a question of "when" there were delays, but
> when *weren't* there.

During those crucial two weeks, when Matsumoto was dependent on the military couriers to deliver the "pool products," delays were never less than twenty-four hours, and sometimes as long as three days.

> Pool tapes had to be driven three and a half hours to the east of the 24th Division's HQ to King Khalid Military City (KKMC) for a flight back to Dhahran. Only first, the tapes had to be driven an hour and a half west, in the *opposite* direction, to the 18th Airborne Corps HQ. This meant the tapes had to travel back east, over the same 150-odd kilometers, past the 24th I.D.'s HQ, towards KKMC. As a result, instead of taking three and a half hours to get the tapes to the airfield, it took five hours minimum. It often took more. If a Division courier missed his drop time, he often missed the Corps courier on his way to KKMC. There was only one Corps run to KKMC a day. Being late five minutes could delay the tape 24 hours . . . which was often the case.

It is hardly as if the journalists had not seen it coming. "We petitioned," Matsumoto told Russert. "We argued. We pleaded . . . in that order. None of our requests were acted upon." Russert might have clued his correspondent in to the futility of negotiating with the Pentagon, based on his own experience in the fall. That would have been the only way for Matsumoto to have learned that the game was rigged from the beginning.

In the end, Matsumoto explained, "Our presence at the front was somewhat 'academic.' We'd shoot the action, but there was no way to get the videotape back. Fine for the Library of Congress, a disaster for Nightly News." But even if the couriers had been swift and sure, the pool arrangement would have yielded poor footage. "We were in the vicinity," said Matsumoto, "but didn't have ringside seats—this was due to a combination of accident, incompetence . . . and design."

On February 18, says Matsumoto, a reconnaissance mission into Iraq was "scrubbed because the PAO, Major Tom O'Brien, got us lost in the desert. For nearly five hours, we sat in the back of a cargo Humvee zigzagging across the desert, asking every sentry we happened upon for directions . . . We were convinced this was DOD's 'final solution' for the press . . . a truck ride to nowhere to suck lungfuls of moondust . . . the next best thing to Zyklon-B." They never found the reconnaissance unit.

For February 19, Matsumoto's pool was scheduled for another cross-border reconnaissance mission, but General Schwarzkopf canceled it. The next day a different PAO, Captain Steve Taylor, could not find the 18th Airborne Apache Squadron, so the pool missed out on a scheduled helicopter assault inside Iraq. There were more missed connections and scrubbed missions before and after "G Day," the formal start of the ground assault on February 24. But G Day itself was part of the Administration's disinformation campaign. Matsumoto learned later that allied divisions had crossed the Saudi–Iraqi border before the twenty-fourth and set up bases inside Iraq: "This was being done during the week we were conveniently lost by our PAOs, or had our missions scrubbed by Schwarzkopf."

Matsumoto's crew, delayed by a sandstorm as well as its military minders, did not catch up with a combat unit in Iraq until February 27, when the "fighting" was virtually over. Arriving at the Jalibah Airfield after the allies had seized it, the "quick reaction" pool was allowed an interview with the commanding officer but was prevented from filming surrendering Iraqi soldiers one hundred yards away. Officers said there were no American casualties at the airfield; the reporters later found out that at least one U.S. soldier had died and several others were wounded in a friendly blunder—an M1 Abrams tank had fired through the rear ramp of a Bradley Fighting Vehicle, killing the driver and injuring some infantrymen.

With such poor access to soldiers and real action, the pool reporters never turned in much that was worth censoring down at the JIB in Dhahran. But the censors stayed busy nevertheless. Assigned to an air base, Frank Bruni of the *Detroit Free Press* described the mood of returning pilots as "giddy." His military editor changed the adjective to "proud," and ultimately they compromised on "pumped up." Bureaucrats being what they are, there was also a great deal of redundancy in the censorship system. Matsumoto of NBC said his tapes had to be reviewed by three separate censors before they could be released to the bored reporters back at the Dhahran International Hotel: first the PAO from the 24th Mechanized had to look at them, followed by someone at the 18th Airborne Corps headquarters, and finally a censor at the JIB in Dhahran would clear them for release. The already tepid material may not ultimately have been edited at all, but the extra delay made it even more worthless.

After the war, Pete Williams liked to point out that only five stories were referred for clearance to Washington by the JIB in Dhahran, and that just one of them was kept from the public by a news organization, a case of self-censorship. In Williams's perception of events, there was therefore no government censorship in the Gulf War. If the Bush Administration's censorship by delay; censorship by direct intimidation of soldiers and interference with pool reporters doing interviews; censorship by outright arrest of unilateral reporters; censorship by preventing reporters from seeing anything interesting; and censorship of pool dispatches such as Bruni's is accepted as standard press relations, we are in great danger indeed.

The suppressed story Williams cited reveals something of the censors' mentality. On February 11, *Washington Times* reporter Michael Hedges filed a story out of Combat Correspondents Pool #1 that described the work of a First Infantry Division intelligence officer named Lieutenant Colonel Bill Moore. In it, Hedges explained that in performing their jobs, Moore's troops traveled into enemy-held territory, "intercepted" and translated Iraqi radio transmissions, used electronic signals to deceive the enemy about the location of impending attacks, and employed canvas and plywood models of vehicles and generators to fool Iraqi pilots about the whereabouts of the real U.S. military encampments. The JIB censors didn't like what Hedges wrote and sent the story to Washington. Five days later, on February 16, Pete Williams got around to writing a memo to then *Washington Times* editor-in-chief Arnaud de Borchgrave requesting— after expressing regret for the delay—that he not publish the rapidly aging story.

"Our intelligence officers consider this information to be of the most sensitive nature," wrote Williams. "They believe its publication could put field intelligence officers at risk." Attached was a copy of the story, with nine bracketed sections that the Pentagon wanted removed. Williams assured de Borchgrave that "the final decision rests with the news organization, not the Pentagon." Someone in Williams's press office must have been confused, or ambivalent, because at the bottom of the memo (acquired through a Freedom of Information Act request) an anonymous handwritten note asks: "Does this mean if they [the newspaper] reject the brackets, it's still OK to print?" De Borchgrave readily agreed to run the story in its Pentagon-edited form.

This example of censorship by delay begetting self-censorship is also significant for its echoes of the war in Vietnam. Again and again during Operation Desert Storm, Pete Williams and other Administration officials reassured the public that censorship was being practiced only to protect military secrets and thus American lives. The vicious implication of this argument was that reckless and ignorant reporters had gotten soldiers killed in Indochina by revealing military secrets. Once again, the facts diverge from the political rhetoric. Barry Zorthian, who spent four and a half years as spokesman for the U.S. Mission in Saigon, reported that violations of ground rules by the media were virtually non-existent during the war. In a deposition taken by the Center for Constitutional Rights, Zorthian said he knew of "at most . . . five or six cases" where reporters had their credentials taken away for violating military ground rules. "In most of these cases, the violations were accidental or based on misunderstanding." In none of these cases, he said, were the lives of American soldiers or the security of military operations put "in jeopardy." In a February 20, 1991, hearing of the Senate Committee on Governmental Affairs chaired by John Glenn and Herbert Kohl, Zorthian chastised the architects of the Pentagon's Gulf press policy for misreading the media's effect on Vietnam.

"The lesson of Vietnam," he said, "is a critical need for accurate and credible coverage by both the government and media which together present a complete picture for the public; not reliance on the presentation essentially of only one side."

Needless to say, there were no genuine violations of security by reporters in the Gulf. Colin Powell claimed that news reports of air force tactics used to locate and destroy Iraqi tanks *were* a violation of the ground rules. But given the virtually unimpeded destruction of thirty-seven hundred Iraqi tanks claimed by the Pentagon, this is a fanciful notion.*

Moreover, several journalists, including de Borchgrave, and Andrew Glass of the Cox chain, told me they had learned that the threatened amphibious landing on the Kuwaiti shoreline was a decoy to distract attention from the eventual ground assault. NBC correspondent Mike Boettcher, assigned to the First Marine Division, said he reported nothing about the allied battle plan—including the feigned amphibious landing—despite being fully briefed on the strategy by a unit commander four days before the ground invasion began.

---

* John Simpson writes that the Iraqis had only two thousand tanks in the field.

Likewise, reporters traveling with the huge armored convoy to the west of Kuwait—the Schwarzkopf "left hook" that was genuinely preparing to invade Iraq—kept silent about the military's plan. The always obfuscating Pete Williams told me that he had heard of a reporter who almost gave away the surprise maneuver, but he said he didn't know the journalist's name. In any case, two ex-military policemen, Michael Strozier and Chuck Akers, said it was unlikely, given the enormous amount of dust and noise created by transporting 100,000 armored troops bumper-to-bumper in broad daylight, that the Iraqis were oblivious to what was coming. How bad could their intelligence have been?

Yet, after the war, there were those in the Defense Department and the press, including Williams and de Borchgrave, who insisted that the Iraqis were taken completely unawares by Schwarzkopf's "Hail Mary" play. If this is true, then why weren't the military commanders up in arms about a *Newsweek* map published in the February 11 issue, at least two weeks before the ground assault, which speculated on the allied invasion plan? The map depicted the "multi-pronged flanking maneuver" by the U.S. 18th Corps and 7th Corps into western Iraq that would cut off Iraqi escape routes from Kuwait. Thus, if we believe Williams and de Borchgrave, *Newsweek*'s apparently well-informed breach of security made no difference whatsoever in the outcome of the war. Perhaps the Pentagon was grateful for the magazine's unstinting patriotism and ignorance of Iraqi military capability. In the same issue, the *Newsweek* staff informed its readers that "Saddam Hussein's soldiers . . . are among the world's best, and they have had six months to prepare for this battle. They can be expected to fight stubbornly . . . daring their enemies to engage in . . . brutal trench warfare . . ."

Writing immediately after the war, Andrew Glass confronted the myth of the unpatriotic reporter. It was Glass who had made the famous "trust us" speech in the final meeting between Pete Williams and the Washington media bureaucrats that sealed the censorship plan. Again he was at pains to remind the public that reporters are patriots, too:

> Before long, we found VII Corps headquarters. We learned the command had shifted 100,000 troops, the cream of the Army, well to the west of Kuwait. The bold plan called for jumping the vaunted Republican Guard from behind. We returned to Riyadh and told an officer who worked for . . . Schwarzkopf . . . what we had seen. "So you guys are going to blow the whole thing," the officer said. "Are you also going to write that the Marine [amphibious brigade] thing is a deception?" he asked sarcastically.

Glass, of course, made himself the hero of the story. He was, after all, a man who could be trusted:

> It's true that reporters will do most anything for a story. But it's also true that in wartime, most are patriots.

Would that they were reporters as well as patriots. For the most part, the journalists in the Gulf were reduced to the level of stenographers. By the time of the cease-fire on March 1, some pool reporters appeared to have lost the habit of working without help from their military minders. Several TV crews and reporters, including Bob McKeown of CBS and Forrest Sawyer of ABC, had broken away from the pools during the invasion and filed uncensored reports from the desert; McKeown got credit as the first television reporter to file with pictures from liberated Kuwait City, where he and other correspondents arrived ahead of most allied troops. But initiative was still scarce on VK Day. According to Tony Horwitz, the *Wall Street Journal* unilateral, pool reporters seemed disoriented by their newfound freedom. At the gates of Kuwait City, he recounted:

> We were waiting for Kuwaitis to have their triumphant reentry into Kuwait, and there were a couple of pool reporters . . . who had arrived there at the same time looking at us. "Who are you?" they asked. "Where's your pool? Where's your escort?"

Then, reinstalled in their natural habitat, a Kuwait City hotel lobby, the poolers found it difficult to rouse themselves from their briefing-induced stupor. While some reporters fanned out into the capital in search of stories, Horwitz said, "Most people . . . hung around, reporting on the hotel or something, waiting for briefings."

The best story of media role confusion concerns Tom Brokaw. Nosing around the capital the day after the liberation, the NBC anchorman experienced a run-in with the military that may well have epitomized the supine posture of the media in the Gulf War.

> I came back to [my] hotel and they [the marines] had sealed off the intersection . . . They had a fifty-caliber [machine gun] pointed at us and said, "Stop the vehicle there," and we did, and I got out . . . I was a little impatient, and I said, "We've been here longer than you have," and the guy [a marine sergeant] locked and loaded on me . . .

Brokaw was rescued by a media-savvy captain who recognized him as the famous anchorman. The guns were lowered and a grateful Brokaw returned a little later to pass out Cuban cigars to the formerly menacing marines.

I expressed astonishment at Brokaw's near encounter with friendly fire and asked if he reported the event. After all, U.S. marines threatening an unarmed network anchorman at gunpoint seemed like a pretty good story in a war with very little real news. It also neatly summed up the tension between the military and the media.

"No," Brokaw replied. "It was just one of a thousand incidents that happened in Kuwait City that day."[3]

CHAPTER 6

Taking the Fifth

The press has its pimps as it has its policemen. The pimp debases it, the policeman subjugates it, and each uses the other as a way of justifying his own abuses. Those gentlemen vie with each other in protecting the orphan and giving her shelter, whether that shelter is a prison or a house of prostitution. The orphan, indeed, is justified in declining such eager offers of help and in deciding that she must fight alone and alone resolve her fate . . .

. . . But in another sense the press is better than intelligence or progress; it is the possibility of all that and of other things as well. A free press can of course be good or bad, but, most certainly, without freedom it will never be anything but bad.

—ALBERT CAMUS
Homage to an Exile, December 7, 1955

AS I PURSUED the story of the government's conscription of the media in the Gulf War, I kept an eye open for journalists and news executives outraged by their humiliating defeat. But they were hard to find. Despite the public statements of some, I came increasingly to believe that the media were themselves largely indifferent to their stunning loss of prerogative.

It is true that a new committee was formed to protest the Pentagon restrictions and that this time it did include two owners, Katharine Graham, chairman of the Washington Post Company, and Donald Newhouse of the powerful Newhouse publishing family, as well as two important CEOs, Louis Boccardi of the Associated Press and James K. Batten of Knight-Ridder. On September 12, 1991, representatives of this latest ad hoc assembly met with Secretary of Defense Dick Cheney to make their case against the Pentagon's conduct toward reporters in the Persian Gulf. The formal rhetoric of protest remained rather timid, however; in a June 24 letter to Cheney outlining their complaints, the seventeen signatories employed the bland and indirect language of the previous fall. The attached "statement of principles" related hardly at all to principles of press freedom. The committee, contrary to Stanley Cloud's advice, accepted the continued existence of the Department of Defense National Media Pool system and asked that the Sidle commission recommendation of temporary pools (the committee wanted them to be disbanded after the first twenty-four to thirty-six hours of war) be respected. As a result, Pete Williams and friends, armed with the media's willingness to play pool in the early stages, could always invoke the exigencies of combat to justify extensions. If the typical American war was to be a police action, then most of the important news would take place in the first day or two when pooled reporters remained under the supervision of the Pentagon. Furthermore, the committee actually *wanted* pools under certain circumstances:

> Some pools may be appropriate for events or in places where open coverage is physically impossible. But the existence of such special-purpose pools will not cancel the principle of independent coverage. If news organizations are able to cover pooled events independently, they may do so.

As for the censorship of dispatches, photographs, and film, the committee adopted the Pentagon's own Orwellian term "security review" in noting that they didn't want it anymore. Would they accept censorship then?

Not surprisingly, Cheney seemed unimpressed by the arguments of the media bosses. The committee's designated liaison to the Pentagon, Lou Boccardi, reported back to his colleagues that the Defense Secretary "persists in calling [the Gulf conflict] 'the best-covered war in history' " in spite of their assertions to the contrary. The most Cheney would say, according to Boccardi, was that he was "not committed to duplicating Gulf policy" in the future.

"[Cheney] knows that public support is with him at the moment," Boccardi wrote. "It would take a degree of naivete that none of us possesses to think that the effort of the next few months will be easy." But like the previous fall, naïveté (or else deep-seated cynicism) was precisely the problem. The newly skeptical Boccardi explained that the "effort will now go forward with our Washington Bureau chiefs engaging Pete Williams & Co." This was a bit like sending Saddam's "elite" Republican Guard into battle against the U.S. Third Armored Division. The media establishment was right back where it started in August 1990. The middle managers were left holding the bag once again.

On the day of the meeting, as if to underscore the fraudulence of the Administration's claim that the Pentagon withheld no information to which the public was entitled, *Newsday* published the first report of how three brigades of the First Infantry Division, contrary to army doctrine, had literally buried alive hundreds and possibly more than a thousand Iraqi soldiers with plows and earthmoving machinery as they crossed the border from Saudi Arabia into Iraq. The hapless Iraqi conscripts had put up scant resistance, brigade officers told the paper's Patrick Sloyan. Pool reporters, Sloyan wrote, had been "banned" from the scene of the killing, and Cheney had not seen fit to include this innovative combat maneuver in his interim report to Congress. Up until the *Newsday* revelation, a smug Pete Williams had stuck to his preposterous figure of 457 Iraqi dead, using the number he said were known to have been buried by the U.S. military.[1] (In our interview Williams had assured me that "there was no fighting up-close in this war.")

Like the *St. Petersburg Times* story on the unseen enemy, the *Newsday* scoop seemed to go nowhere. *The New York Times*, for example, didn't catch up with the story until three days later, and relegated its account to the inside pages of its Sunday edition. The army was forced to acknowledge the *Newsday* story of the burials, but a spokesman, Major Peter Keating, minimized the number of deaths by suffocation, calling them "isolated incidents." Williams, in the best tradition of the public relations business, defended the one-step killing/interment process, saying: "I don't mean to be flippant, but there's no nice way to kill somebody in war."

The *Times*'s reaction to the *Newsday* story typified its ambivalent attitude toward censorship during the war. The paper had joined in the tepid protests of the previous fall, and it published a critical piece on censorship in its Sunday magazine by Malcolm Browne just after the fighting had ended. But in other ways the paper of record's coverage of the issue was troubling. Like most of the media, the *Times* barely mentioned the *Nation* lawsuit against the Pentagon, and when it did, it at least twice misreported its purpose. (The foreign-news editor later refused to run a correction.) Curiously, when the *Times*'s only full-time unilateral reporter, Chris Hedges, was detained by U.S. military officials for six hours, stripped of his credentials, and escorted back to his hotel in Dhahran, *The Washington Post* played the story bigger—they put it on the front page—than the *Times* did. (Hedges's transgression had been to report, unescorted, on price-gouging of American GIs by Saudi shopkeepers.)*
Similarly, Katharine Graham signed the June protest letter

---

* Hedges was one of at least twenty-four journalists detained by the military during Operation Desert Storm. Another detainee, New York photographer Wesley Bocxe, was blindfolded and held for thirty hours by the Alabama National Guard.

to Cheney for the *Post*, but *Times* executive editor Max Frankel, rather than chairman and then-publisher Arthur O. Sulzberger, was the signatory for America's preeminent newspaper.

Because of its influence and its pretensions to completeness, *The New York Times* receives a disproportionate amount of attention from ideologues and press critics on the left and right who ascribe virtually all that is bad about the media to the influence and actions of the so-called "gray lady." There is even a left-wing newsletter called *Lies of Our Times*, devoted entirely to exposing the paper's alleged perfidy. No doubt many of the criticisms are justified, but more scrutiny should be paid to the other media conglomerates and well-known journalists who purport to inform the public in a timely fashion and don't, either because of censorship or self-censorship.

Consider the case of *The Washington Post*'s Bob Woodward, the epitome of the aggressive investigative reporter. After the war, in his book *The Commanders*, Woodward scored a major scoop by revealing that President Bush was prepared to go to war against Iraq as early as August while General Colin Powell privately favored continued economic sanctions throughout the late summer and fall. Woodward reported that Powell made the "pitch" within the Administration for "containment" of Iraq while mutely opposing an attack to drive Iraq out of Kuwait. Within Woodward's obtuse account of events leading up to the war was the important information that America's top military man was a dove, and, alone among Bush's advisers, profoundly skeptical of the use of military force in the Gulf. "No one," wrote Woodward, "including the president, embraced containment. If only one of them had, Powell was prepared to say that he favored it."

Why, one may ask, didn't Woodward report this in *The Washington Post* when he learned it in the fall? Perhaps

Powell spoke to Woodward on the condition that he not reveal the general's position until after the war, but that was not Woodward's explanation when he was challenged about his delay by Bob Edwards of National Public Radio. Edwards, perhaps the antithesis of the aggressive investigative reporter, had wondered out loud whether Woodward wasn't uncomfortable about "sitting on information" for so long when his principal occupation was reporting for a daily newspaper. Woodward replied that "the war only ended two months ago, and if there was something that was so crucial that I felt that this had to be in the newspaper right away, I would have gone to the sources I have and said that. Happily, that wasn't the case." Edwards talked back to the journalistic icon, arguing precisely to the point:

> But if you could have published this stuff at the time you learned it, it has much more impact—it's like your Watergate reporting; every new element that you published produced a turn in the story.

To which Woodward answered:

> In Watergate we were talking about crimes. In this case, we're talking about no crimes. There's no portrait of somebody with their hand in the cookie jar or doing something illegal. There's a lot of emotion and there's a lot of debate and . . . anxiety, uncertainty . . .

It *sounds* like a front-page story: disagreement about war policy at the highest level of the Bush Administration; an anxious Joint Chiefs of Staff chairman who really doesn't want to fight; a President eager to go to war before having thought through the consequences. Internal Administration policy debates routinely appear on the front page of *The Washington Post*. If our premier investigative reporter won't tell us the uncensored news he knew in time for us to debate the war policy, then how seriously can we take the media's stated commitment to overcome government censorship in order to tell us what's really going on?

Over at ABC, the executive producer in charge of Gulf War coverage, Jeff Gralnick, displayed an equally disturbing indifference to the public's right to know promptly. Echoing Pete Williams, he told *The New York Times* that ABC's coverage of this heavily censored war was "as close to perfect as we can get." With virtually no access to the fighting and such egregious delays in deliveries of pooled videotapes, how could this possibly be so? In a later interview, Gralnick haughtily dismissed such skepticism: "Criticism such as it is comes from people who a) don't understand live coverage, b) don't understand war, and c) don't understand war zones."

Other media stars were ambivalent about the impact of censorship and the need to reverse the Administration's encroachment on freedom of the press. The most famous American newspaper editor, Ben Bradlee (immortalized by Jason Robards in *All the President's Men*), on the verge of retirement from *The Washington Post* in July 1991, downplayed the significance of Operation Desert Muzzle; he seemed, in fact, to share Pete Williams's faith that the truth will out— eventually: "It does not serve their ultimate purpose to control information because the one verity in this business is that the truth emerges. It damn well does."

Bradlee seemed cynical when I asked about the importance of active press opposition to the policy:

Once these assholes did this there seemed to be no point in editors moaning and groaning and saying how terrible it is and how they're chiseling away at the great First Amendment, freedom of the press, the public's right to know. Baloney. What you have to do is get people over there and work and then when it's all over point out all the frailties of the system.

So why hadn't Bradlee, with his great stature, protested in the late summer of 1990, just eight months after the frailties of the system were exposed in the Panama invasion? Bradlee replied that he had "too high a profile" and "wasn't the right person to stand for that [issue]." Like Evan Thomas of *Washington Post*–owned *Newsweek*, he didn't think protesting would do much good anyway. "They were going to have a pool system, and they were going to have monitors," Bradlee said. "There was nothing we could do about them —nothing." He dismissed the value of institutional opposition to the policy from groups such as the American Society of Newspaper Editors: "Excuse me; I just don't think that's a very influential organization. They can scream all they want, but they don't get anywhere."

Overall, Bradlee seemed to shrug at the threat to the First Amendment posed by the Gulf War press censorship. "At best," he said, "[the military] can delay it a few days. Tell me now how society was poorer by the report coming out two days late or three days late." (Bradlee abruptly changed his tack when he realized he was excusing the Pentagon's censorship-by-delay tactic, and reverted to an institutional persona: "I don't want to pursue this argument because I'm going to end up against my side. I don't believe that anything gets served by delaying it two days. I think you should get the Goddamn thing out.")

Bradlee considers himself a pragmatist first and foremost:

> When I was a foreign correspondent I was always told the first thing you do when you get to a new place is find out where you're going to file. How are you going to file. When does the PTT [telephone and telegraph office] shut? . . . That to me is the first object. The first object is not to wrap yourself in the First Amendment and go up there and make a speech. Who are you going to sue?

(I reminded Bradlee that a group of magazines, writers, and journalists had indeed sued the Pentagon over the policy on First Amendment and Fifth Amendment grounds; he seemed genuinely surprised that the *Post* had not at least filed a friend-of-the-court brief in support.)

I asked if it would have done any good to bring in the big guns of management, either publisher Donald Graham or his mother, Katharine Graham, who at the time held the position of chief executive officer as well as chairman. Bradlee most emphatically did not want to involve the owners in politics.

> Modern editors, the best of us, have told, urged, begged their publishers to knock that shit off. . . . Because we don't want them to make deals with the powers that be in private, and keep this person off the ticket and put this person on the ticket. We believe that publishers and editors, everybody, should try to stay off the stage . . . The idea that we are activists in one cause or another . . . I don't like that.

Among publishers, Katharine Graham *has* been something of an activist for the cause of defending the First Amendment, so I asked her directly why she hadn't made any private or public protests about the censorship before or during the war. (In pursuing this interview I had again bumped up against the amorphousness of responsibility within large media organizations—publisher and newly appointed CEO Donald Graham declined to speak with me, but Mrs. Graham reluctantly accepted my request, all the while insisting that I really should be speaking to her son and to foreign-news editor Michael Getler.) Her answer was that nobody had asked her:

> I mean, you rely on people to come and say, "Hey, we need you" . . . I wasn't aware of this anywhere. And

secondly, I really wasn't aware that the situation was as
bad as it seems to have turned out to be . . . I'd read
about Grenada and Panama. Everybody had. But I rather
thought that whatever was wrong there had gotten fixed
. . . I have to say this issue was not on my screen. Maybe
it should have been on my screen, but it wasn't.

Katharine Graham seemed measurably more upset by
the Pentagon's victory over the media than Bradlee did. She
called the censorship policy "antidemocratic" and said that
the public had the mistaken impression that coverage of the
war had been thorough. "I think it was very bad," she said.

I think that they effectively blocked very good coverage
of the war, and [the war] was popular. And the issue has
become very murky to the public because they've said,
"Well, we got [coverage]"; they saw those pictures of
the Scuds . . . and CNN on the top of the hotel floor and
they said, "Okay, we know what happened; so what's
the big deal?" They don't realize that what they know
they know despite the government attempts to delay and
disrupt the coverage.

Graham's old-fashioned commitment to press freedom was
heartening, yet there was something unsure in her tone of
voice. Perhaps all the advice from people like Bradlee to
butt out of politics and "issues" had weakened her self-
confidence, or perhaps it was just that she was trying, as best
she could, to retire from the scene and turn things over to
her son. (I somehow lacked the heart to tell her that he had
refused to be interviewed.) I read her what Bradlee had said
about having too high a profile to make a stink, to which she
responded, "You know, Ben has not been involved in the
issues as much as he is in [specific] cases. All his life he really
hasn't." Realizing she might have sounded ever so slightly
critical, Graham then tried to take back what she had said.
In the end, Graham, like so many others, lapsed into

the higher institutional voice and offered me questionable advice about this book. She wanted me to be fair to the military, she said, because it was concerned about "valid security issues."

"You don't want to come on as a partisan in this," she cautioned in a reprise of Bradlee's apolitical ethic. "You want to come on as an American who cares about press freedom."

Katharine Graham was not alone in her skittishness about strong opinions. Mainstream media critics also waffled on the issue of censorship. Throughout the war Graham's employee Jonathan Alter, of *Newsweek*, took a generally anticensorship position, but like others, he hedged his bets. In the magazine's January 14 issue Alter wrote:

> Contrary to popular impression, most reporters actually support certain wartime restrictions . . . Obviously, there are some legitimate concerns about the role of the news media during combat. If Vietnam was the first TV war, this could be the first live one, thanks to satellite technology. Live means no editing, a careless kind of journalism. And the presence of global networks like CNN is dicey in wartime . . .

What restrictions do most reporters support, I wondered. I certainly didn't support any *government* restrictions; I favored the Vietnam ground rules, general guidelines that called for sensible behavior on the part of accredited journalists. Alter and *Newsweek* correspondents Tony Clifton and Ray Wilkinson evidently could not bring themselves to invoke the word "censorship," so it is difficult to know what they meant. For example, did Alter find Edward R. Murrow's live radio broadcasts of the London blitz "careless"? I suppose Nazi agents in America might have been listening to the broadcasts and cabling damage reports back to Berlin, so perhaps Murrow should have been gagged. In the context of the Gulf War, what did "dicey" mean, and what is "dicey" about being "global"? Did Peter Arnett's censored reports from Baghdad give aid and comfort to the enemy?* Did CNN cause the deaths of allied soldiers, and we simply haven't heard? Surely Pete Williams would never have allowed such events to be overlooked.

After the war, *Washington Post* columnist David Broder was downright unenthusiastic about the desire by reporters to move about freely on the battlefield; he came right out and challenged the press's need for freedom of movement. Without criticizing the pool system he chastised reporters who complained about being stuck in the hotel: "Their gripes are out of line." Presumably Broder hadn't heard how the pools had prevented coverage of the war; it is the only conceivable explanation for the bizarre sentences that followed: "If the 160 'pool' reporters with combat units were not capable of describing the look, the sound and the feel of the war, the news organizations that hired them should replace them. But in fact they proved their capability." Furthermore, wrote the widely syndicated political pundit,

> the press will gain public support, not by complaining about Pentagon controls but by staying with the story until the public knows what really happened—a far more complex and contradictory tale than the government wanted or permitted to be told at the time.

Should Katharine Graham and her colleagues have aborted their mild protest mission to Cheney and just simply have shut up?

During the war, *Washington Post* ombudsman Richard Harwood had ridiculed the imprisoned press corps while at

---

* Ironically, the first fourteen days of CNN's live coverage from wartime Baghdad consisted of audio reports without live pictures. During that period, the images on CNN were taped, so in a sense viewers were "watching" the radio. Satellite coverage with live pictures did not begin until 8 p.m. (EST) on January 29.

the same time finding it impossible to embrace the concept that the Pentagon was practicing censorship. In Harwood we hear the voice of the antiskeptic:

> They spend hours bitching at their lot, nurturing paranoias . . . There is a lot of harrumphing about "censorship," but there is no claim that anything of significance to the "public interest" has yet been suppressed.

After the war, Harwood attacked the efforts of some reporters to make a First Amendment issue out of the Gulf War press censorship:

> Their highly publicized efforts to transform petty professional jealousies and minor inconveniences into great issues of constitutional law were absurd. It is difficult to persuade skeptical and not entirely ignorant publics that 48-hour delays in the publication of feature stories on female truck drivers or mess hall crews from Montana threaten the nation's survival and the "people's right to know."

Former *Miami Herald* editorial-page editor Don Shoemaker felt that the *Nation* lawsuit against the Pentagon was a bad idea. "Lawsuits such as these," he wrote in the *Herald*, "do not help matters." He praised the military briefers: "Senior-senior officers who are now doing the briefings, and Gen. H. Norman Schwarzkopf, a sensitive and level-headed commander, are improving the situation." And he exhorted the press to "pay more attention to accuracy than [to] spasm about ethics." To be accurate inside an information vacuum, a reporter would presumably need to remain silent, but Shoemaker wasn't offering any tips.

In the TV ranks, Sam Donaldson stands out for his aggressive posture in questioning politicians. But Donaldson, as was noted earlier, had ducked on the story of the satellite pictures and the unseen enemy. In our interview, he seemed pleased with his performance as ABC's special Scud correspondent and said nothing critical about military censorship, which he believed was here to stay. Pete Williams had told me that Donaldson had called him at a certain point to praise his work, a gesture that didn't square with the reporter's adversarial reputation. I asked Donaldson about this, and he hesitated, first inquiring, "When was I alleged to have made this phone call?" then acknowledging, "I'm sure I must have told him that something he did I liked . . . I know that I appreciated his cooperation, and told him so . . ."

My quest for outrage eventually took me to the offices of the three major network anchormen. Peter Jennings told me candidly that he didn't follow press issues very closely. The good-natured Tom Brokaw blandly suggested that the press and the military needed to find a "middle ground." Only Dan Rather, the most overtly patriotic anchorman during Desert Storm, seemed angry about censorship and the general conduct of the media during the conflict. Like Bob Woodward, Ben Bradlee, and Sam Donaldson, Rather enjoys the status of journalistic icon. He has earned a reputation for toughness for at least appearing tough in comparison with his colleagues; his well-publicized confrontations with Richard Nixon during Watergate, and with George Bush over the then Vice President's role in the Iran-contra scandal, have contributed to his no-nonsense image. Rather has always struck me as the most cerebral of the three anchors, but I'm not sure why. Perhaps he seems a little more serious, and anxious, than the others, and caving in to politicians doesn't square with his style.

Rather told me he had been warned not to meet with me because the word was out that my book was going to be "critical" of the media. Fortunately, he was feeling rather critical himself that day and decided, to my relief and pleasure, to shed the institutional voice. He told me frankly that

he "probably didn't do enough; we [at CBS] probably didn't do enough" to combat the Pentagon censorship plan. The war, Rather said, "blew up very suddenly," and he and others were only "vaguely aware that the rules and regulations were coming."
However:

I'm not the vice president in charge of excuses here . . . I don't want to duck and I gently encourage the people around here, "Don't duck." But some of what happened was because there was a lack of will, a lack of guts to speak up, to speak out, speak our minds, and for that matter to speak our hearts. I've got a reputation of being corny about these things, but about that I have no apology . . . I think—and without getting philosophical about this because I don't consider myself a particularly philosophical person—that you would be wise to consider the possibility that this fits into a general trend of American journalism over the last five to ten years that you can see in the coverage of political campaigns, in the coverage of domestic issues such as race and the economy, just to pick two, and manifested itself in the intensive coverage which is an inevitable consequence of war. It is: just get in the middle and move with the mass; don't cause any trouble; don't ask any tough questions; don't take the risk—I'm not talking here about physical risk . . . Not too long ago in this country, a reporter who expected to be judged by his peers as worthy [of the] name [was] expected to ask the tough question. It wasn't so much seen as a popularity contest as it was a responsibility. I'm not saying this as well as I'd hoped to . . . But it's fitting into a trend. Obviously politicians, and I'm one who thinks being a politician is a high calling . . . have learned ways to intimidate individual reporters, news organizations, and the press in general.

I thought he said it very well, and certainly better than anyone else in the mass media had said it over the past year.

After all the cant about press "responsibilities" and military "rights," I had finally found someone in power who seemed actually committed to freedom of the press and the public's right to know. And he wasn't finished. Rather proceeded to invoke the dreaded word "outrage."

> We did not meet our responsibility in the Persian Gulf as well as I wish we had, and that begins with me. We should have been more alert after Grenada . . . About that I did speak out, and a number of people have [including] Jack Nelson of the *Los Angeles Times* . . . But [Grenada] was an outrage. It should have been an outrage to any thinking American citizen . . . I didn't see it as a Democratic or Republican or Mugwump issue . . . But if you stop and think about it . . . Grenada was really messed up.

Too often, Rather said, the press, the politicians, and the military used "national security" and protecting the troops in the field as a guise "to protect the reputations of the decisionmakers in a military operation":

> Grenada was not well done. We now know this. Part of the reason we didn't know at the time was because Admiral Poindexter, since become well known in another context, decreed that nobody was going to know anything except him and a few other people. He succeeded with that. The record is now very clear. Such things as the army assault on the western side of Grenada stalled [and] was a mess. Most of [those] killed in action [were] killed in there, but [there] were maybe twelve men who were let out under the wrong conditions, in the wrong places. The marines had to be brought all the way around from the eastern side of the island . . . to the western side of the island to pick up the momentum . . . [And] the

ridiculous thing about the forward artillery [spotter] who had to go to a pay phone [and] use his credit card to phone the Pentagon to call in offshore fire.

As for the remedy for the Grenada news blackout, the DOD National Media Pool, Rather contemptuously called it "legislation for the preservation of the Pentagon correspondents; basically, what that turned out to be was like Congress passing laws to help lawyers." However, "it was the best we could get, and it wasn't on the face of it, on paper, too bad. The implementation was the point." But implementation of the pool system in Panama, Rather said, "matched the early work of the Marx Brothers. All they needed was a duck flying through the room and they could have made a real Marx Brothers movie out of the thing. It was ridiculous."

Rather was not entirely critical of the media and the military; he thought the Persian Gulf coverage was better than in Panama (how could it have been worse?), but was at a loss to explain the lack of access and the long delays in returning pooled tapes to Dhahran. He preferred to assume good intentions on the part of Generals Powell and Schwarzkopf, but allowed that he could be wrong. When we returned to the subject of press behavior in general, however, Rather's anger burned through even more brightly than before:

We begin to think less in terms of responsibility and integrity, which get you in trouble . . . and more in terms of power and money. I do not except myself from this criticism, by the way . . . That increasingly anybody who subscribes to this [idea that] the job is not to curry favor with people you cover . . . finds himself as a kind of lone wolf [who] probably ought to wear one of those shirts that says "last of the independents," and will be in the minority. In the best halls of American journalism not too long ago those who subscribed to what I've described to you earlier were clearly in the majority. If you wanted into the club, that's how you got in, and you had to prove it. Now those are like the yellow-banded bower-birds or wolverines or some other endangered species in which their part of the forest gets smaller and smaller, and they're rarer and rarer to see. And probably most important, I do subscribe to the idea that journalism with guts starts with a publisher who has guts . . . [Nowadays] the publisher [or network equivalent] says, "Listen, I've got to have circulation, I've got to have ratings, I've got to have numbers . . . You know, I've taken a look at X, I've taken a look at the station in—name the place— California, and you know [X] just makes people feel good. Why can't we have a broadcast like that?" Or why can't we have a newspaper like that? Max Frankel is an old, dear friend of mine. I not only love him but I respect him as a journalist, as I do very few people . . . But there are days when I see the *Times*, when I see *The Washington Post*, days when I see the *Los Angeles Times* with something on the front page . . . White House coverage—when I covered the White House you'd get hooted out; you certainly wouldn't be able to drink with the big boys if you caved . . . Now read the best papers in the country . . . Suck-up coverage is in.

As we talked, I began to get the feeling that Rather would really like to change things but he felt powerless. Strange as it may seem that a $3-million-a-year anchorman could be without influence, he is probably right. If Rather went on the air with anything approaching the tone he used with me, he wouldn't be broadcasting the following evening. He doesn't own CBS, of course, and he assiduously avoided criticism of network chairman Laurence Tisch (who declined to be interviewed for this book) and CBS News president Eric Ober. Attached to Rather's desk is a small makeup table and mirror which serve as a reminder of his primary responsibility to his employer. Still, I pressed him further on what he could do personally to fight the trend toward more and more supine coverage:

> To change the atmosphere is the challenge. How to do it, I don't know. Part of it is to . . . have a little more intestinal fortitude and a little more will ourselves.

But, he said, "until and unless the audience and the readership begin to say to the people who own the entities [that] this isn't the best way," things are not likely to change.

> I can't make this case too strong, but it is not the role of the press to be an attack dog in my view, but it's damn well not being a lapdog. These days the lapdog is in. These days if you want to "make it," the belief runs strong that you can make it faster by convincing the audience that you're really on good terms with the mayor, or the sheriff, or fill in the blank.

And so it was that Dan Rather was genuinely angry about censorship and "suck-up coverage," but said he had little power to object to it, while Katharine Graham had the power to do something but respected the wishes of her employee, who didn't want her to use it.

New York Times publisher Arthur O. Sulzberger, now retired, declined to be interviewed for this book, but Harrison Salisbury, still aggressive and alert at eighty-two and presumably with nothing to lose, was happy to give me his frank assessment of the *Times*'s posture toward the government and the general timidity of the media. He was a student of the *Times*, having written its history, and he knew all the principal players from his years as a *Times* editor and correspondent. I asked him why he thought none of the major media had joined the *Nation* lawsuit against the Pentagon:

As far as the [TV] nets are concerned, they're looking
for favors. All they want are good photo shots. If they
get in bad with the Pentagon, they're going to miss out
on something.

In general, Salisbury said, "the bottom-line boys" were in
control of the media, and he lamented the passing of an era
when, he believed, owners and editors took their First
Amendment responsibilities to heart:

You do not have in this country today important, big
spokesmen for the press. Editors, managing editors, executive editors are not big people in Washington, as they
were during the period when I was an active newspaperman. They don't pretend to be. When something like
this [Administration censorship] happens, and the American Society of Newspaper Editors meets and takes some
action or passes some resolution, nobody knows who
these guys are . . . outside of Ben Bradlee, who doesn't
stand up as far as big issues are concerned. Max Frankel
of the *Times* [is] big in name, but he has never been
known to take a stand on anything; he doesn't even participate in professional organizations . . . You take Abe
Rosenthal, who is a very flamboyant editor—did a lot of
good things, did a lot of bad things—but didn't speak
out on these issues of the press.

Salisbury said the current breed of editor simply didn't measure up to the likes of former *Times* executive editor Turner
Catledge and managing editor Clifton Daniel, "who were in
Washington all the time and were always speaking up and
getting . . . fellow editors to speak out on these basic
issues . . ."

As for old-time stalwarts among publishers, Salisbury
admired the late John S. Knight and the "absolute Nean-
derthal" Colonel Robert McCormick, the publisher of the
Chicago Tribune until his death in 1955. "Jack Knight was

a newspaperman as well as a publisher," Salisbury said. "Beginning with World War II he always took a position; you knew he was there, and he brought other businessmen, executives, along with him. But the guy [James Batten] who runs the Knight-Ridder team now is not involved in [press issues]." The bigoted McCormick backed the First Amendment lawsuit by the bigoted Minneapolis publisher Jay M. Near, which resulted in the 1931 landmark Supreme Court decision that outlawed prior restraint of publication by the government. As the author and former *Washington Post* columnist Nicholas von Hoffman wryly remarked to me, "McCormick was a tiger on the First Amendment, because, unlike most people, he had uses for it."[2]

Salisbury found "Punch" Sulzberger's performance on free press issues mixed: "Punch [has] never been an up-front guy. If you know him at all, you know he is not going to be there. He's taken pretty good stands on principle, and he's backed up things that his editors have done, but he himself likes to be a little bit in the background."

Salisbury seemed perplexed by the silence of newspaper executives on issues bearing on freedom of the press. "I don't know why [they don't protest]. Who *is* speaking out on the issue of the press?" he asked me. "Name one."

Until the Gulf War, I subscribed in part to the notion that, even lacking principled objections, the media's economic self-interest would force them to take an aggressive stance in defense of the First Amendment. If news was a moneymaking product, then profit-driven businessmen would naturally fight tooth and nail for their constitutional right to sell the most interesting news they could find. Contrary to this belief, Harrison Salisbury and Nicholas Horrock argue that "bottom-line" interests prevented certain media companies from paying close attention to First Amendment issues and sometimes caused them to sell out their independence to the government. Yet the big three television networks together lost tens of millions of dollars in their vain efforts to "cover" the Gulf War, and their protests to Pete Williams were tepid and tardy. Uncensored coverage would presumably have been better coverage, and better coverage would have attracted more viewers and more advertising revenue. Similarly, but on a smaller scale, newspapers and magazines motivated by profit should have rationally desired the ability to earn scoops, free from the pool system, in order to boost circulation. If they wouldn't fight the Pentagon for love of freedom, why didn't the networks and the press fight the Administration for love of money?

My effort to understand this paradox took me to the Rockefeller Center office of NBC president Robert Wright. Of the four major news networks, NBC was said to be the most vulnerable to government intimidation because the Pentagon is a major customer of the network's parent company, General Electric. In our interview, news division president Michael Gartner had dismissed out of hand the contention that General Electric interfered with coverage or policy, but deep down I couldn't abandon the image of a heavy-handed corporate owner issuing subtle hints, at the very least, through Gartner to his news executives.

With all this in mind, I expected Wright to be defensive, but instead found him to be frustrated and angry with censorship, the advertising business, and, I concluded, his own newspeople. The more Wright talked, the more I began to wonder if he was not simply a straightforward businessman rather than a vulnerable tool of corporate interests. It took a while for him to warm up, but I noted that he didn't seem as anxious as Katharine Graham that I be fair to the military public relations team. Wright had no difficulty assigning most of the responsibility for the pool debacle on the government: "That blame has to fall on the Pentagon or the U.S. military forces." He also said he didn't like censorship, and he called the Israeli shutdown of NBC's Martin Fletcher "offensive."

Nor did Wright shrink from the analogy between his job

and that of a newspaper publisher; unfortunately, like Katharine Graham, he said he relied on his executives to ask
for help if they needed it in their negotiations with the
Pentagon.

> Nobody came and said, "Can we mobilize NBC or NBC's
> affiliates in some sort of way to improve the situation?"
> . . . Unless the news division feels strongly about some-
> thing like that, and unless I have separate information
> which leads me to believe that they should feel more
> strongly, which I didn't, there's really no reason for me
> to do that . . .

With Michael Gartner so admiring of Pete Williams, it is not
difficult to see why nobody in the news division asked Wright
to intervene. But Gartner's boss had ample reason to be
unhappy with the outcome of the deal Gartner and Tim
Russert cut with the Pentagon; the entire war effort lost NBC
$55 million—about $35 million in extra production costs and
$20 million in withdrawn advertising. Wright had assumed
that the journalists on the third floor of 30 Rockefeller Plaza
knew what they were doing; he believed that playing by the
Pentagon rules would at least yield some decent pictures.
Imagine his surprise, and horror, when on the first day of
the ground assault, Sunday, February 24, he turned on the
television at his suburban Connecticut home and observed
NBC's massive investment going down the drain:

> The first footage I remember seeing was [ABC's] Forrest
> Sawyer standing by a mound of sand somewhere near
> the lines but well behind them, not part of the pool,
> saying, "Tanks went by here . . ." I remember calling
> up [Don Browne] in our own news department. I said,
> "What the hell is this? Why is ABC on here with Forrest
> Sawyer and they're saying this is the first footage from
> the war." I said, "This isn't a war; he's just standing next
> to a pile of sand. It could be anywhere in Saudi Arabia.

There's no indication that there's a war going on, and
they're saying this is the war." I said, "Is this pool coverage?" Browne said to me he's not part of the pool.
They just sent him out because they didn't have any
footage. I said, "How long is this going to go on?" He
said our footage should be coming back any minute now
. . . it wasn't until another twenty-four hours . . . that
there was some CBS footage that was from the pool.

Wright showed up at the office the next day hoping for something better than Sunday's fiasco. Things got worse:

Now it's almost twenty-four hours later, and basically
there was some CBS footage, supposed to be from the
pool, and again it was the same sort of thing. There was
another person standing next to a hill of sand. Tanks
were going by, but it was like you were in a parade. They
could have been five hundred miles from the front . . .
Now I'm down in the newsroom watching this thing. I
said, "This can't be pool coverage." They said, "It is,"
but it isn't. I said, "Where the hell is Arthur Kent? Where
is he?" The answer is, "We can't find him."

Wright was justifiably angry, but I think his anger was
misdirected. It is, after all, the nature of the government and
the military to keep secrets, and sometimes to lie. The Pentagon had done it in Grenada, Panama, and now the Persian
Gulf. But it is the journalist's job to expose the secrets and
lies of the government. Hadn't Wright wondered about the
competence of his news executives? After all, nobody had
warned him that this might happen. He hesitated—for he
was still a corporate man—but he came as close as any boss
I interviewed to placing at least some of the blame for the
success of military censorship in the Gulf on his own
journalists:

They took the position that "we'll get it straightened out"
. . . I think that they could have raised their hands in my
direction and said, "We need every bit of effort we can
get; we really sense that this is an intentional problem
rather than an accidental problem." But they did not
take that position . . . In hindsight it's hard to debate
that.

I admired Wright's candor, as well as his news judgment.
Gartner insisted to me that all the money the network spent
was worth it. Wright clearly realized that most of it had been
wasted. In the end, Wright, not Gartner, took much of the
blame for the huge financial loss, and pointed to a problem
faced by news organizations that few outsiders understand.
"We really got the cold shoulder [from advertisers during
the war]," he said.

I kind of feel in my case that I fell down on that . . . If
we had been able to get underwriters [for war coverage],
then it would have taken an awful lot of pressure off us
for the future . . . The [advertising] agencies said no,
absolutely no way . . . I think that was a terrible mistake
for U.S. advertisers. I think it was an unfortunate over-
reaction to events in Vietnam that took place twenty-five
years ago. I mean, my God, how many times do we have
to relive this issue? Nobody wants to be associated with
body bags.

Public reaction didn't help. Paradoxically, while NBC's
heavily censored coverage was failing miserably to inform
Americans of the real war, "the vast majority of the mail we
got was negative from the standpoint that we were not being
patriotic [and] weren't being supportive of the troops and so
forth." Nevertheless, Wright's studies showed that "American viewers would not have been offended at all by [com-
mercial] sponsorship" of war news and that advertisers were
not harmed by their association with news in general. "The

results were overwhelmingly supportive" of those advertisers that took the risk. "I always feel like I'm screaming this: CNN has been on the air for ten Goddamn years. How long does it take you [advertising agency] guys to figure out that advertisers aren't hurt by being associated with the news?"

Wright was also bitter about what he considered to be the extortionate pricing by the Saudis and Israelis for special phone and satellite links. "Everybody made a buck on the war," he said ruefully. "The nature of a war is everybody makes a buck . . . except the networks."

In the end I sympathized far more with the businessman Wright than I did with the blind mice on the news side who purported to know the score. CBS News had beaten NBC in the ratings in the final two weeks of Desert Storm, and Wright wondered out loud if he shouldn't have urged some of his journalists to defy the pool system. Another businessman running NBC might have fired somebody for blowing the coverage and wasting so much money, but this is not the way things work in a modern corporation.

Writing this book made me feel at times that the world was upside down: the confusion of the institutional and honest idioms; the failure, with the exception of Ted Turner, of owners and top executives to take responsibility for their companies, as well as their refusal to be answerable for the failures of their employees; the unwillingness of journalists to fight for their lifeblood, the First Amendment; the withdrawal of American reporters from Baghdad; the lack of interest in the matter of the unseen enemy; the inability of anyone to call Pete Williams a liar. What had happened to Thomas Jefferson's and Thomas Paine's legacy?

When Dan Rather had said he worried about the effect of "suck-up" journalism on young reporters just starting out, I had suspected him of posturing—a grizzled veteran admonishing the young pups. But I have soberly reconsidered: Rather is absolutely right to be worried.

Every spring, the White House Correspondents Association (WHCA) celebrates the professed power of the capital's press corps by throwing a gigantic black-tie banquet at the Washington Hilton. The Radio and Television Correspondents Association holds its own dinner around the same time, and I suppose that in our electronic age, it may well have become the more important of the two events. For reasons of tradition and prestige, however, the WHCA dinner seemed to me the place to be after Desert Storm. I still imagined that the press had more integrity than television, and that the print-dominated WHCA would present a prouder face in the aftermath of the Pentagon's smashing victory in Desert Muzzle.

For the inquiring reporter, journalism banquets can also be useful for their occasionally bizarre manifestations of the institutional voice. At the Overseas Press Club (OPC) awards dinner in 1990, for example, former Gannett chairman Alan Neuharth announced to an uncomprehending audience that "there are no more secrets anywhere in the world, from the largest cities to the smallest villages, from the highest mountain to the lowest valley." Addressing the OPC in 1991, Ted Turner made a rambling speech in which he described his reaction to death threats over his decision to let Peter Arnett remain in Baghdad: "Everybody dies sooner or later; we decided if we were going to get blown away, we're going to get blown away."

This year's WHCA dinner displayed a decidedly military flair, befitting the capital's festive "We kicked butt" mood after Desert Storm. The twenty-four hundred or so guests who packed the enormous International Ballroom were treated to a dazzling display of marching prowess by a joint armed-forces color guard while a marine band blared the five service anthems. The after-dinner entertainment was provided by President Bush and "Sinbad," a gentrified Eddie Murphy knockoff. Bush tried hard to be funny: "I wonder if this very minute Saddam Hussein is appearing before the Baghdad Revolutionary Palace Press Corps and his wife is sitting in the limo saying, 'Try to be funny, sweetie.' " The crowd erupted in laughter.

To experience the behind-the-scenes action at the WHCA dinner, you must arrive early and stay late, for the truly interesting conversations and power surges take place in the numerous "hospitality suites" set up by the larger newspaper and magazine companies. Here, the capital's press grandees can make a show of their magnificence; a publication's perceived influence rises and falls depending on which celebrities of the moment drop in, and for how long. New publishing blood can stir excitement; this year, for example, British press baron Robert Maxwell, now deceased, was playing the debutante as the new owner of the New York *Daily News*, and he had rented an eighth-floor presidential suite for the occasion.

Before the dinner began I struggled down the densely packed corridor past the various newspaper parties, searching for the vortex of power. President Bush would later address the banquet, but a President does not generally press the flesh with journalists unless he needs something badly, and Bush, at the height of his popularity following Desert Storm, would not make an appearance in this mob scene. On the right side of the corridor, the *Baltimore Sun* appeared to be making a respectable showing, although it seemed a little too easy to enter the room for theirs to be considered a truly important suite. Farther down and across the hall, at the right-wing *Washington Times* suite, I caught the first whiff of genuine celebrity heat. *Times* editor Arnaud de Borchgrave greeted me at the door—I had interviewed him about his unilateral reporting with the Egyptian army—and he explained excitedly that I had just missed the two chief stars of the evening. (The Sun Myung Moon–controlled *Times* wields influence out of proportion to its small circulation because of its fidelity to Ronald Reagan and its location in the capital.) I hurried out of the suite and pressed on into the wake of celebrity. An energy beam seemed to be pulling me toward the end of the hallway, and I quickly decided that must be where the action was. I arrived at last at a dead end and found a suite with a sign out front that announced: "*U.S. News* party—By Invitation Only."

I had crashed many events in my years as a reporter and I knew I had to crash this one, for here was surely the center of media power on this glittering evening. I met no resistance as I headed for the door, and, to my surprise, out came Colin Powell in a formal white uniform, causing me to halt and stare. He seemed embarrassed by the attention he was getting, and I sensed he was relieved to escape the clutches of his admirers as he hurried past me with his head slightly bowed.

Once inside the suite, I realized I had found the action. In the middle of the room, bathed in a riot of photographic flashes, was the massive, beaming, larger-than-life General H. Norman Schwarzkopf. Hero of Desert Storm; celebrity of the moment; contender for *People*'s Sexiest Man Alive; coarchitect of Desert Muzzle. Schwarzkopf appeared to be swimming in the adulation that swirled around him as he smiled for the cameras and signed autographs.

By the general's side—below him may be more accurate—stood the lucky host, Mortimer Zuckerman, the real-estate man turned owner and editor of *U.S. News & World Report*. Zuckerman had scored a tremendous publicity coup by snaring Schwarzkopf for his party as well as for the *U.S. News* banquet table. What price—financial or spiritual—Zuckerman may have paid for the honor was not known. What was known was that Zuckerman had refused to waffle on censorship and had actually *endorsed* it. (Zuckerman told an audience at Ogilvy & Mather on March 8 that he was "astonished by the availability and the access that we

have had both to the Pentagon and to the information we
feel we needed to cover the war. The press . . . is petulant,
self-concerned, self-centered, and really downright silly, particularly when you compare the rather mature intelligence
of some of the military briefers . . . to the stupidity of some
of the questioners . . . We had information pouring into us
that we couldn't believe. I don't know what in the world they
were complaining about.") In the French vernacular of his
native Montreal, Zuckerman had become *un vendu.*

The crush of frenzied admiration around Schwarzkopf
brought to mind the final scene from Nathanael West's *The
Day of the Locust*; journalists, public relations people, and
photographers jockeyed strenuously for proximity to their
hero. One by one the lesser stars of the evening approached
to pay their respects, among them wide-girthed Robert Maxwell, who seemed shrunken in the glow of Schwarzkopf's
medal- and ribbon-covered magnificence. Republican media
manipulation king Roger Ailes entered the room. After a
suitably hushed conversation with Andrew Rosenthal of *The
New York Times*, the goateed Ailes congratulated the hottest
new media property in town. Ailes may well have been covering his flank; Democratic National Committee chairman
Ron Brown had already presented himself to take the pulse
of Schwarzkopf's political ambitions.

"This guy's got heavy-duty charisma," confided one excited guest to another. A young woman exclaimed: "Did you
see him? He's such a sweetheart." A female *U.S. News* staffer
was content to keep her distance: "I'm just standing here in
awe," she told me.

One *U.S. News* reporter, Gloria Borger, could not restrain her admiration. She lunged at the general and de-
manded his autograph. "I want one for my son," she
squealed, and Schwarzkopf was happy to comply. Borger
later confided to friends that the general had declined to sign
her commemorative card of an M1A1 tank "because the
lawyers told him not to; it would create a market."

It was a disturbing scene. Reporters and publishers were paying homage to a general who clearly despised the press, to the representative of an Administration that had succeeded in relegating them to almost complete compliance with its propaganda aims. The Fourth Estate was bowing to a man who had treated it with the contempt normally reserved for enemy soldiers.

Something even more distressing was shortly to follow. Into the room strode the only well-known reporter who had maintained an image of independence from the Bush Administration during the war: Peter Arnett of the Baghdad dateline. Arnett walked up to Schwarzkopf, into the limelight, and vigorously shook the general's giant hand: "Congratulations, General, on a very fine effort," he said. "I know you didn't mean all those things you said about me." Then, like any media-trained celebrity, Arnett tossed a quip to the assembled guests: "He tried to kill me," he joked, gesturing at Schwarzkopf. The general said nothing, but continued smiling.

I lingered for a few minutes, absorbing the conversations around me. At last Schwarzkopf, Zuckerman, and their entourage moved out in a convoy of regal splendor. Small knots of people stayed on to gossip. "Maureen Dowd [of *The New York Times*] was here," said one delighted *U.S. News* staffer, as if that capped the success of the party.

Just before I left, I eavesdropped on a conversation among four people I assumed were journalists. One man was eagerly recounting the action to the others. "There was an amazing moment when Ron Brown, Roger Ailes, Schwarzkopf, and Zuckerman were posing for pictures," he said. The storyteller suddenly observed me taking notes and asked abruptly: "Hey, do you work for the government?" I mumbled that I didn't and walked out of the room. I should have asked the same question of him.

IN THE MONTHS following the June 1992 publication of the hardcover edition of this book, the American news media continued to mutter their disapproval of Gulf War censorship while swearing, at least in some quarters, never to be fooled again by the likes of George Bush, Pete Williams, and General Norman Schwarzkopf. The mood of establishment discontent revealed itself when Patrick Sloyan of *Newsday* was awarded the Pulitzer Prize in April 1992 for his post-war discovery of the First Infantry Division's secret burial—using earth-moving equipment—of live Iraqi soldiers dug in at the Saudi Arabia–Kuwait border. Later that year, the *New York Times* complained of the government's methods in uncharacteristically aggressive fashion—first by publishing Mark Crispin Miller's June 24 op-ed page exposé of Schwarzkopf's false claims about the destruction of mobile SCUD launchers, and then, more dramatically, by reporting on August 16, 1992, President Bush's secret plan to "provoke a confrontation" with Saddam Hussein over the dictator's purported interference with United Nations weapons inspectors. According to the *Times* story, the White House apparently meant to synchronize the bombing of Baghdad with Republican convention festivities at the Houston Astrodome, thus providing suitably martial background music for the launch of the president's re-election campaign. The Administration denied stooping to such crass political tactics, but Baghdad went unbombed for the moment, and the president went down to defeat in November. (This did not, however, prevent Bush—clearly raw with spite—from pointlessly bombing Iraq twice more before leaving office. To Bush's chagrin, Hus-

sein proved more resilient than Manuel Noriega, another
friendly dictator turned restless, and the Iraqi leader was able
to answer present at the creation of the New World Order.)

The media's superficial bravado did nothing to resolve the
familiar conflicts between institutional ideals (as advertised by
the media themselves) and institutional reality. In the spring of
1992, the barons of the nation's press and television networks
once again lost their argument with Pete Williams over proposed changes in the ground rules governing combat coverage.
Williams departed the Pentagon with the election of Bill Clinton, but as of this writing the Bush/Pentagon's National Media
Pool system remains in place, with a few toothless qualifications, and no one has been hinting that in the event of another
war the Clinton administration might behave any differently
than its predecessor. Nor do the media exhibit the slightest
inclination to exploit the new political environment and shake
free of their Pentagon shackles. Their docility is in keeping
with the general lack of media self-examination after Desert
Storm. Outside of the occasional academic seminar, hardly
anyone in a big news organization has discussed seriously the
demerits of the pool system, military censorship, or the failure
of the media owners to fight back. One minor exception was
John Fialka of the *Wall Street Journal,* a Gulf War pool reporter
and occasional pool coordinator. Fialka's university press
monograph, *Hotel Warriors,* was generally critical of government behavior toward the media and rightly noted the special
access to troops that was granted military cheerleaders like
Schwarzkopf's Vietnam crony, Joe Galloway of *U.S. News and
World Report.* But Fialka didn't object to the pool system per
se, merely what he considered its inefficiency and favoritism.

Just as important perhaps, the system of rewards in
mainstream journalism—so forcefully denounced by Dan
Rather—persists in its comic self-delusion. While the Pulitzer
Prize jurors did take note of Sloyan's sensational (albeit
delayed) revelation about the Army's one-step killing/burial
innovation, many American newspaper editors failed to recog-

nize the pointlessness of their own Gulf War "coverage": a well-placed source on a Pulitzer Prize committee told me that "at least" thirty of the sixty-six entries in the International Reporting category were for "reporting" on the Gulf War.

The hubris of the newspaper establishment is remarkable, but it pales in comparison with the effrontery of the major television networks. CBS News hired General Schwarzkopf to host documentaries* and NBC engaged General Tom Kelly (the Pentagon's military spokesman during the Gulf War) as a military "analyst" in its news division. Then, in March 1993, NBC outmaneuvered ABC for the journalistic services of none other than Pete Williams, the front man for the White House censorship apparatus and a hero of Operation Desert Muzzle. Not content with their acquisition of Williams, NBC simultaneously added to its news-department roster a former National Security Council staff member, Richard Haass. Haass's qualifications were no doubt enhanced by his co-authorship of the patriotic essay signed by George Bush and published with great fanfare in *Newsweek* in the fall of 1990.

The hiring of Williams and Haass illustrates perfectly the media's confusion about public relations, propaganda, and journalism. During our interview in 1991, NBC news president Michael Gartner suggested they were one and the same. The bow-tied news bureaucrat had expressed his great admiration for Williams's work and his earnest desire to hire the bespectacled public relations man as an NBC newsman. Gartner did not keep his job long enough to see his hope fulfilled, being forced to resign over the scandal involving NBC news's concoction of a General Motors pickup truck explosion. But Timothy Russert, the network's Washington bureau chief and himself a former P.R. man (for New York governor Mario Cuomo), quickly lifted his fallen leader's standard and engaged Williams to cover the Justice Department. A senior NBC producer, Steve Friedman, gleefully announced that Williams would also co-host a new "magazine" show. *Newsday*'s television critic,

Marvin Kitman, suggested instead a program entitled "Meet the Press Agent."

Was there a more fitting, or more absurd, irony with which to cap discussion of the media's complicity with Gulf War censorship and propaganda than Williams's ascension to the capital's journalistic pantheon? Perhaps only this one: Early in 1993 the Committee to Protect Journalists (CPJ) released its comprehensive annual survey of attacks against the press around the world. The CPJ report provided all manner of depressing stories about the killing and intimidation of reporters, including an interesting chart that listed the ten countries holding the most journalists prisoner. Predictably, as the world's most populous country, the People's Republic of China stood as the undisputed leader in the competition to incarcerate reporters, with a total of twenty-seven as of February 1993. In second place, with a considerably smaller body of citizens than its principal rival's (0.1 percent), was the emirate of Kuwait—the seat of liberty that the American media had so recently championed and done so much to preserve. Little Kuwait could take pride in its eighteen journalist prisoners, for on a per capita basis the emirate was peerless in its detestation of freedom of the press.

New York City
April 1993

---

*In June 1993, Dan Rather, critic of "suck-up" journalism, hosted the elegiac CBS documentary "Schwarzkopf in Vietnam: A Soldier Returns," starring General Schwarzkopf.

NOTES

1. Cutting the Deal

1. At Time Warner, the confusion over corporate authority has been purposely institutionalized, in theory to protect the editorial side of the company from interference by the business side. Time Inc. Magazines editor-in-chief Jason McManus does not report to Time Warner chairman and chief executive officer Steven Ross, who McManus insists is a "colleague," not his boss; McManus reports directly to the Time Warner board of directors, on which he sits, and technically McManus cannot be fired by Ross. Thus, Ross is not really the equivalent of a publisher, but neither is McManus, who also must work with Time Inc. Magazines president Reginald Brack.

2. Congress also was reluctant to debate the Pentagon censorship policy. When it finally did so, on January 16, the discussion centered on a feeble resolution introduced by U.S. Representative Louis Stokes (D-Ohio), which called on the Secretary of Defense to "limit restrictions [on the media] to those required for operational security and protection of classified information." Two days later, U.S. Representative Barbara Boxer (D-Cal.) proposed a tougher resolution directing the Pentagon to "cease the imposition of military security review panels that could result in unwarranted censorship of the news media." Boxer, however, stopped short of demanding an immediate end to the combat pools, asking that they be suspended "when they are no longer absolutely necessary . . ." Both resolutions died in the House Armed Services Committee.

In the debate on Pentagon censorship, U.S. Representative Bruce Vento (D-Minn.) made a far more impassioned defense of First Amendment rights than the major media bureaucrats ever mustered during the entire Gulf crisis: "There is no place in a free society for this 'see no evil, hear no evil, speak no evil' Pentagon policy. We cannot tolerate the Pentagon dictating the words and images the public is allowed to receive . . . The Administration is not entitled to prior restraint, censorship, sanitization, or spin control of the news . . . The destructive weapon of censorship the Pentagon is employing to control the press is rapidly chiseling away at our democratic rights."

3. Federal judge Leonard B. Sand dismissed the suit in April 1991 on the grounds that the end of the war and lifting of official restrictions on the media removed the urgency, or live controversy, from the case. But much of the language in his opinion was favorable to the plaintiffs' argument, and provided a solid basis for a legal challenge to future government censorship in wartime. Judge Sand rebuffed the government's contention that the President's war power under Article II of the Constitution was superior to the press's freedom under the First Amendment. He also rejected the government's argument that a court could not mediate a dispute between the military and the press over First Amendment rights during a war.

2. Selling Babies

1. The Reagan Administration tilt toward Iraq—both military and diplomatic—was as cynical a display of realpolitik as one can find in recent U.S. history. It began in March 1982, when the United States removed Iraq from the State Department's list of nations that support international terrorism, and twenty-two months later added Iran to its terrorist blacklist. This permitted the Administration to guarantee U.S. bank loans to Iraq for the purchase of American grain and opened the door to future sales of military technology at the same time that the Administration's Operation Staunch was attempting to slow worldwide arms sales (notwithstanding Oliver North's future efforts) to Iran.

Following a meeting between Reagan and Iraqi foreign minister Tariq Aziz in November 1984, according to Dilip Hiro's *The Longest War*, the U.S. set up direct links between the CIA and the American embassy in Baghdad to aid the Iraqi war effort; thus, the intelligence shared with the Baghdad government helped defeat the Iranian offensive of March 1985. Collaboration between Washington and Baghdad increased to the point where, by early 1987, U.S. Navy ships were guiding Iraqi missiles to Iranian targets, according to BBC correspondent John Simpson. In his book *From the House of War*, Simpson reports for the first time that the USS *Stark* was hit by two Iraqi Exocet missiles on May 17, 1987, because the Iraqi pilot "homed in accidentally on the radio beam from the Stark which was directing the pilot to his [Iranian] target." The incident killed thirty-seven American crewmen and, Simpson writes, the White House "did not even ask Iraq for compensation . . ." On May 29, Hiro says, Assistant Secretary of Defense Richard Armitage stated publicly, "We can't stand to see Iraq defeated."

2. On May 3, 1990, Patrick Tyler reported in *The Washington Post* that Pentagon analysts had "assembled . . . conclusive intelligence that . . . the [Halabja massacre] was caused by repeated chemical bombardments from both belligerent armies." Tyler cited a Pentagon "study" based on "highly classified sources." Tyler's information was similar to that found in a study done by a U.S. Army War College investigative team, but his source appears to have been different. The report of the War College team, first revealed by *Newsday*'s Knut Royce on January 19, 1991, was more equivocal than the conclusions drawn by Tyler's sources, noting only that the investigators could not prove that the Kurds were killed by Iraqi gas.

3. Glaspie told Hussein that "We [the United States] have no opinions on the Arab-Arab conflicts, like your border disagreement with Kuwait." Later, upon her return to the United States, Glaspie said in an interview published in the *New York Times:* "Obviously I didn't think, and nobody else did, that the Iraqis were going to take all of Kuwait."

4. In U.S. History, the Gulf War public relations effort is closest in tone and content to the Spanish-atrocities propaganda that fueled American intervention in Cuba in 1898. During the two years leading up to the Spanish–American War, however, it was William Randolph Hearst's *New York Journal* and Joseph Pulitzer's *New York World* that trumpeted the most anxiety-arousing horror stories. It was not the McKinley White House, which for a time resisted newspaper and congressional pressure to go to war against Spain.

"The horrors of a barbarous struggle for the extermination of the native population are witnessed in all parts of the country," screamed the *World* on May 17, 1896. "Blood on the roadsides, blood in the fields, blood on the doorsteps, blood, blood, blood! . . . Is there no nation wise enough, brave enough, to aid this blood-smitten land?" Stories of slaughtered babies were popular as well in the late nineteenth century. On June 3, 1896, the *World* reported the alleged death of a Cuban infant at the hands of the Spanish monsters: "The woman tried to shield her child with her own body, but the merciless bullets did their work . . . The baby was not killed outright and one of the soldiers, moved by a kind of barbarous pity, crushed the little one's skull with the butt of his rifle." The "Free Cuba" PR effort of the 1890s bears a striking resemblance to Hill and Knowlton's work a century later on behalf of Citizens for a Free Kuwait, albeit on a more modest financial scale. Then, a certain Tomas Estrada Palma performed the equivalent function, running the Cuban propaganda operation out of donated office space in lower Manhattan and feeding all manner of fake atrocity and battle stories to eager reporters. The Spanish were the era's Iraqis, with the military governor of Cuba, General Valeriano Weyler, assigned the role of Saddam Hussein. The *Journal* labeled the general "Butcher" Weyler, so that, like the "Butcher of Baghdad," he would cease to seem human. Whoever wrote the following passage for Hearst's flagship paper in 1896, taken from W. A. Swanberg's brilliant *Citizen Hearst*, could well have been a model for A. M. Rosenthal, William Safire, and Alfonse D'Amato ninety-four years later: "Weyler the brute, the devastator of haciendas, the destroyer of families, and the outrager of women . . . Pitiless, cold, an exterminator of men . . . There is nothing to prevent his carnal, animal brain from running riot with itself in inventing tortures and infamies of bloody debauchery . . ." No comparison could be made with Adolf Hitler, who was still a young boy.

God, too, was enlisted into the cause of Cuban revolution, just as He would be in 1990 on behalf of Kuwait. Church ministers across the U.S. were urged by the Cuban League to conduct their services on July 4, 1897, "so as to influence public opinion favorably toward the struggle of the Cubans for independence." (For more on the campaign for intervention in Cuba, see Marcus Wilkerson's book *Public Opinion and the Spanish–American War*.)

The public relations assault against the Spanish administration in Cuba was not aimed solely at the popular imagination. Highbrow periodicals like *Harper's Weekly* joined the fray with somewhat more sophisticated justifications of U.S. intervention that were aimed at better-educated readers. After the war commenced, in its June 4, 1898, issue, *Harper's Weekly* haughtily dismissed complaints from European commentators that America was indulging ignoble urges by invading Cuba:

> In France and Germany, this country is openly charged with having a land-grabbing spirit, with being actuated by the desire to take advantage of Spain's present distress for the purpose of depriving her, by force, of her last colonial possessions. This accusation falls naturally from the lips of a Spanish statesman like Sagasta, or a Spanish butcher like Weyler, but it is not true. Indeed, it is so far from being true that no one can make it—no one, we mean, not blinded by the cruel prejudices of war—without laying himself open to the accusation of mendacity or of gross ignorance, for of all countries of modern times the United States has shown the least inclination to add distant territories to her possessions.

(The editors of *Harper's Weekly* evidently did not consider the seizure of large portions of northern Mexico and the Indian territories of the West to be distant land grabs.)

In another parallel between the Spanish–American War and the Gulf War, the Spaniards, like the Iraqis, turned out to be paper tigers. Poorly armed and badly organized, the Spanish generals held out for just twelve weeks, not that much longer than Hussein. In both conflicts U.S. casualties were light, and the celebrations of painless victory back home were similarly bellicose and jingoistic.

5. California rice growers and other American agricultural exporters were then benefitting from U.S. government loan guarantees for grain sales to Iraq. These federal export credits permitted the Atlanta branch of the Banca Nazionale del Lavoro to safely lend $5 billion to Iraq (which was considered a poor credit risk) for purchases of American grain. That some of the loaned money was used illegally by Saddam Hussein to buy military equipment did not concern the Bush Administration, which evidently viewed the arrangement as a fine

method of providing secret foreign aid to its second favorite (after King Fahd) Middle Eastern despot. After the Gulf War, thanks to the tireless efforts of U.S. Rep. Henry Gonzales (D-Texas) and *New York Times* columnist William Safire, and the federal prosecution of BNL's Atlanta branch manager on charges of fraud, this additional, and politically embarrassing, example of Administration coziness with Hussein was revealed to the public. The alleged efforts by the U.S. Justice Department to delay the indictment of the BNL Atlanta manager, Christopher Drogoul, until the Gult War was nearly over—as well as the Administration's secret acquiescence to Hussein's diversion of loan money to weapons (this in spite of its knowledge of the Justice Department and FBI investigations of Drogoul)—is what has come to be known as "Iraqgate."

6. In her spoken testimony, Nayirah departed from her written statement and did not specify the number of babies allegedly killed, referring only to "babies." But the discrepancy didn't diminish Hill and Knowlton's passionate commitment to her story. Following publication of this book, in an angry phone call denouncing my reporting, Lauri Fitz-Pegado told me that Nayirah had, in fact, specified 15 babies to Hill and Knowlton before the hearing, and that no one had seen fit to question the gap in Nayirah's public statement. Perhaps Nayirah had, at least partially, lost her nerve. According to Fitz-Pegado, "She [Nayirah] was extremely emotional; she did not read word for word at that testimony." Whatever it was that caused the omission, Fitz-Pegado stood by her client to the bitter end. "I believe what Nayirah told me in 1990," she said. "Come on, John. Who gives a shit whether there are fifteen [babies] or two?" For her part, Nayirah never agreed to be interviewed.

7. Mrs. Mutawa possessed a keen sense of the dramatic. Not only were Saddam's soldiers agents of a new Hitler, but according to Mrs. Mutawa, they were also inspired by Dracula: "A Moroccan lady . . . told me she had taken both her daughters to the hospital for a simple treatment. Instead of providing the treatment, the Iraqis forcibly removed blood from her tiny children in order to give blood to injured Iraqi soldiers."

8. The debate over Hussein's nuclear weapons program raged on well after the war had ended. Before the war, facts were hard to come by and the political propagandist's hand could be seen in the wildly varying estimates of Iraq's alleged drive toward a radio-

active Armageddon. In its November–December 1990 issue, *Proliferation Watch*, a newsletter of the Senate Committee on Governmental Affairs, published a chart exhibiting the range of "expert" opinion on the matter. At one end, Paul Leventhal, director of the Nuclear Control Institute, said Hussein would possess what the newsletter termed a "crude nuclear apparatus, difficult to deliver," within one to three weeks; closer to the middle of the pack, William Safire predicted the dictator would have a usable nuclear explosive in a little over two years, while former Defense Secretary James Schlesinger said it would take about five years. At the far end of the spectrum, *The Australian* of Canberra quoted an Australian intelligence estimate that Hussein would not have a deployable nuclear device for another fifteen years. (At a Foreign Policy Association forum in April 1991, *New York Times* science writer Malcolm Browne said Iraq was ten years away from building a nuclear weapon with practical uses.)

The United Nations, with some difficulty, investigated Iraq's nuclear weapons program after the war, and in early August 1991 found that Saddam's scientists had extracted some plutonium—not nearly enough to make a nuclear weapon—from spent fuel at one of its nuclear installations. Nuclear expert Paul Leventhal told *The New York Times* that eight kilograms of plutonium were required to make a successful nuclear device; the Iraqis had so far managed to collect three grams, or .0375 percent of the required amount. Iraq had earlier admitted to secretly producing about one pound of slightly enriched uranium not previously disclosed to international authorities. According to Leventhal, twenty-five kilograms (fifty-five pounds) of highly enriched uranium is needed to produce a nuclear bomb.

A month later, the Saddam nuclear bomb threat of the fall began to look more like a scare story intended to drive the United States into war. On September 26, Andrew Rosenthal, son of the apocalyptic A. M. Rosenthal, said in a front-page *New York Times* news analysis that "American officials, including Gen. Colin L. Powell . . . acknowledged . . . that [Iraq's nuclear threat] is not any real threat—in the short term or even medium term."

Eventually, the assumption that Saddam's pre-war A-bomb program posed an immediate threat seemed to unravel entirely. On May 20, 1992, in the midst of several highly publicized confrontations between U.N. inspectors and Iraqi officials in Baghdad, *The New York Times'* Paul Lewis reported on a "secret gathering" of nuclear weapons designers convened a month earlier in Vienna to review data on Iraqi nuclear capabilities. Lewis quoted an anonymous official of the International Atomic Energy Agency saying that the designers concluded that pre-war Iraq was "at least" two to three years away from manufacturing an atomic bomb—not, as President Bush had claimed as a possibility in November 1990, six months away. Lewis' revelation raised the obvious question of how Hussein could have achieved his (alleged) deadly ambition in the face of the very aggressive U.N. trade embargo in effect during the fall and winter of 1990–91. With all their design flaws and technical insufficiencies, the Iraqis surely would have needed expert advice from the outside, not to mention spare parts and more uranium or plutonium. It's unlikely anybody or anything that important could have gotten through the U.N.'s cordon sanitaire.

Without the threat of an imminent nuclear holocaust, yet another of Bush's rationales for pushing war over continued sanctions appears to dissolve. What, we are left to ask, was the rush?

Another revelation on nuclear weapons capability in the Middle East occurred in October 1991 when Seymour Hersh reported in a new book, *The Samson Option*, that Israel possessed "hundreds" of nuclear weapons, as opposed to the official U.S. intelligence estimate of fewer than one hundred. Hersh said that the Israeli government went on full nuclear alert once during the Persian Gulf war, actually placing nuclear missiles on launchers while Iraqi Scud missiles were striking Israel.

(Having already branded Hussein a nuclear terrorist as well as a Hitler, it wasn't difficult for the White House to then dress him in the costume of "environmental terrorist." In the case of Iraq's "deliberate" oil spill in the Persian Gulf on January 25, reality once again diverged from propaganda. Initial reports said that the Iraqis had "dumped" 11 million barrels of oil into the Persian Gulf. Images of oil-soaked cormorants enraged environmentalists around the world. Three days later, the gigantic oil spill [the *Exxon Valdez* leak amounted to 250,000 barrels] was acknowledged to be smaller than advertised, and allied officials said that it may, at least in part, have been caused accidentally by Iraqi shelling on the first day of the war. Greenpeace reported after the war that at least some of the spill was caused by allied bombing of Iraqi oil tankers. In May 1991, Saudi Arabia formally told an Extraordinary Session of the Regional Organization for Protection of the Maritime Environment [the Gulf States version of the Environmental Protection Agency] that Iraqi forces "caused" 6 million barrels of oil to be "released" into the Gulf. "According to the best available information," the Saudi government reported, "the leakage source could be traced primarily to the Sea Island Terminal and to some Iraqi oil tankers in these waters . . . Of this, three to four million barrels came from tankers. The balance came from land sources and/or terminals." The Saudis said that through April 1991, "an additional 3,000 barrels of oil continued to be spilled daily from damaged tanks, ruptured pipelines, and tankers." In retrospect, it appeared, the allies were partners in Hussein's environmental disaster.)

9. Citizens for a Free Kuwait ended their contract with Hill and Knowlton on January 8, 1991, to the chagrin of H&K's management. One theory for the abrupt dismissal was, surprisingly enough, that the Kuwaitis considered the PR firm too high-priced. According to a former H&K vice president, Steve Meeter, H&K had pitched its services to the Kuwaiti government before the Iraqi invasion and were rejected "because I believe they thought we were too expensive." Another H&K executive, who asked not to be identified, theorized that the newly restored Emir and his ministers may have resented the success of Dr. al-Ebraheem, who was thought to have acted too independently. Still another theory, according to this executive, was that al-Ebraheem had earned the Emir's displeasure by associating himself with the pro-democracy movement in Kuwait after the liberation. It was possible, the executive said, "that Ebraheem and all those guys were pushing a little too strong for democracy . . . al-Ebraheem [may have been] trying to take advantage of his success to sort of push his agenda, and the Emir didn't like that." In any event, the executive explained, Citizens for a Free Kuwait had been paying H&K almost entirely with Kuwaiti government money, so the termination of the firm's services was the government's decision to make.

If there had been a loss of trust, it didn't take the Emir long to overcome his suspicions about H&K; Kuwait soon hired the firm for a return engagement: a one-shot project in September 1991 when the Emir traveled to New York City for the opening of the United Nations General Assembly.

Gary Hymel, the H&K vice president who lobbied Capitol Hill for Citizens for a Free Kuwait, was disappointed and perplexed that H&K had fallen from favor with the Kuwaiti government. "They got their country back, and we thought we educated the American public," he said. "We did a hell of a job for them." Referring to Kuwaiti torture, execution, and intimidation of alleged collaborators after the liberation, Hymel said, "That's when they really needed the PR, as you saw." But the Kuwaitis were famously indecisive, he said: in the months following the war, the government switched PR firms two more times before hiring H&K for the Emir's visit to the U.N. "Somebody told me that's exactly what Kuwaitis do," Hymel noted. "They hire, they can't make up their minds, they can't get direction. You know, they can't focus, and then it just kind of fritters away."

In the end, the Kuwaitis' inability to "focus" apparently caused them to be defrauded by another American friend of Kuwait, Sam H. Zakhem. As President Reagan's one-time ambassador to Bahrain, Zakhem was well placed to offer promotional services to the exiled government of Kuwait, which he performed in his role as co-chairman of The Coalition for America at Risk (CAR) and the Freedom Task Force (FTF), both of which masqueraded as U.S. citizens' lobbies *a la* Citizens for a Free Kuwait. The Kuwaitis entrusted Zakhem's front groups with $7.7 million for advertising and lobbying on their behalf and CAR/FTF did place full-page ads in newspapers, including the *Washington Post,* espousing a vigorous anti-Saddam message. On July 7, 1992, however, Zakhem was indicted, along with two associates (William R. Kennedy, Jr., and Scott Stanley, Jr.), for failing to register as foreign agents and allegedly stealing all but $2 million of the Kuwaiti slush fund. In a 1991 interview with my researcher, Scott Anderson, Zakhem said that contributions to CAR "almost" came in "by the thousands . . . but they were all small. I'm told the biggest was $50 and smallest one $1."

Zakhem explained that CAR's and FTF's supporters were thoroughgoing American patriots. They were "people [who] . . . knew the score . . . they knew that really it was not just Kuwait that we were fighting for; that it was America's national interest and America's

... heritage of support for the weak and standing up for the cause of the individual."

10. My own research found far more skepticism than support for the baby incubator story. Andrew Whitley, executive director of Middle East Watch, called it "farfetched" to suggest that there were as many as 312 incubators in Kuwait at the time of the Iraqi invasion. After August 2, only "a handful of babies" were in incubators at the principal Kuwait City maternity hospital (where two-thirds of the country's incubators were installed), Whitley said. According to the human rights investigator, there were unconfirmed reports that 2 incubators out of a total of 130 in Kuwait had been stolen during the occupation. "Iraqis did many terrible things," Whitley said, "but they did not interfere with medical treatment of people in hospitals . . . Somebody decided [the incubator atrocities story] would be a fine line to peddle."

Dr. Nasser al-Busairi, an obstetrician and gynecologist at the maternity hospital in Kuwait City, said in an interview in November 1991 that he was certain the Iraqis had not removed any babies from incubators. He agreed with Icelandic doctor Gisli Sigurdsson's assertion that the Iraqis were indirectly responsible for the deaths of babies because they caused foreign medical support staff and doctors to flee the country.

Yet in the late fall of 1991, Dr. al-Ebraheem continued to insist that the baby incubator atrocities had occurred. He urged me to call a Dr. Abdullah al-Hammadi for confirmation, but repeated phone calls over several days to al-Hammadi at the maternity hospital in Kuwait went unanswered. Finally, in January 1992, an envelope from the Kuwaiti Association to Defend War Victims arrived at my office; it contained ten color photographs of unidentified adult corpses and a handwritten report entitled "Kuwait's Ordeal: An Eyewitness Account," allegedly written by Dr. al-Hammadi. Nowhere in the "account" were the baby incubator atrocities even mentioned.

Then, in February 1992, after *The New York Times* published my op-ed piece revealing the true identity of Nayirah al-Sabah, the U.S. government joined the Kuwaitis and Hill and Knowlton in what seemed a desperate last effort to prove the existence of the baby incubator atrocity. It was damage control at its most heavy-handed. In a February 4 cable sent to the State Department, but obviously addressed to the media, America's ambassador to Kuwait, Edward W. Gnehm, tried to salvage the shredded credibility of the war propagandists by citing accounts by three "witnesses" to the removal of babies from incubators. In addition, he railed against the "smug and cynical" human rights investigators and journalists who had challenged and refuted the incubator story, calling them "revisionist historians." (The sobriquet "revisionist historians" appears to have been inspired by a letter to *The New York Times* from Representative Tom Lantos in which he defended his decision to conceal Nayirah's identity, while at the same time insisting that her filial relationship to the Kuwaiti ambassador to the U.S. actually "enhanced" her credibility.) Unfortunately for historians, revisionist or otherwise, Gnehm blacked out the names of his "witnesses" in the cable. I called the U.S. embassy in Kuwait to ask Gnehm about the omissions, but he declined my request for an interview.

The Gnehm cable forced Middle East Watch into publicly defending its own research. In a report issued February 6, the organization demolished Gnehm's diplomatic tantrum in a paragraph-by-paragraph textual analysis. Virtually nothing Gnehm wrote in the cable, it seemed, was backed up with hard evidence; it wasn't hard to see why. Until my op-ed piece appeared in *The New York Times* on January 6, no one in the U.S. government had attempted to contradict either the reporting of John Martin and Middle East Watch or the Amnesty retraction of its support for the incubator story. On the contrary, when Middle East Watch investigators met with Gnehm and his staff on March 21, 1991, they heard no argument whatever against their initial finding that the baby incubator atrocities had never occurred. According to Aziz Abu-Hamad: "Our preliminary conclusion, that we could find no basis to the incubator deaths allegation, was presented in the course of a broader discussion about our documentation of Iraqi atrocities during the occupation, as well as ongoing human rights abuses in Kuwait. Those conclusions were not contested by Embassy staff at that time or in subsequent meetings with Middle East Watch in March and May 1991."

The Kuwaitis had one more card to play, but it was a bluff that ultimately backfired. In the aftermath of the Nayirah scandal, the royal family hired Kroll Associates, a New York private detective agency, to find, in effect, some plausibly dead babies and rescue the tarnished reputation of the al-Sabah clan. Kroll accepted the assignment for an undisclosed sum of money, although in its final report the agency insisted that the Kuwaitis had guaranteed the independence of the investigation. Whatever the arrangement, the Kuwaitis and Hill and Knowlton can not have been pleased with the results. The Kroll report on the baby incubator affair was dated April 1992, but never formally released. However, copies began to leak out in June, which is when I obtained one.

Most importantly, the Kroll investigators announced that Nayirah had never volunteered at al-Addan Hospital (she just happened by one day) and had not witnessed babies being removed from incubators:

The other misunderstanding is that her observation was based on a significant period of observation as a volunteer at al-Addan Hospital. In fact, her testimony was based on a single incident that took place only minutes after her arrival at al-Addan, which coincided with a confrontation between armed Iraqi soldiers and hospital personnel involving the removal of babies from incubators.

This scene is detailed and substantiated later in this report. A key point, however, is that Nayirah's experience of it amounted to a glance or 'snapshot' impression that included chaotic commotion and the sight of one infant on the floor and the presumption that other infants, not seen, had also been removed from incubators.

Having witnessed this scene for no more than seconds, she hurried out of the hospital, realizing that it was unsafe (given her identity) to be present during such volatile activity.

Translated, the preceding passage means that Nayirah never saw anything, but that she should be taken off the hook for the faked incubator propaganda. However, the destruction of Nayirah's credibility didn't prevent Kroll from trying to save face for the Kuwaitis in general. In the end, the investigators managed to conclude that "seven babies died directly because of the looting of incubators and ventilators from pediatric wards at al-Jahra and al-Addan hospitals." This

was patent nonsense, and once again Aziz Abu-Hamad and Middle
East Watch were called upon to straighten out the Kuwaiti disinformation. In its July 16, 1992, rebuttal the human rights organization
stated:

> Kroll did not find evidence to support these reports [of seven babies
> killed]... In arriving at this figure Kroll had to change the issue to
> be investigated: the charge had been that Iraqi troops had pulled
> babies out of incubators causing them to die. But only one of the
> seven reported by Kroll fit this category. The other six, according
> to the report itself, died because of lack of equipment or because of
> a decision by an Iraqi doctor to move incubators from one ward to
> another, in an attempt to consolidate civilian wings. Similar inci-
> dents had been reported before by Middle East Watch and other
> human rights organizations. While we have held Iraqi authorities
> responsible for such actions, these actions may not be reasonably
> considered the same as pulling babies out of incubators, which is
> tantamount to murder.
>
> The claim that one baby reported by Kroll to have died in
> August 1990 as a result of being taken out of an incubator is based
> on the testimony of Salwa Ali Ahmad, a nurse who said she had
> witnessed the incident. However, this nurse's testimony as reported
> by Kroll is contradicted by other more reliable witnesses at the hos-
> pital. In some key aspects, her testimony as reported by Kroll is also
> at variance with testimony she herself had given before, including
> in a published report by Reuters from Kuwait earlier this year.
>
> We recently re-interviewed a number of al-Addan Hospital's
> staff. They again denied that the incident as described could have
> happened at al-Addan. They questioned the nurse's contention that
> she could not report it to the hospital administration or note it in
> the records. They said that despite Iraqi interference, hospital
> administration remained largely in Kuwait hands and that the hos-
> pital staff reported everything that happened in the hospital. The
> fact that she waited all this time to come forward with this report
> cast serious doubt about her recollection, they said. As for not
> being able to note such developments in the records for fear of Iraqi
> retribution, they pointed out that the hospital records from the
> period contained information more damaging to the Iraqis than
> what she claimed to have witnessed, including reports of execution
> and torture by Iraqi troops.

Ahmad's sudden recollection of incubator deaths was likely colored by political pressures of the moment. According to Middle East Watch:

> Kuwaiti health workers have reported to MEW that tremendous pressure has been put on them to testify in support of the incubator death allegations. A number of them reported that they were severely reprimanded for denying to reporters and human rights organizations any knowledge of the incubator deaths. Some were pressured to recant.
>
> Several doctors quoted by Kroll as claiming knowledge of the incubators story had previously flatly denied the story when they were interviewed by Middle East Watch, Physicians for Human Rights and others, immediately following the liberation of Kuwait.

3. Designing War

1. J. B. Kelly's *Arabia, the Gulf and the West* explains that in the 1930s, before the full potential of its oil riches was known, Kuwait considered itself poor in contrast with Iraq. The then–Iraqi king, Ghazi ibn Faisal, exploited the economic disparity, as well as centuries of close commercial ties, in arguing for union between Iraq and Kuwait as well as with the other Gulf states. Britain's divide-and-rule approach to the region could not permit such an arrangement, and, according to Kelly, the Kuwaiti ruler, Sheikh Ahmad al-Sabah, "was made to dismiss his advisory council and disown the resolutions" advocating union. "Riots followed in Kuwait, and Ghazi wanted to intervene and occupy the sheikhdom. Pressure was exerted upon him to refrain from doing so, and the affair came to an abrupt end in April 1939 when Ghazi killed himself in a motorcar accident."

2. When it appeared in October 1992, Schwarzkopf's book, "It Doesn't Take a Hero," rocketed to number two on the *New York Times* bestseller list, apparently unaffected by a revelation, published four months earlier in the *Times*, that should have damaged the general's nearly unquestioned reputation for candor and honesty. In a June 24

op-ed piece, Professor Mark Crispin Miller of Johns Hopkins University revealed that Schwarzkopf's repeated assertions that U.S. aircraft had destroyed all of Iraq's mobile and fixed Scud missile launchers were false. Miller quoted former Marine Corps analyst Scott Ritter (now with the United Nations) as saying "No mobile Scud launchers were destroyed during the war," and furthermore that just 12 of the 28 fixed launchers were eliminated. Miller reported that Schwarzkopf made one of his bogus announcements after a meeting in which two expert analysts told him that the destroyed targets seen on an Air Force video tape were in fact trucks, not Scud launchers. Evidently carried away by their enthusiasm, Schwarzkopf's military briefers had, by the end of the war, claimed the destruction of 81 Scud launchers—an amazing accomplishment given their original assertion that the Iraqis possessed just 50 Scud launchers in total. These contradictory figures presented a historical irony—perhaps lost on Schwarzkopf—since the Desert Storm commander had publicly stated his disgust with the hugely exaggerated U.S. estimates of enemy casualties in the Vietnam war.

3. The charges that Peter Jennings has an anti-Jewish bias, or a pro-Arab bias, are based on rather thin evidence. In the May 24, 1991, *Baltimore Jewish Times*, Arthur J. Magida purportedly tried to get to the bottom of the story, but he didn't find much. The "verbal smoking gun," according to Magida, is to be found at around 3 a.m. Munich time on September 6, 1972, during the incident in which eleven Israeli Olympic athletes were murdered by members of the Palestinian extremist group Black September. Jennings covered the crisis for ABC. In a discussion with colleagues before the fate of the hostages and their captors was known, Jennings, Magida wrote, "questioned Palestinians' commitment to die for their cause." Then, Jennings said: "It's often hard to convince people that Arabs are not fighters and don't like to fight." The previous day Jennings had remarked: "There is in the Palestinian people a strange streak which has never made them successful in being outright killers." These comments supposedly proved Jennings's "sympathy" for the Palestinians, but it seems a shaky contention. Presumably Jennings's Jewish critics think he was implying that the Palestinians were somehow more pacific than the Israelis, despite the ongoing campaign of terrorism against Israeli civilians by Palestinian paramilitary groups. But another interpretation

could be that Jennings was questioning the courage and fighting ability of the Palestinians and other Arabs, if not outright calling them cowards. It was probably foolish of Jennings to express such generalizations about Arabs during a breaking news story, but it hardly proves an anti-Jewish bias. Paradoxically, Jennings told Magida that he made the comments in an effort to counter generalizations about Arabs: "At that point, the tendency was to see all Arabs as *all* Arabs . . . The point I may have been trying to make was that the kind of violence exhibited by certain Palestinians did not necessarily reflect the character of the Palestinian people."

Another mark against Jennings in the eyes of his Jewish critics is that his first wife, Anouchka Malouf, was a Lebanese Christian. This sort of guilt by ethnic association is reminiscent of the charges of enemy sympathizing laid against Peter Arnett because he was married to a Vietnamese woman. That Jennings's current wife, Kati Marton, is Jewish has evidently failed to cleanse his original sin.

4. *Vietnam Syndrome*

1. Like his former White House subordinate, CNN president Tom Johnson, and unlike many in the military, Bill Moyers emerged from the Vietnam horror a wiser man. After the Gulf War he narrated and co-wrote a public television documentary that was sharply critical of the Gulf War itself, as well as some of the patriotic hype that passed as news coverage.

2. During the Nixon Administration, when negotiations in Paris toward "Vietnamization" of the war and heavy bombing of the North became the government's principal strategies, Knightley writes, "The war seemed to fade away . . . editors and producers became less willing to devote space and time to a war that the Administration assured them was as good as over . . ." This occurred despite the fact that roughly one-third of the Americans killed in the war died during the Nixon years.

5. *Operation Desert Muzzle*

1. In the end, Clifton did manage to witness some fighting from a combat pool that accompanied a light armored marine unit

called the "Tiger Brigade." His story, appearing in the March 4 issue of *Newsweek*, was rather flat, and gave the impression that he had observed the tank and mortar battle that took place somewhere near the Saudi–Kuwaiti border on Friday, February 22 (a day before the government said the ground invasion had commenced), from a great distance. Clifton's experience was exceptional in that he saw anything at all during the ground fighting.

Significantly, the pool photograph that ran with Clifton's dispatch depicted a marine combat exercise, not the battle Clifton watched.

2. After the war, Knut Royce of *Newsday* quoted an unnamed U.S. official who bluntly described the poor state of Iraqi military readiness based on his knowledge of interviews with Iraqi officers taken prisoner by the allies: "The [Iraqi] general officers knew they couldn't win the war and weren't planning to fight a war . . . They didn't expect to fight a war because they knew damn well they'd be creamed . . . [they] assumed Saddam was playing a game of chicken and would turn off the road at the last minute or reach a political compromise." The official said the Iraqi officers estimated their average regimental and divisional strength at 80 percent when they arrived in Kuwait. Thus, according to Royce's source, the total allied force of 540,000 troops faced as many as 432,000 Iraqi troops before the bombing began on January 16.

But in fact 432,000 was a gross exaggeration, even by Kuwaiti (and Hill and Knowlton) standards. On April 23, 1992, the House Armed Services Committee released a study that estimated Iraqi troop strength in Kuwait and southern Iraq at 362,000 on the first day of the bombing campaign. When the ground campaign began thirty-eight days later, the study found, just 183,000 Iraqi troops remained. The study estimated that during the bombing 153,000 Iraqis deserted, 17,000 were wounded and nine thousand were killed. Of the 183,000 who stayed in place to meet the allied ground assault, the study said, 63,000 were taken prisoner; the rest either escaped or died.

As for the quality of the Iraqi army, the BBC's John Simpson was properly contemptuous. In his book *From the House of War*, he wrote: "The Republican Guard, which journalists and politicians insisted on describing as 'elite,' was increased by several divisions during the period of the crisis, largely by means of taking men from regular units and giving them red berets. Anyone who could march in step was considered eligible. The officers of the Republican Guard were usually better trained, but that generally meant that they too had to be taken from other units. The mass dilution meant that the Republican Guards' standards, which in the war against Iran had been above average, were little different from those of the rest of the Iraqi army . . . When the ground offensive came, the 'elite' Republican Guard showed little more inclination to fight than the regular army divisions and reservists." Simpson cited British military correspondent Robert Fox's opinion of the Iraqi army's capabilities: "His overall impression was that most of the Iraqi soldiers had come to the desert to get away from Saddam Hussein. It was certainly true that even the punishment squads positioned behind the lines with orders to shoot deserters had little interest in obeying. Many of them were themselves deserting."

3. Four freelance journalists went to extraordinary lengths to get the real story of the war—namely, violence and death—and they deserve mention. The first, Paul William Roberts, a British journalist based in Toronto, lived up to the reputation of the fearless foreign correspondent by sneaking into Iraq on camelback from Jordan and making his way to Baghdad during the height of the allied bombing. His account of the journey, published in the May 1991 issue of the Canadian magazine *Saturday Night*, is the only piece of printed war reporting I have been able to discover that is worthy of special praise. A short excerpt tells volumes about why governments want to censor war correspondents:

> Seconds later, that ominous and now familiar thunder swept above us. The room lit up, the building shook. Seizing my arm, the old man virtually dragged me from the room and down a crumbling flight of stone steps into a musty cellar colder than most fridges . . . Clutching blindly, screaming with fear, a dozen or so children had just been woken yet again that night.
>
> The noise of explosions was unimaginably terrifying. The whole world seemed about to collapse, to fold up, give in, go home. Yet in the midst of this, accompanied by some women who were also there in the dark and cold, the imam started singing what I presume were children's songs, loudly and tunelessly. The louder the explosions, the louder he sang,

until everyone was singing. *These fragments shored against my ruins . . .* I remember thinking.

It was over quickly. What followed was worse. Upstairs flashlights waved, voices called out. The confusion was absolute. In the imam's hallway lay a small girl whose left leg had been ripped off above the knee; standing over her a woman in torn clothes screamed unintelligibly, beating the walls. Then a man in some kind of nightshirt slapped this woman hard around the face twice, shouting and pointing at the girl, who lay mute and staring on the cold stone, thick blood pulsing from her leg.

"Get a fucking *doctor* here," I shouted usefully.

"No doctors," the imam said, calm, almost stern.

From television, only Jon Alpert, a freelance producer and cameraman, brought back images comparable to Roberts's prose. But none of it was aired on NBC, Alpert's principal outlet. When I asked why, NBC News president Michael Gartner told me that the videotape was tainted by the fact that Alpert had traveled to Iraq with antiwar activist Ramsey Clark at the invitation of the Iraqi government. Gartner said Alpert also had lost credibility at the network for getting the U.S. embassy to restage a flag-lowering ceremony for filming in Afghanistan, an event Alpert acknowledged occurred. The gruesome images of wounded and dead civilians in Alpert's videotape did not appear staged, however, and Gartner's argument seems specious when one considers the enormous volume of Pentagon videotape broadcast by NBC. Gartner said he never watched the Alpert video, but that his subordinates had assured him it wasn't of a quality worthy of airtime.

In the United States, one freelancer broke the Pentagon rules in unique fashion. Posing as a mortician, Jonathan Franklin succeeded in being hired temporarily at Dover Air Force Base, the receiving facility for American dead from the Persian Gulf. The Administration had banned journalists from Dover because in 1990 the networks had broadcast the embarrassing split-screen images of a Bush speech glorifying the Panama invasion alongside rows of coffins of soldiers killed in the fighting. Franklin's description of the mangled faces and bodies of dead soldiers was a journalistic tour de force, not war reporting, but it was better than nothing.

Franklin wrote: "As a journalist, deception is not a step I take lightly. It was only because of the Pentagon's extraordinary efforts to sanitize the war through military censorship, the feebleness of the media protests, and my deep belief that the public must understand the realities of war that I decided to go undercover. I believe I am the only journalist to see the dead returned from the Gulf." Franklin's report from the morgue at Dover appeared only in alternative newspapers such as *The San Francisco Bay Guardian* and *The Boston Phoenix*.

During the allied ground invasion a British freelance cameraman named Vaughan Smith got better footage than the competition by dressing in his old regimental captain's uniform and talking his way onto a Bradley Fighting Vehicle. According to the BBC's John Simpson, Smith filmed the destruction of two Iraqi tanks and witnessed the deaths of "three or four" U.S. soldiers when their vehicle was hit by Iraqi fire. Smith's daring masquerade was successful, but not timely. "The best television pictures of the entire war were late in coming to people's screens," Simpson wrote in *From the House of War*.

6. Taking the Fifth

1. One of the most sinister aspects of the Gulf War censorship campaign was the deliberate obfuscation of Iraqi casualty figures by the Administration. Thus, the estimates of Iraqi war dead ranged from Pete Williams's own 457 ("That's the number that we buried," Williams told me) to the widely quoted but unofficial and unattributed Defense Intelligence Agency (DIA) estimate of 100,000 (300,000 wounded), with a margin of error, above or below, of 50,000. Williams, in our interview, ridiculed the DIA analyst who came up with the 100,000 figure, calling it "crazy." According to Williams, the analyst was employing "estimates of the accuracy of our weapons based on his experience in Vietnam," where "the weapons were totally different." They weren't totally different, of course, because B-52 bombers played a major role in both wars.

"He just doesn't know," Williams said of the DIA analyst. "There's just no way to know." Williams would not arrange for me to meet the analyst, nor would he reveal his name.

General Schwarzkopf was no help either. The American commander was said to be almost phobic about body counts because of his bitter experience in Vietnam, where, under pressure from his superiors, he and other officers had reported false and possibly exaggerated enemy casualties.

The BBC's cautious and generally reliable John Simpson believed the DIA estimate was too high, saying the actual figure was probably "much lower: maybe 30,000 killed and 50,000 wounded, though this can only be a guess." After the war, the Iraqi embassy in Washington would not even venture a guess. (Paradoxically, the most visible, and therefore most memorable, scene of "military" destruction—the "turkey shoot" on the highway between Kuwait City and the Iraqi border—took the lives of only about four hundred Iraqi soldiers, according to Simpson.) As Simpson wrote in *From the House of War*: "Western assumptions may have put [the number of Iraqi dead] much higher than it actually was. Allied claims about the number of tanks destroyed were hopelessly inflated. The Iraqi army was not drawn into battle and destroyed; it melted away. Men deserted in great numbers when the Allied bombardment was at its height. Often they simply headed back to their homes."

The civilian death toll in Iraq was also difficult to ascertain. Greenpeace estimated it at somewhere between twenty-five hundred and thirty-five hundred killed directly by the bombing, while Alexander Cockburn of *The Nation* (based on the reporting of his brother, Patrick Cockburn of London's *The Independent*) was less conservative, estimating forty-five hundred. On June 23, Caryle Murphy of *The Washington Post* cited a "preliminary estimate by Iraqi officials" of seven thousand civilian dead from the bombing. Simpson reported "unofficial estimates" in Baghdad of two thousand, and Middle East Watch put the "upper limit" of civilian dead at twenty-five hundred to three thousand. The most memorable scene of civilian deaths for television viewers (once again because it was the most visible)—the U.S. bombing of the Amiriya bomb shelter in Baghdad on February 13—was responsible for between two hundred and five hundred deaths, a small minority of the total number of civilians killed.

More frightening was the October 1991 report by a group of Harvard researchers, which estimated the number of Iraqi children killed by the "indirect effects" of allied bombing. In the report, the group, calling itself the International Study Team, said about forty thousand Iraqi children under five had died from January to

August 1991 from a combination of disease and malnutrition caused by the United Nations economic embargo and the allied destruction of electric power generators, which rendered water and sewage treatment plants useless. After the war ended, Greenpeace said that between twenty thousand and thirty thousand cubic meters of raw sewage was flowing into the Tigris River daily.

2. I asked Time Inc. Magazines editor-in-chief Jason McManus how he thought Henry Luce would have dealt with the Administration's censorship policy had he opposed it. McManus told me Luce would have skipped the formalities with underlings like Williams and Cheney and simply called Bush directly to complain.

"I'm sure the call would have gotten through," McManus said. "And [Luce] would have explained to the President, 'This is no way to run a war or a railroad.' He would have offered to come down and talk about it . . . and probably a vigorous discussion, at which he was good, would have ensued. He certainly argued with Kennedy, Eisenhower, and Presidents in the past . . . Luce, in particular, would have taken it on as a matter of citizenship and argument . . . He would have said, 'We're both important Americans concerned about this war, Mr. President. I believe in this war, Mr. President. You know that . . . Have you thought through the consequences of this policy?' "

Had Bush refused Luce's entreaties, McManus said, Luce would have faced the choice Time Warner confronted in the Gulf War, between boycotting and cooperating. Referring to the possibility of a boycott, McManus said, "I think the journalists would have told him, 'Well, we love the gesture, but it may put us out of business entirely.' "

APPENDIX

Portions of a December 11, 1990, memorandum from Robert K. Gray of H&K to Dr. Hassan al-Ebraheem reveal some concerns and advice worth recording: ". . . A natural attrition has set-in after the early bravado in American attitudes . . . the potential for a protracted battle becoming more real to Americans over time as deadlines draw near, the approaching holiday season, the isolation of the armed forces from their surroundings and the indigenous

population, all serve to underscore . . . the lessening of the U.S.
public's enthusiasm for pursuing a military option before exhausting
other remedies . . . The relatively limited knowledge of the American public about the countries in the Gulf region also is a problem
for Kuwait, which does not fit into the neat definition of democracy
as most Americans understand it . . . While President Bush seems
to have increased his support . . . through what is viewed as a tough
policy that has enabled the hostages to come home, at the same
time the key reason providing justification for many Americans to
pursue military action is depleted . . . [Americans] want to give
the sanctions more time to work (since the present policy of sanctions and the threat of military action seems to bring desired results
and Americans don't have to die)." How to counterattack? Push
the " 'human face' " of Kuwait. ". . . CFK must keep hammering
away at the brutality of Saddam Hussein . . . the people/human
rights message must be told over and over. Kuwait is 'people' who
still are suffering under the boot of an oppressor. As U.S. diplomats
and hostages return home from Kuwait, this should be underscored
further by 'eyewitnesses' . . . to the extent comfortable, discuss the
new Kuwait: rebuilding, further democratization, more assistance
to neighbors in need, etc."

The December 28, 1990, contract between "author" Jean Sasson
(a propagandist for hire) and Knightsbridge Publishing (a fly-by-
night front organization) reveals more about the Kuwaiti government/
White House axis of manipulation. The resulting Kuwaiti-financed
collaboration, a lurid and wildly inaccurate paperback titled *The
Rape of Kuwait*, embellished on Nayirah's tall tale of atrocities and
actually rose to number two on the March 3 *New York Times* bestseller list—just above *Saddam Hussein and the Crisis in the Gulf*, a
book co-written by the sometime journalist, sometime propagandist
Judith Miller: "With regard to the *Rape of Kuwait* . . . the embassy
of Kuwait is purchasing 300,000 copies. . . . 250,000 are for distribution abroad and 50,000 are for distribution to the U.N., Em-
bassies, etc. in the United States. . . . The embassy of Kuwait has
agreed to pay $1.80, FOB, Tennessee, plus related shipping costs,
payable to you [Knightsbridge] on release of copies of the
book. . . . These terms shall be kept confidential between the parties." Uncounted thousands of American G.I.s received complimentary copies.

CHRONOLOGY
OF THE 1991 GULF CRISIS

July 17, 1990 President Saddam Hussein accuses Kuwait and the United Arab Emirates of plotting with the U.S. to keep oil prices low by flouting their OPEC export quotas.

August 1 Kuwait talks break off concerning oil and border disputes.

August 2 Iraqi troops and tanks storm the border of Kuwait. President Bush orders economic sanctions against Baghdad.

August 6 The U.N. authorizes a trade and financial embargo of Iraq.

August 6–7 Bush orders American military forces to Saudi Arabia to defend its oilfields from Iraqi attack.

August 8 Saddam Hussein annexes Kuwait.

August 15 Iraq offers Iran a peace deal.

August 20 Bush declares Americans held in Iraq to be "hostages."

August 22 Bush calls up U.S. Reserves.

November 8 Bush orders a major U.S. buildup of troops in Saudi Arabia.

November 29 The U.N. authorizes the use of force against Iraq if it does not withdraw totally and unconditionally from Kuwait by Jan. 15, 1991.

December 1 Saddam Hussein accepts Bush's proposal for talks, but no date is set.

December 6 Saddam Hussein orders all hostages freed.

January 9, 1991 U.S. Secretary of State Baker and Iraqi Foreign Minister Aziz hold more than six hours of talks in Geneva, but make no progress. Aziz refuses to deliver a letter to Saddam from Bush.

January 9 U.S. press rules finalized.

January 10 Congress opens debate on giving Bush authority to use military force against Iraq.

January 12 Congress grants Bush the authority to use military force against Iraq.

January 10–12 Western envoys leave Baghdad.

January 15 Bush gives written authority for an attack of Iraq unless Iraq begins a withdrawal soon after the midnight U.N. deadline to withdraw from Kuwait.

January 16 The U.S. begins launching an attack on military targets in Iraq and Kuwait. Bush addresses the nation.

January 17 The first Iraqi Scud-type long-range missiles hit Israel.

January 16–17 The Cable News Network (CNN) broadcasts live from Baghdad.

January 24 CBS News reports that veteran foreign correspondent Bob Simon and three other crew members are missing.

January 25 U.S. charges that Iraq deliberately created an oil spill in the Persian Gulf that grew to be among the largest on record.

January 26 Tens of thousands join in an antiwar protest in Washington, D.C., the biggest protest of the war.

January 29 Iraq begins an incursion into Saudi Arabia in the first major ground offensive of the war.

January 30 Eleven Marines become the first U.S. soldiers killed in ground fighting.

January 31 Allied forces retake that Saudi town of Khafji.

February 13 As many as several hundred Iraqi civilians die when U.S. bombs destroy a Baghdad building where people are sheltered. U.S. says that the building was being used for military communications.

February 15 Iraq announces that it will consider withdrawing from Kuwait, but imposes strict conditions. Bush calls the offer a "cruel hoax."

February 22 Bush sets a noon, Feb. 23 deadline for Iraq to begin a "large scale" withdrawl from Kuwait or face a ground assult by the multinational coalition.

February 23 Bush announces at 10:00 p.m. that the allied ground offensive has begun.

February 25 An Iraqi Scud missile kills 28 U.S. soldiers in a barracks in Dhahran, Saudi Arabia. Baghdad announces orders for Iraqi soldiers to withdraw from Kuwait, and troops begin to leave Kuwait City.

February 28 Iraq announces a cease-fire and agrees to a meeting of military commanders to arrange terms.

March 2 Bob Simon and his CBS crew are released in Baghdad.

March 3 The U.N. approves a resolution backing Bush's insistence that allied troops remain in Iraq until Iraq has complied with cease-fire terms.

March 4 Iraq accepts all of the allied terms, including the release of all prisoners. Civil unrest spreads in Iraq.

March 9 The first American troops return to jubilant, flag-waving, horn-honking crowds. Forty journalists held captive in Iraq for almost a week are turned over to the International Red Cross in Baghdad.

Index